Changing services for older people

Changing services for older people

The Neighbourhood Support Units innovation

ALAN WALKER
and
LORNA WARREN

Open University Press
Buckingham · Philadelphia

Open University Press
Celtic Court
22 Ballmoor
Buckingham
MK18 1XW

and
1900 Frost Road, Suite 101
Bristol, PA 19007, USA

First Published 1996

A catalogue record of this book is available from the British Library

ISBN   0 335 19137 1 (pb)   0 335 19138 X (hb)

Library of Congress Cataloging-in-Publication Data
Walker, Alan.
    Changing services for older people: the neighbourhood support units innovation /
Alan Walker and Lorna Warren.
        p.   cm.
    Includes bibliographical references and index.
    ISBN 0-335-19138-X. — ISBN 0-335-19137-1 (pbk.)
        1. Aged—Home care—Great Britain—Case studies.   2. Social case work with
    the aged—Great Britain—Case studies.   3. Volunteer workers in social
    services—Great Britain—Case studies.   4. Community organization—Great
    Britain—Case studies.   I. Warren, Lorna, 1962– .   II. Title.
    HV1481.G52W35   1996
    362.6—dc20   95-26371
                                                                                              CIP

Typeset by Type Study, Scarborough
Printed in Great Britain by St Edmundsbury Press, Bury St Edmunds, Suffolk

E0004234679001.

To the older people and their informal and formal carers in Manor and Southey Green

Contents

List of figures and tables

Figures

Tables

Preface

The story of the project on which this book is based is a long, sometimes convoluted, often immensely frustrating and, ultimately ironical one. It serves as yet another warning of the dangers involved in conducting research into social policy and particularly social services innovations. The project began as a logical follow-on to the Family Care of the Elderly Project (Qureshi and Walker 1989) and was generously funded by the Joseph Rowntree Memorial Trust (JRMT). Unfortunately the Elderly Persons' Support Unit that was to be the original focus of evaluation was delayed (by a public consultation process) and, in fact, was never built. After a year of preparation the project went into limbo and the co-director, Hazel Qureshi, departed. The project was revived in 1989, when Lorna Warren was appointed as Research Fellow, but the planned experimental evaluation design was abandoned and the focus shifted to the Manor Support Unit which had the great advantage of being built and in the process of becoming operational. The support units innovation itself was overtaken by events, particularly the severe constraints on local authority social services spending and various changes in policy within Sheffield's Family and Community Services (F&CS).

With such a large and long drawn out venture it is inevitable that there will be many debts to acknowledge. Hazel Qureshi played a key role in planning the project and in preparing some of the instrumentation. Robin Guthrie of JRMT was a tower of strength when the project encountered its initial difficulties, as was his successor Janet Lewis (Director of Research) and Rowntree adviser Tilda Goldberg, when it later ran into choppy social services waters.

As well as ourselves the project team comprised Andrew Pattenden (research assistant) and Marg Walker (project secretary). Andrew prepared some of the material used in Chapters 4 and 5 and conducted interviews. Marg has been responsible for technical, clerical and secretarial assistance over the whole life of the project. The skilled team of interviewers employed to assist with the collection of survey data included Win Powell (coordinator), Cherie Neale, Sandra Davies, Colleen Clarke, Hazel Watson and Pat Buckley. Julie Calladine contributed observational data on one of the day centres held at the Manor Neighbourhood Centre and assisted with some data analysis.

We relied heavily on the cooperation of staff at all levels of F&CS and the Health Authority. We are particularly grateful to Robert MacDonald (chief assistant, service development), Mick Bond (research officer) and Nic Ralph (principal research and information officer) also, in the health service, to Diane Walker and Judy Gollins (senior nurse managers) and the other members of the health team. The heaviest burden of the evaluation fell on the General Managers of the Neighbourhood Support Unit (NSU), Janice Griffin and Doreen Cook, the Team Leaders, Kath Cotton, Jenny Underhay and Steve Clayton and the Clerical Officers, Janet Weinmann and Pat Clarkson. Our sincere thanks to all of them.

Above all we could not have conducted this research without the collaboration of older service users in Manor and Southey Green, their informal carers and the support workers and home care staff of the two areas. This book and the story it tells is devoted to them.

During the protracted preparation of this book Jacinta Evans and Joan Malherbe at Open University Press have both been patient and supportive. David Phillips provided helpful comments on parts of the manuscript and Kai Leichsenring and Marja Vaarama kindly assisted in the preparation of Chapter 2.

A final acknowledgement is to Margery Warren, who fell ill with terminal cancer during the course of the project, and to Frank Warren, who cared for her, for their unfailing love and support to their daughter.

Abbreviations used

EMI	Elderly Mentally Ill
EOC	Equal Opportunities Commission
EPICS	Elderly People's Integrated Care System
EPSU	Elderly Persons' Support Unit
EU	European Union
F&CS	Family and Community Services
GHQ	General Health Questionnaire
HC	home care
M	Manor
NHS	National Health Service
NSPCC	National Society for the Prevention of Cruelty to Children
NSU	Neighbourhood Support Unit
PGCMS	Philadelphia Geriatric Centre Morale Scale
SG	Southey Green
SPAS	Survey Pyschiatric Assessment Schedule
SSD	social services department
UKCC	United Kingdom Central Council

1

Introduction

The narrative at the heart of this book concerns the attempt by one local authority social services department (SSD) in England to introduce a new approach to the care of disabled older people. The local authority is Sheffield, the SSD is called Family and Community Services (F&CS) and the innovation in question began its life with the title Elderly Persons Support Unit but was subsequently renamed Neighbourhood Support Unit.

Why should this particular story have general, including international, relevance? In the first place, attempts to introduce more flexible, involving and empowering approaches to social care are being made not just throughout the UK but, as we show in Chapter 2, in Europe as well. Indeed, the recent combination of pressures – socio-demographic, fiscal, ideological and grass roots – has begun to produce reforms or proposals for reform in all established welfare states. The social services systems of European Union (EU) countries are in transition; for example there is the creation of more mixed economies of welfare, the separation of provider and funding roles, care packaging, case management and the tailoring of services to users (Friedmann *et al.* 1987; Evers 1991). In the UK this transition was given impetus by the NHS and Community Care Act (1990) which emphasized the development of domiciliary services, flexible and sensitive support to meet the needs of individuals and their informal carers and an increasingly mixed economy of welfare (Chapter 2).

Second, the NSU innovation is located centrally in the policy towards the care of older people that has been adopted in all advanced industrial societies, variously called community care, the promotion of independent living or 'ageing in place' (Walker 1982, 1993a; Tinker 1995). As well as this general relevance to the development of community care policy and practice the NSU project has special relevance in the UK. There is a longstanding suspicion that community care is favoured by policy makers because it is regarded as a 'cheap' form of care ('cheap' in the very narrow sense of cost to the Exchequer). This suspicion was heightened in the 1980s when, under the ideological engine of neo-liberalism, the Thatcher government began to promote what were seen as low cost approaches to the care of older people (Walker 1993a). For example, the Kent Community Care Scheme, which utilizes case management methods to maximize informal and quasi-formal support from friends and neighbours, was given extensive backing by the Department of Health and was the subject of a very large scale evaluation (Challis and Davies 1986). In contrast the NSU innovation, though reflecting a similar case management orientation to the Kent scheme, represented a substantial investment in public provision. Thus, rather than focusing primarily on the extension of care *by* the local community, NSUs were concerned with support *in* the community by trained and salaried staff (Bayley 1973; Walker 1982; Bulmer 1987). The reasons why Sheffield F&CS swam against the ideological tide of the 1980s are discussed in Chapter 3.

Third, NSUs may be used to exemplify the process of innovation in the social services and, as we show throughout the book, there are both positive and negative lessons to be learnt. Some policy experts might argue against the classification of NSUs as an innovation, regarding it as merely a reform or even a development of existing provision, for example (Hall *et al.*: 19). However in terms of both the novel way in which services were delivered and the assumptions underlying the support units policy it did represent a distinct departure from previous practice (Chapter 3). Moreover, although there were bound to be elements of policy succession (Hogwood and Gunn 1984) in any change within an established social services department, the NSU initiative involved not only changing existing organizations and roles but also creating new ones.

Fourth, this book has broad relevance to policy makers and all those with an interest in the care of older people because, as well as being a scientific record of inputs and outcomes, it represents a series of personal accounts. The reporters of these accounts comprise the older people, on whom the service innovation was focused primarily; their informal (unpaid) carers who were also recognized in the aims of the NSU; and the paid support workers whose task it was to translate the high aspirations of the social services planners into practice. Thus this book is both a case study of a particular innovation in a British SSD and an example of the impact of the general trend of change on the users of the services themselves and their informal carers. In the variety of methodologies we adopted (see appendix) and in the distillation of the data for this book we have used every opportunity to let the older service users speak for themselves. Indeed we have followed the same principle with regard to the other two groups of respondents, informal carers and support workers.

Neighbourhood Support Units versus home care

Key aims of the NSUs were to break down the traditional division between domiciliary, day and residential care and to make services more user-oriented with respect to older people and their carers. Originally it was planned to conduct a quasi-experimental evaluation, looking at older people before and after the implementation of the NSU. However, as is often the case with innovations in the social services, this plan had to be abandoned when the building of the NSU that was to be the focus of the evaluation was delayed. In fact that unit was never built and it was decided to play safe (or safer) and concentrate instead on one that was already operational. Thus the evaluation was based on the second NSU which was opened in the Manor area of Sheffield, in October 1988. It was considered unwise to centre the evaluation on the first NSU, in Ecclesfield, partly because it was the first one and partly because it had several unusual factors, including a small catchment area. In place of the experimental research design, we used a comparative framework involving another part of Sheffield, Southey Green, which was well matched with Manor in demographic and socio-economic terms, but which operated a more traditional home care service for the care of older people. (Manor and Southey Green are the actual names of the two estates in Sheffield. We have also used the real names of senior management. The names of the users, carers and support workers are disguised.) Full details of the design of the evaluation are contained in the methodological appendix.

Manor NSU

Neighbourhood Support Units aimed to replace the traditional tripartite division of services for older people – domiciliary, day and residential care – with a more integrated and flexible deployment of resources. The Manor Unit was locally situated and was the physical base for the services that were delivered in older people's own homes, as well as being a day centre and a community resource. The services provided from the unit itself included a weekly lunch club, twice-weekly meals on wheels, twice-weekly day care as well as a club for older people with mental disabilities, a laundry service, bathing facilities and shopping trips.

The key departure from traditional practice in service delivery was the organization of staffing. Teams of community support workers replaced wardens and home helps. They undertook caring duties fulfilled by staff in day centres and some duties undertaken by social work assistants. Workers had been encouraged to break away from the traditional and much-criticized approach to assessment conducted in terms of needs for specific services. They were required to respond flexibly to the fluctuating support requirements of individuals, based on overall assessments of their needs and resources. There was to be a rota system in operation so that, if required, support workers were available at any time to provide a seven day a week, 24 hours a day service (though this was never operationalized chiefly because of the cost). It also provided staff at evenings and weekends according to users' needs. Teams met weekly to sort out care rotas. The teams were expected to evolve their own ways of working according to local conditions, demands upon them and the skills and experience of particular team members.

The Manor NSU was, at the time of the evaluation, a joint initiative between health and social services. This being so, in addition to the three teams of community support worker staff of the Family and Community Services Department, there was a multidisciplinary team of community health personnel – senior district, psychiatric and auxiliary nurses, health visitors, a dietician and an occupational therapist. Among other things, members of the team provided medical services, counselling and advice on aids and adaptations to older people living in their own homes. The team also operated a screening programme of people aged between 75 and 85 in the community to identify individual levels of disability and need.

Official communications between health and social service staff were well established and frontline workers were encouraged to liaise as much as possible. However, the physical separation of the two groups – health staff did not operate from the Manor but had a physical base which was approximately a kilometre from the centre – presented practical as well as symbolic barriers to communication.

Southey Green

The services provided to older people in Southey Green were representative of the traditional home care system operating in all areas of Sheffield outside those served by NSUs. Here, frontline care was provided by home carers and home wardens. The groups were distinguishable chiefly by the hours which they worked: while most home carers were employed on a part-time basis and may have worked a variety of different morning, midday or afternoon shifts, their hours largely fell within and constituted the equivalent of a traditional nine-to-five shift. Home wardens, on the other hand, were employed on a more flexible basis. As a general rule, they worked between the hours of 8.00 p.m. to 1.00 p.m. and 6.30 p.m. to 9.30 p.m., though these times varied where, for example, people needed assistance early in the morning to get ready for a hospital appointment or attendance at a day centre. Weekend and night shifts were covered by wardens who additionally had to be available, on a rota basis, to provide emergency cover to users. Unlike home carers, home wardens were not expected to do any housework. Both groups were employed at the same basic rate of pay, though home wardens received an extra 'split duty payment' as well as an increased rate for weekend and evening hours.

Home carers and wardens were accountable to organizers. The Southey Green area was covered by two full-time home organizers and a senior home care organizer. At the time the evaluation commenced, policy had recently been introduced by F&CS which encouraged frontline carers to begin to work in groups to arrange provision of support to users. Home care organizers in Southey Green were attempting to establish such a system, though a number of problems were being encountered. Chief among these was an absence of guidelines. The area was also felt to lack suitable venues where group meetings could take place. The home care organizers were housed in offices which were not central to the Southey Green patch. Partly as a result of this, it was the usual practice for carers and wardens to send in their time sheets. Consequently there was little incentive for staff to liaise (face to face) on a regular basis. In theory, monthly meetings should have been held between organizers and frontline workers, though this target was rarely met due to demands on the time of the former.

Plan of the book

The primary aim of this book is to describe the impact of the NSU innovation on older people and their informal carers. But, as indicated already, there are various subtexts that run throughout the book. Most important of all are the related issues of flexibility, user involvement and empowerment. One of the aims of the Manor Unit was 'to make services more user-oriented' – an aim that is mirrored in social care provision in many different parts of the UK and also the EU. This policy and the effectiveness of its implementation forms a continuous thread linking each of the subsequent chapters. It is, we believe, one of the most important issues confronting all social services systems.

Chapter 2 places the specific NSU case in the wider context by looking at, on the one hand, the changes that are taking place in the social services systems of the other EU countries and, on the other, the various pressures creating those changes. In Chapter 3 we outline the history of the NSU innovation, the day to day operation of the Unit and staff attitudes towards it. Chapters 4 and 5 examine the impact of the Support Unit from the perspective of the older service users involved and, therefore, represent the largest section of the book. The views of informal carers are discussed in Chapter 6 and, in Chapter 7, those of the support workers on whose shoulders the NSU project rested. Chapter 8 provides an assessment of the extent to which the Manor Neighbourhood Centre and the support unit concept succeeded in achieving the key goal of user involvement. Finally, Chapter 9 consists of our conclusions and policy proposals.

The South East Essex
College of Arts & Technology

2

Changing social services in Europe

Introduction

This chapter provides a broad, European, context for the changes underway in the British social services and introduces the key issue of user involvement. In specific terms, we examine the nature of recent developments in policy and practice with regard to the home care of older people in the countries of the European Union (EU). This is followed by an outline of the main challenges facing the social services in all EU member states which also provides the background to the Neighbourhood Support Unit (NSU) project and other innovations like it. Finally we contrast the two different approaches to user involvement found in discourse and policy on the care of older people and other groups in need and examine their implications. We begin with a brief summary of the main organizational features of home care in EU countries and some thumb-nail sketches of the current stages of development of such services.

Organization of home care services in the EU

What does recent research tell us about the current situation of home care in EU countries? There is considerable institutional variation between member states, including a range of different funding arrangements, so caution is necessary in making international comparisons. Also, until recently, there was very little comparative information on personal social service provision in the EU. That deficiency has been rectified to a considerable extent by a series of cross-national research projects on the care of older people in EU countries, most of which were sponsored by the Commission. These include the joint Leuven-Amsterdam comparative study of services in the 12 countries of the European Community (Nijkamp *et al.* 1991); the Age Care Research Europe project covering nine countries (Jamieson and Illsley 1990; Jamieson 1991); the European Centre's study of service innovations in the Netherlands, Sweden and England and Wales (Kraan *et al.* 1991); the Hoger Institute's research (Pacolet *et al.* 1994); and the early stages of the comparative research of the EU's own Observatory on Ageing and Older People (Walker *et al.* 1991, 1993b; Alber 1995).

The common method of organizing domiciliary care in the EU is for these social services to be clearly differentiated from medical services and under the control of local authorities. Home care services in the EU are at varying stages of development and three broad groups of countries may be distinguished: those with fully developed services in terms of scope and coverage, those with partially developed domiciliary service infrastructure; and those where services are underdeveloped. As will be seen later in this chapter, even in those countries with fully developed home care services by no means all domiciliary care needs are being met and regional disparities in provision are common.

Looking first at those countries with fully developed home care services, in Belgium services have been organized on a regional basis under the control of local authorities and non-profit voluntary associations since 1982 (while health care is centralized). The main domiciliary services are home helps and cleaning services, district nursing, meals on wheels and day centres.

Denmark and Sweden have the most fully developed system of domiciliary care services in the EU. The main services provided are home helps, district nursing, meals on wheels and social work. All services are coordinated and administered by local authorities and financed from taxation. The home help service covers household management tasks, such as cleaning, and personal care including hairdressing, assistance with eating and dressing. In most municipalities the home help service is available on a 24-hour basis and is combined with district nursing in the same organizational unit.

Finland also has a highly developed home care system with comprehensive coverage (though subject to cuts in recent years). Responsibility for provision lies with the municipalities, working under skeletal national regulations. The public sector dominates provision (90 per cent) though there are significant voluntary and private sectors. Funding comes from general taxation and, until recently, user fees were negligible. There is operational cooperation between home care and home nursing.

The development of home care services in France may be split into two periods, before and after 1983. Since 1983 these services have been increasingly regionalized under the control of local branches of national government. Home helps are financed from social assistance and pension insurance.

In Luxembourg home help and home nursing have been long established as the main domiciliary services and they are run almost wholly by private and non-profit organizations. The Family Ministry coordinates and partly pays for services going to low income families. The major providers of home nursing services are religious orders, the Red Cross and two municipalities. Meals on wheels have been introduced recently but day centres are scarce and emergency telephones are found only in the capital.

Until recently the bulk of social services expenditure in the Netherlands went to residential care but increasing amounts of home care are being provided to substitute for residential care. Domiciliary care is supplied by local non-profit associations and financed (up to a limit) by an exceptional medical expenses scheme with private cost-sharing. The United Kingdom would be classified as a country with a fully developed social services system.

Turning to those countries with partially developed systems, in Austria home care is administered and funded locally by the provincial authorities. They have tended to contract out most care services to the voluntary sector. There are wide variations between the nine provinces in terms of regulations, standards of service and coverage. Formal provision has been dominated by large nursing homes, with a community care policy being of only recent origin. There is a lack of day care and respite care and, consequently, heavy reliance on the family.

In Germany (former FDR) home helps are financed by means-tested social assistance and provided by the voluntary sector with public subsidies.

Italy is still in transition from institutional to community care. Domiciliary services are organized by local health units, financed from regional funds. Provision is patchy and inadequate in many places, especially in the south.

Community care policy towards older people in Spain developed in three stages: prior to 1972 there were no social policies for older people; between 1973 and 1979 policy concentrated on residential homes; and from 1979 local personal social services have been created, including home helps and day centres. Domiciliary services are organized by local authorities and voluntary associations and financed by municipalities for low income users.

Finally there are two countries with underdeveloped domiciliary services. In Greece there is a lack of up-to-date information on services. The last decade has seen the development of community services around the KAPI system (i.e. decentralized community centres and informal care) supplemented by district nurses, home helps, meals on wheels and physiotherapy. Provision is minimal, however.

Portugal has placed increased emphasis on day centres for older people (there are 530 such centres) but domiciliary services are in very short supply. Where these services exist they are financed partly from social security and partly from private charges.

Home care in the EU: current trends

Despite considerable institutional variations between EU countries, particularly on the north/south axis, it is possible to identify five major common trends and themes in the current development of policies towards the care of older people.

The state preference for community care

Not only are home care services for older people available in all EU countries but all governments are expressing a preference for this form of care as opposed to residential or hospital care. In some cases this preference has been a long term one. The reasons for this policy are outlined below but, for the moment, it is important to recognize that because the motivations behind this policy vary between countries the nature, the pace and scale of the changes underway, or being contemplated, differ significantly between countries. Thus, among the long established institutional welfare states of the northern part of the EU, we may contrast the market-orientated thrust of the British government's community care policy – privatization, the creation of quasi-markets in social care and the withdrawal of local government from the direct provision of services – with the careful attempts to reform the state agencies in Denmark.

These sorts of variations derive from fundamental differences in ideologies between the governments in power in member states, rather than from any intrinsic features of their social services. In addition, as shown above there are considerable differences between EU countries in the organization and level of development of social services. For example, in administrative terms, the home care services in Greece and Portugal are combined with district nursing and, in Belgium and the Netherlands, there are separate cleaning services. There are also some variations in the classification of home care tasks as being either primarily nursing or domestic in nature. The dominant model of home care in the EU appears to be the conventional home help role consisting of, on the one hand, practical care and tending, primarily in household management and domestic tasks and assistance with other activities of daily living; and on the other, emotional support, being concerned, befriending, acting as adviser or confidant (Warren 1990). Moreover, in the majority of EU countries home care provision is either public or predominantly public: at the present time there are very few for-profit agencies. The Swedish model of home care appears to be more flexible, covering housekeeping and personal care as well as some straightforward medical tasks.

The clear preference on the part of EU governments for the community-based care of older people is also shared by EU citizens. In the recent Eurobarometer survey, in all 12 member states a large majority of the general public (four out of five) thought that older people should be helped to remain in their own homes (Walker 1993b: 29). The only countries wherein more than one-fifth of the general public preferred residential accommodation to community care were Denmark and Portugal.

Shortages of Community Care Personnel

While there is a clear convergence in political rhetoric concerning community care, there are wide variations in provision between EU countries. The range stretches from more than one home help for every five households headed by a person aged 65 and over in Denmark, to one in 10 in France, three in 100 in Ireland, to one in 100 in Spain and Portugal. Denmark, Finland, the Netherlands, Sweden and, to a lesser extent, the UK seem to be the countries with the most extensive infrastructure of services among the northern EU countries (Kraan *et al.* 1991). For example, Denmark has 27,000 people employed in home care services (35 per 1000 people aged 65 and over), whereas in Germany there are only 22,000 full-time equivalents (2.4 per 1000 people aged 65 and over). The proportion of older people in receipt of services is smaller than these figures suggest because the home care jam is not spread uniformly across the older population in any country.

Thus, even in some of the major EU countries, the levels of domiciliary care services are not sufficient to keep pace with the rising need created by socio-demographic change. In other words there is a 'care gap' between the need for care among older people and the supply of both informal and formal carers (Walker 1985a; Qureshi and Walker 1989). It has both demand side and supply side components (Nijkamp *et al.* 1991: 270). This care gap is a feature of the majority of EU countries including Sweden (Kraan *et al.* 1991: 190); all of them except Denmark and Luxembourg report excess demand and there are growing concerns about the lack of specialist home carers for older people with dementia.

The continuing failure to provide sufficient community care services obviously means that some frail older people and their family carers are put under intolerable strains which, in turn, threaten the viability of their caring relationships. It means too that the home care services cannot realize their full potential in the prevention of dependency, but instead are forced to act in a reactive or casualty mode – a point we return to later.

Territorial inequalities

There are considerable territorial variations in the coverage of community care services *within* EU countries. In some cases these regional disparities appear to be of the same magnitude as some of those between the north and south of the EU. For example, in Italy not all of the country's 21 regions have a full home care service, and in Austria, Finland, France and the UK there are wide differences in provision between different areas. Geographical isolation is a factor in such territorial inequalities, as is the rural/urban divide in general, but these are not the major ones. For example in the UK there is wide variation in home help numbers between local authorities depending on their political complexion: within London some boroughs provide three times as many home helps per 1000 older people as others. Even in Denmark and Sweden there are regional variations in home care provision, partly resulting from their highly decentralized system.

Fragmentation of community care

In most EU countries there is fragmentation of community care policies between public, private and voluntary agencies, and, often as a consequence, a lack of coordination between domiciliary care and other services. Most important of all there is the separation between health and social services. Whereas health services are financed from social insurance or general taxation, social services are usually administered and financed either by local government or by various voluntary organizations or a combination of both.

So the necessity of integrating the services is impeded by the organizational separation of responsibilities for funding and management. Most countries report problems of coordination between health and social services and these appear to be particularly acute in Belgium, Germany, the Netherlands and the UK. The main exception is Ireland, where health and social services are managed by the same department at local level.

The problem of lack of coordination in the face of ever-increasing demand has led to adaptations being made to services in some countries. For example in Italy some social workers are acting as social network organizers. In Belgium cooperation initiatives between GPs, home help services and district nursing have been introduced. In France there are regional coordinators; in Luxembourg the integration of all services in regional centres for older people is intended to enhance cooperation; and in the Netherlands there are neighbourhood health centres.

Service innovations

What is, perhaps, most striking about the comparative EU research is that despite, or rather because of, shortages of funding, the social services are in a state of purposive development (for reviews of other UK innovations in community care see Association of County Councils 1979; Durward and Morton 1980; Bayley 1982; Goldberg and Connelly 1982; Ferlie 1983; Clarke 1984; Isaacs and Evers 1984; Salvage 1985; Renshaw 1988; Barritt 1990; Robbins 1993). Examples include:

- service buses – Ireland, the Netherlands;
- the spread of alarm systems – Belgium, France, Luxembourg, the Netherlands, Spain, Sweden and the UK;
- hospital at home/terminal care schemes – the Netherlands;
- hospital discharge schemes – the UK;
- the increasing recognition of and support for informal carers including self-help groups in Belgium and Sweden; carers' support groups in Belgium, the Netherlands, Sweden and the UK; family placements/boarding out in

Germany, Greece, Ireland and Italy and the UK; respite care in Belgium, the Netherlands, Sweden and the UK; sitting services in Belgium and the UK;

- short term or supplementary home care – the Netherlands;
- new community resources in support of home care, such as day centres in Belgium, France, Ireland, Luxembourg, the Netherlands, Portugal and Sweden and the KAPI in Greece;
- housing improvements – Denmark, the Netherlands and the UK;
- new forms of service integration and coordination – Belgium, France, Ireland, the Netherlands and the UK;
- new training regimes to improve the quality of home care services – Denmark and Luxembourg.

While there is plenty of evidence of considerable innovatory zeal throughout the European Union it is important to guard against the danger of overemphasizing the impact of service innovations, as we pointed out in Chapter 1. Despite the existence of high profile innovations throughout the EU (and beyond) the dominant model of social care remains that of the traditional home help. In other words the experience of the majority of older people who are fortunate enough to be receiving social services amounts to one or two hours per week of a home help. Change is taking place even within the social services, for example the enhanced home care/community support worker role in the UK and Denmark, but the 'spotlight effect' of innovations should not mislead us into imagining that they are universal. The majority of older people in need of care in the European Union are not getting sufficient support from the formal services. The Eurobarometer survey emphasized the relatively minor role of the formal services in the care of older people; only 13 per cent of those receiving some form of care were being helped by the public services and only 11 per cent by paid private helpers, though of course the role of the formal services increased with the age of the older person (Walker 1993b: 28).

Pressures for change in social services

This brief review of current trends in the provision of domiciliary care reveals both convergence and divergence; there is a remarkable degree of similarity between member states in the sort of traditional services available to older people but considerable disparities in the *levels* of such services. With the exceptions of Denmark, Finland, the Netherlands, Sweden and the UK, the northern EU states are characterized by minimal home care provision (with a wide variation in the definition of 'minimal'); while the southern states and Ireland suffer from underdevelopment in all social services. Nonetheless it is possible to discern similar trends and service developments within the EU as a whole. This is not surprising perhaps because some of the pressures for change facing member states are common ones. There are three main sources of pressure and, as we show in the next chapter, each of them contributed to the thinking behind the NSU innovation.

Socio-demographic pressures

The European Union is ageing rapidly. At present there are 48 million people aged 65 and over in the EC; 20 million of them are aged 75 or over. By the year 2000 they will represent more than one-fifth of the population and by 2020 they will comprise more than one-quarter. All EU countries face similar demographic patterns: lower fertility rates coupled with higher life expectancies – though they have different starting points. There is considerable convergence between member states in the proportion of their populations aged 65 and over.

The facts of the demographic revolution are well known so we will not labour the point, but it is important to guard against the tendency to regard population ageing automatically as a problem (Henwood and Wicks 1984; Phillipson and Walker 1986). Ageing populations are a sign of success – mainly on the part of national health services and especially public health measures – in overcoming many of the causes of premature death that cut short people's lives in the last century. Moreover, even among very elderly people it is still only a minority that require care (one-third of those aged 80 and over in Germany and the UK).

Population ageing does present a challenge to the social services, however, partly because of the association between disability (including dementia) and advanced old age and partly because this change is coupled with other socio-demographic changes. Most importantly there is the fertility trend towards smaller family size. This means that by far the main source of care for older people in need – their own families – are having to face, more and more, the prospect of caring for older relatives for longer and with fewer potential family members to help. Moreover since women are the main source of care within the family, smaller families mean that more and more women are being forced to shoulder both the labour and the responsibility for caring on their own (Qureshi and Walker 1989). This development is of profound importance for both families and the providers of home care and other services.

It means that family members are entering new intergenerational caring relationships – new in terms of both their intensity and duration – with both sides having to bear the strains these relationships can generate (Walker 1993a). The inevitable result is that these caring relationships will break down with increasing frequency, due to carer fatigue. Alternatively, given this prognosis fewer and fewer women will be prepared to enter such long term caring relationships. Either way, the result is increased demand for service provision (often residential). There are very few examples of care systems having fully adjusted to the implications of the demographic revolution that we are experiencing in the mid-1990s.

The trend towards increased female participation in the labour market (often in roles, such as home care, that mirror their domestic one) puts additional burdens on the female dominated informal care sector. Although there is no widespread evidence at present that women are giving up family care for the labour market, the case of Denmark gives some indication of the potential conflict between full-time paid employment and unpaid domestic labour. In 1960 one-quarter of women aged between 25 and 34 were employed. By 1986 this had risen to 89 per cent (Dooghe 1991). At the same time Denmark is the one EU country to report relatively low 'family' participation in care (Walker *et al.* 1991). The example of Denmark gives some flavour of the distaste of Scandinavian women for the full-time housewife role (Waerness 1990) and, therefore, the enlargement of the EU is likely to emphasize further the social distance between north and south. The growth in divorce and family break-ups is also important because there is evidence that divorced children give less help to older relatives than those in stable marriages. As well as providing less direct personal care they are less likely to have social contact with their older relatives (Cicirelli 1983), though, it must be said, more recent research in Britain has reached a more positive conclusion (Clarke 1995).

There is one further point of importance in this socio-demographic matrix. In all EU countries an increasing proportion of older people are living alone. This is partly a function of demographic change and geographical mobility, but it also appears to reflect a desire for separate dwelling places on the part of both older and younger people. The variation in the EU is from a low of 17.5 per cent of people aged 65 and over living alone in Ireland to a high of 49.3 per cent in Denmark. Again it is necessary to be cautious about this trend. There has been a great deal of speculation about the break-up of the family which is simply not borne out by the evidence. What the research shows is that, although they may live in separate households, older people and their adult children are still in close contact – they prefer 'intimacy at a distance' (Qureshi and Walker 1989; Walker *et al.* 1991).

So caution is necessary, but the widespread trend towards living alone has service implications; older people living alone are likely to be poorer than couples and in some countries, such as the UK, home care has traditionally been targeted on (or rationed to) those living alone.

Political/economic pressures

In all EU countries economic concern about the cost implications of population ageing – in terms of pensions, health and social services – is coupled with political worries about the fiscal implications of increased welfare spending. In some countries this has led to a high level of pessimism about the so-called 'burden' of societal ageing (Walker 1990). In general, economic concerns about the cost implications of population ageing are universal – however the more extreme forms of pessimism are associated primarily with those governments that, for ideological reasons, have adopted an anti-welfare state posture.

The service implications of these political/economic pressures are, as far as the mild form found in most EU countries is concerned, a cost effectiveness imperative that, for example, establishes the principle that older people should stay in their own homes for as long as possible and promotes a search for cheaper forms of care. In the extreme pessimistic form of these pressures, there is a desire to place even greater responsibilities on family members and to encourage the growth of the private and voluntary sectors in substitution for the public sector. Scandinavian countries are not immune to these pressures but, so far at least, they have taken the relatively mild forms of action with regard to social care (Waerness 1990; Kraan *et al.* 1991).

Within the EU the specific service implications of these political/economic pressures include: strict financial limits on care (Belgium, Finland, France, Greece, Ireland, Italy, the Netherlands, Sweden and the UK); a shift or a planned shift from residential to community care (all countries but most radical in the Netherlands because the proportion of older people in residential care has been, on average, twice as much as other countries); deinstitutionalization (Ireland, Germany, the Netherlands and the UK); increased expectation of financial contributions (Belgium, Finland, Germany, Italy and the UK); decentralization (Germany, Ireland, Italy, the Netherlands and the UK); encouragement of family and informal service networks (Germany, Ireland, the Netherlands); failure to improve training and pay for home care staff, which reinforces staff shortages (most countries); local experimentation with cheaper forms of care (most countries); and encouragement of the private sector (Italy, Luxembourg, the Netherlands, Portugal and the UK).

Thus, although they are not the only factors underlying the new agenda in services for older people, political and economic pressures are key inspirations behind innovation and experimentation. In other words, if necessity is the mother of invention, then the primary necessity in EU countries is shortage of funds for community care.

Grass roots pressures

In the northern EU states, with long established social services systems, a certain disillusionment with these services has set in, particularly with regard to monolithic public services. These services, including traditional home care services, have been subjected to four sorts of criticism (for a full account see Walker 1987).

First, more and more users of the social services have been complaining about their bureaucratic organization, complexity and lack of responsiveness to felt needs. In fact there is a long series of research studies pointing to the divergence between the perceptions of need held by users and professional providers in the social services (Mayer and Timms 1970; Sainsbury 1980; Fisher 1989). Some groups of users – such as people with disabilities – have formed self-advocacy movements to press their case for greater influence over their own lives and the services they use. At the present time groups of older people are not at the forefront of pressure for change in the social services, but the recent emergence of grey political parties and the strengthening of EU-wide organizations of older people suggests that this may change in the future.

Second, there is the distinct feminist critique of the gendered nature of care which has developed, since the late 1970s, into a devastating indictment of both informal and formal care. Feminists have been primarily responsible for demonstrating that community care is, in fact, mainly care by female kin and also that care consists of two dimensions: labour and love (Land 1978; Finch and Groves 1980; Walker 1981), though it must be said that most emphasis by feminist researchers has been given to the former dimension. This has led to a demand for alternative approaches that do not exploit women (Dalley 1983; Finch 1984; Waerness 1986). Of course this criticism is of direct relevance to traditional home care services because they are modelled largely on the female domestic or housewife role and are staffed mainly by women. Furthermore many innovations in social care rely on the unpaid or low paid services of women and therefore they may be subjected to the same feminist critique as traditional social services.

Third, out of this feminist critique has come a specific case mounted by those people responsible for providing informal care. During the 1980s, in Britain and the Netherlands, carers began to form self-help and pressure groups to support themselves and represent their views. Together with researchers they have shown, for example in the UK, that community care policies have paid very little attention to the needs of carers and the state has done very little to support the activities of the six million carers (Oliver 1983; Wright 1986). The EU is likely to see the emergence of more politically active informal carers as more women enter the labour market and more men take on caring roles. Their pursuit of their own and their relatives' interests will inevitably put further pressure on services.

Informal (unpaid) carers are part of the taken-for-granted context within which services are provided (Twigg *et al.* 1990). For example the provision of home care is based to some extent on assumptions about the availability of informal carers and their domestic duties towards the person in need of care. Thus the scope of home care is determined frequently by the activities performed, or assumed to be performed, by a caring relative. If home care services are targeted on those living alone and without relatives living nearby, then those carers often under the greatest strain (those living with a frail older person) will not receive the support they need.

In this instance, as in the UK, there is an inverse relationship between the severity of the problems faced by carers and the likelihood of the person they are caring for receiving home care. Thus, according to Levin *et al.* (1983: 3),

> the elderly persons most likely to have home helps were those whose supporters, in the light of several measures, carried the least heavy loads. Supporters (carers) who gave most practical help with personal care were far less likely than others to have home helps. So too were those

who coped with severe dementia, those who coped with faecal incontinence, those who coped with many 'problem behaviours', those who faced a high number of key problems and those who showed signs of severe strain.

Fourth, users and carers from ethnic minority groups have begun to criticize the social services in general and the home care services in particular for failing to recognize their specific needs and the extent to which their cultural background and their experience of racism should be reflected in service provision (Atkin 1991; Fatimilehin and Nadirshaw 1994).

These four criticisms are contributing to a disillusionment with social services, including traditional home care services, and, in combination with the demographic, political and economic factors, have created significant pressures for change in the organization and delivery of services. They have set a new agenda for the care of older people and other groups (Evers 1991). Some changes are already underway, for example,

- standard, off-the-peg services are being replaced by more flexible, tailor-made and coordinated care services;
- the role of the informal sector is becoming more explicit and attempts are being made to better integrate the formal and informal, rather than seeing them as substitutes for each other;
- in some cases the service user as a passive recipient is being replaced by the idea of an active co-producer of welfare;
- symbolically the term 'client' is being replaced by 'user'.

These are, of course, desirable changes because they mean that services can begin to better reflect the needs of users and informal carers (Barnes and Walker 1995). But the progress of change across the EU, and in the UK itself, is patchy and still the majority of older people who are fortunate enough to receive services will not be aware of any new agenda. This raises questions about the prospects for the emergence of an EU-wide convergence in policies on the care of older people.

User-oriented policies on the care of older people

The goal of extending domiciliary care for older people is explicit throughout the EU. At the same time, however, we have seen that home care services are in short supply in virtually all EU countries and only in Denmark and Sweden is there a widespread 24-hour service. Thus there is a continuing care gap and many home care services are still stuck in a rather traditional mould. At the same time most older people in need of care have very little choice, if any at all, about the service they receive (both in terms of the type of service and its intensity). The signs of overburdening can be seen in the incidence of physical and mental ill health among informal carers (and in sickness rates and absenteeism among paid home carers).

How should Britain and the other EU countries respond to the pressures we have outlined? What is the role of the Commission itself in encouraging convergence towards best practice in the social care of older people? It must be recognized that the primary motivations behind change in the social services are political and economic rather than grass roots. Thus one of the most important and difficult challenges facing policy makers and service providers is how to create a more equal and effective partnership with the citizens they serve. Of course the answer to this challenge has profound implications for the meaning of citizenship to older people and their carers and, in particular, how much power and autonomy they are able to exercise in making decisions about their own needs and the sorts of services they require. In other words, how far can the political and economic pressures for change be steered in the positive direction of empowering service users and carers, or are these elements of the new agenda entirely incompatible?

This dilemma poses a fundamental question to proponents of community care: what is its purpose? Merely to keep people in their own homes – ageing in place – or are there other goals? If there are wider goals what is the social philosophy underlying innovations in home care? By examining the two contrasting approaches to user involvement we can prepare the way for a detailed analysis of the NSU initiative. Then, in Chapter 8, we will review the achievements of the NSU with regard to the goal of user involvement. However it must be borne in mind that the NSU innovation occurred before the empowerment movement had come fully to fruition – its focus was on involvement and consultation – and, therefore, we will not fall into the ahistorical trap of judging it according to a standard it was not designed to aspire to.

Consumerism or empowerment?

At the moment there are two distinct models of user involvement within social discourse and social services practice: consumerism, or what Percy-Smith and Sanderson (1992: 49) call 'pseudo-market empowerment', based on analogy with the market, and user-empowerment based on clearly defined rights (Walker 1989, 1991; Barnes and Wistow 1992; Barnes and Walker 1995).

The first, consumer, model derives from the limited form of supermarket-style consumerism which assumes that, if there is choice, service users will automatically have the power of 'exit', that is, the power to give up consuming a particular product. Of course even if this is true in markets for consumer goods, in the field of home care many people are frail and vulnerable; they are not in a position to shop around and have no realistic prospect of exit. Moreover research suggests that the association between marketization and choice is often false (Bradshaw and Gibbs 1988). Private markets only create choice for those that can afford the full range of goods or services on offer, and private forms of care are no less dominated by bureaucratic rules and professional assessments than their public counterparts. Quasi-markets are difficult to operationalize in the context of a monopoly purchaser and without the wasteful purposive duplication of service suppliers (Hoyes and Means 1991).

Underlying this consumerist model of social care are two questionable assumptions. First, it is assumed that monopolies can only operate in the public sector. However, as far as, for example an isolated and frail older recipient of home care, either public or private is concerned, her provider may well be the monopoly power because she has no realistic alternative. Having a range of theoretical alternatives will not make the consumer sovereign if she cannot exercise effective choice. Second, it is assumed that direct payment confers power. But a financial transaction does not necessarily mean the bestowal on the purchaser of either influence or control over the provider. By definition the relationship between the home care provider and the user is an unequal power relationship and, regardless of whether or not there is an exchange of money, it is the provider that holds the power.

The consumerist perspective derives from a crude and narrow economic rationale and, not surprisingly, the organizational forms arising from it are managerial, displaying for example, overriding concern with cost efficiency and cost containment. This managerialism inevitably reinforces the power of professionals, for instance, through forms of case management which see users as passive receivers of care: 'clients' to be 'managed'. In fact the only way that frail and vulnerable service users can be assured of influence and power over service provision is if they are guaranteed a voice in the organization and management of services. This would, in turn, ensure that services actually reflected their needs (a point we return to in Chapter 8). Because of its restricted economistic underpinnings the consumer perspective also perpetuates very limited constructions of both the needs of older people and the potential of home care. The needs of older people are viewed negatively in terms of dependency and the role of home care is confined to that of maintenance or tending rather than prevention or rehabilitation.

In contrast to the consumer orientated model the user-centred or empowerment approach would aim to involve users in the development, management and operation of services as well as in the assessment of need. The intention would be to provide users and potential users with a range of realizable opportunities to define their own needs and the sort of services they require to meet them. Both carers and cared for would be regarded as potential service users. Services would be organized to respect users' rights to self-determination, normalization and dignity. They would be distributed as a matter of right rather than discretion, with independent inspection and appeals procedures, and would be subject to democratic oversight and accountability.

Although we have distinguished the two models of consumerism and empowerment as if they represent the two extremes of a continuum, in practice they are confused. This confusion may be seriously inhibiting progress towards empowering users because the limited goal of consumer consultation is sometimes mistaken for empowerment or regarded as sufficient, similarly with the goal of home care itself, which we rightly associate with increased user-centredness. Home care, however, can be developed without granting any additional rights to older people (compare this with Kraan *et al*. 1991: 188). Indeed the development of home care may consist of a diminution of rights. For example in Britain the previous right of access to private residential care on the part of poor older people was replaced under the NHS and Community Care Act (1990) by home care which is allocated on the basis of provider discretion. The gulf separating the two models – consumerism and empowerment – and the difference between public services and the market can be illustrated with reference to a supermarket. Consumerism ensures that shoppers have a reasonably wide choice and some safeguards as to safety and quality. It is an entirely different matter, however, to expect that shoppers might be involved in the management and day to day running of the store. In other words, in the market analogy, the user remains relatively powerless.

The NSU initiative was borne on the spring tide of the service user empowerment movement, when involvement and consultation were seen as working goals for service providers. As we will show in the following chapter it was a genuine attempt to take services closer to the people and to involve service users and carers in decisions concerning the provision of care. Therefore in motivation it was closer to the empowerment model than the consumerist one.

Conclusion

The main purpose of this chapter has been to set the NSU innovation in the broad context of a similar trend of change taking place, at different speeds and from different starting points, in all EU countries. As will be clear in the next chapter the pressures for change in social services generally all had an important bearing on the origin of the support unit concept although, of course, local factors determined its particular form. In the next five chapters we will illustrate the achievements and shortcomings of the NSU initiative from the perspective of service users, informal carers and paid carers. In Chapter 8 we return to the specific issues of user and carer involvement and assess the extent to which the NSU enabled these processes to take place. Finally, in Chapter 9, we assess the potential of the NSU initiative as an example of good practice by looking at the role of the EU itself in policy towards the care of older people.

3

Neighbourhood Support Units

Introduction

This chapter provides a detailed introduction to the development and operation of Neighbourhood Support Units (NSUs). First of all we describe the process whereby the NSU concept was introduced, the key figures involved, the main thinking behind the innovation and its novel features. This is followed by a description of the day to day operation of the Manor Unit and includes a comparison of caseloads and tasks between support workers and more traditional home carers. Finally we report the views of the staff themselves about the NSU innovation and how it differs from the services it replaced.

History of an innovation

Local situational factors

The general policy context behind the development of community-based alternatives to the residential care of older people has been outlined in Chapter 2: socio-demographic, political/economic and grass roots. While such factors are instrumental in the creation of a particular policy trend, they do not explain the specific nature of different responses to this trend. As with other forms of policy development or innovation there were local situational factors that had a major bearing on the form and content of the NSUs. Two such conditional factors must be highlighted.

First there was the location of the innovation in Sheffield which has a longstanding tradition of Labour radicalism in its organized political culture

(Pollard 1959; Pollard and Holmes 1976; Smith 1982; Westergaard *et al.* 1989). Apart from brief aberrations, local government in the city has been controlled by Labour for the whole of the post-war era. In the period during which the NSU innovation was first taking shape and subsequently being implemented the political style and activities of the Council gained it the slightly mocking title of 'the socialist republic of South Yorkshire'. Although there is more rhetoric than substance to this reputation, the Labour Council did mount dogged and ultimately tortuous resistance to the Thatcher government's policies towards local authorities in the early 1980s, for example with regard to local budget reductions, rate capping and the abolition of the metropolitan counties. Until it was forced into line by legislation, the Council was also a staunch opponent of the Thatcher government's social policies including those in the field of social care.

Thus when Conservative Secretaries of State for Health and Social Services, first Patrick Jenkin and then Norman Fowler, were exhorting local authority social services departments to involve the private and voluntary sectors while reining back their own direct provision of services (Johnson 1987, 1990; Walker 1989) – a policy that was later enshrined in the NHS and Community Care Act (1990) – Sheffield's Family and Community Services (FC&S) Department was one of very few in the country actively seeking to make a substantial investment in public services. More prevalent in the early 1980s were attempts to enhance existing services by formalizing informal caring relationships. The best known of these was the Kent Community Care Scheme (Challis and Davies 1980, 1986) which employed case management techniques to encourage support for older people within their own local community. This 'cost-effective' approach to community care was, not surprisingly, favoured highly by the government and it pumped relatively large sums of money into the evaluation and proselytization of the scheme. In contrast the policy towards the care of older people pioneered in Sheffield focused on extending the role of the social services themselves and, therefore, the NSU innovation attracted no support from central government.

Because support units were a 'top-down' innovation (Barrett and Fudge 1981; Hogwood and Gunn 1984) the local political culture was crucial in explaining the path taken by the project and, specifically, its oppositional character to the course encouraged by central government. But this does not explain the particular form of the innovation and, to do that, we need to examine the second situational factor, individual agency. Like most innovations in social policy there are usually one or two key figures exerting influence behind the scenes (Hall *et al.* 1975).

The origins of the support units concept may be traced back to the late 1970s when its two main architects were appointed to senior management positions within F&CS. Bob Brown (chief assistant, residential services for adults) and Robert MacDonald (chief assistant, service development) had worked together in Wakefield before being appointed to senior management positions in Sheffield. They were keen to develop flexible community-based alternatives to residential care but recognized that, in order to do so, it would be necessary to alter the traditional tripartite structure of social services for older people – domiciliary, day and residential care. Thus, in early 1980, a process of advocacy began within F&CS to promote the idea of support units. For the reasons outlined in Chapter 2, this initiative caught the changing tide of opinion within the social services which included criticism of both the institutionalized nature of residential care and the inflexibility of traditional domiciliary services and calls for the greater involvement and empowerment of service users. As also noted in the previous chapter, this new tide had brought with it a fashion for pluralistic experimentation and innovation throughout the UK as well as in other European countries.

The first phase of the internal F&CS policy making process culminated in the report to the Social Services Committee in December 1980. This proposed that a site earmarked for an older people's home in the 1982/83 programme be diverted instead to the building of a support unit and attached bungalows. Approval was given and construction work commenced in 1982, and the completed building was handed over in February 1983. Thus the first support unit was born, in the Ecclesfield area of Sheffield, and the much more challenging phase of implementation got underway.

NSU philosophy

The starting point for Brown and MacDonald in advancing their NSU concept was the conviction that older people 'have a right to live in an ordinary home, with all the privacy and choice this implies' (F&CS 1980). Services should be accessible and flexible and should work in partnership with both individuals and communities in identifying and providing for their needs. Thus it was intended that support units would provide a means to involve older service users and their informal carers more directly in decisions about the sorts of support they required. It was argued that care should be provided along a continuum depending on the needs of the user and not prepackaged in service provider categories. Therefore it was necessary to replace the traditional tripartite structure of services for older people, geared to different levels of disability, with an integrated and flexible deployment of resources. Underlying the concept of support units, then, is the belief that formal care for disabled older people can be provided more effectively by placing flexibly deployed staff and other resources in the centre of an area, rather than by waiting for the disability to increase in severity and then removing individuals to an establishment providing total care (MacDonald *et al.* 1984).

Thus there were three separate strands in the policy discourse concerning the care of older people that were woven into the original NSU concept. First there was the preference for community care which stemmed in part from the longstanding critique of the manufacture of dependency in older people's homes (Townsend 1962; Booth 1985) and partly from the Thatcherite 'cost-effectiveness imperative' which was imposed throughout the public sector (Davies 1981; Walker 1981, 1982). Second there was the increasing recognition of the right of service users to be involved in determining their own needs and the sorts of services required to meet those needs, which was destined shortly to turn into a fully blown empowerment movement (Chapters 2 and 8). The third strand consisted of the then growing interest, in the UK and in the US, in the decentralization of social services into small local areas or patches, what was referred to as 'getting back to the people' (Hadley and McGrath 1980; Bayley *et al.* 1981). The Barclay Committee (1982) added its support for this trend towards the construction of a community-centred approach for the social services by proposing a community orientation for social work and emphasizing the importance of informal support networks in the provision of care.

Reflecting these three trends in policy and practice, though with greater emphasis on the first and third elements than the second one, Sheffield's Social Services Committee report in December 1980 outlined the expectations associated with the new service:

> a significant improvement in the quality of care . . . by taking services to elderly women and men in need rather than place the people in the middle of the services . . . what is required is a building which would be a base for staff providing services to all elderly people in a designated community.
> (quoted in Bond and Ferrari 1987: 1; see also Bond and Bennett 1987)

Although much of the initial planning, including both internal documents and community consultations, focused on the building, it was the new role of community support worker that represented the heart of the NSU concept and the main point of departure from previous practice. Support workers were supposed to embody the core NSU philosophy of flexibility. They were to undertake caring duties fulfilled by staff in day centres and some duties undertaken by social work assistants. The aim was to encourage staff to break away from the traditional and much criticized approach to assessment conducted according to older people's needs for specific services (Goldberg and Connelly 1982). They were expected to respond flexibly to the fluctuating support requirements of individuals, based on an overall assessment of needs and resources. The teams of support workers were encouraged to evolve their own ways of working according to local conditions, demands upon them, and the skills and experience of particular team members (see p. 28). In the words of Robert MacDonald (1982):

> In my view we need to ensure that this provision is planned with maximum flexibility in mind. We must be careful that staff are not restricted from developing the service in a way which responds to the changing needs of the people being supported. It is important to understand that the [NSU] approach is a model rather than a specific design.

Community support workers were the key to this flexible approach and it was intended that they would provide the whole range of care services required by older people, from routine domiciliary assistance through to comprehensive care of the same level as that available in a residential setting.

Six units were planned across the city, to be concentrated in the more socially deprived areas with high proportions of older people. The first to be opened, in September 1984, was the Ecclesfield Elderly Persons' Support Unit (EPSU), as the NSUs were labelled initially. Substantial resources were committed to the scheme (the equivalent cost to a 42-bed old people's home and a 16-place day centre) representing a rejection of official belief that alternatives to residential care are necessarily cheaper. The first unit received a lot of attention, both nationally and abroad, following the publication of the Audit Commission's (1986) report *Making a Reality of Community Care* which supported a model of community care (if not the financing of it) very much in line with the Ecclesfield initiative.

Planning within F&CS tended to focus more on the physical structure and use of the building, to the partial detriment of the development of the support worker role. In the case of Ecclesfield it was decided that the aim of preventing admission to residential care required the service to implement five organizational features: the building would be equipped to prepare meals and have communal dining and recreation areas; it would act as a reception point for an alarm and communication system; it would be staffed on a 24-hour, seven day a week basis; intensive care units or sheltered housing with access to support from the unit would be built on the same site; and the unit would be the base for a personal social service for older people in the area (Bond and Bennett 1987: 13).

These basic principles were developed further through the planning process, which included a public meeting in Ecclesfield and the election of a local working group. Not surprisingly the chief impact of this local consultation process was to boost the role of the community itself in the NSU initiative. For example the encouragement of community use of the building and the involvement of community members in the management and monitoring of the project were accepted as basic aims of the NSU (Bond and Bennett 1987: 13). A steering group of local people was established in March 1983 to monitor community usage of the unit.

The implementation of the Ecclesfield unit entailed several departures from the principles set out in the previous paragraph. Although sheltered housing units were built on the site these were managed by the Housing Department. The original aim of providing intensive support to those in sheltered housing altered to a situation in which support was provided on the basis of the user's need. The unit did not become the reception point for an alarm and communication system, nor was the area covered by the proposed city wide alarm system (a casualty of reductions in social services spending). The lack of an alarm system constrained the ability of the unit to provide a 24-hour 'on call' service. However support workers did provide a night sitting service and did visit at weekends and in the evenings. A users' committee was established but the attempt to set up a community management committee failed. In the view of the general manager, this set-back occurred because the attempt was made too early in the history of the unit and the users' committee was already taking up the available time of the small number of local people who were then involved closely with the project (Bond and Ferrari 1987).

Manor Neighbourhood Support Unit

The Manor council estate, incorporating Upper Manor, Lower Manor and Manor Park, was chosen as a potential NSU site having been designated by Sheffield City Council as an area of poverty. Indeed, levels of unemployment and social security benefit receipt were (and still are) very high whilst much of the housing stock, built in the inter-war years, was damp and in a state of decay. The council had begun a huge redevelopment programme which carried implications for the demand for domiciliary services as it was anticipated that by 1986, there were likely to be 250 new dwellings in the area of which about 100 were designed for older people. At the time when the initiative was being considered there were around 3500 pensioners living on Manor. F&CS was already providing home help and home warden services to 271 households with older people and over 80 people were attending day centres at Shireland and Ravenscroft old people's homes.

Lower Manor was selected as the specific location for the project building in part because it lacked any community facilities and inclusion of these in the support unit could enable provision to be made as economically as possible. The nursery facilities were added following proposals to replace a local council day nursery with a series of smaller centres. Two smaller day centres/ community rooms were suggested for sites on Upper Manor, where there was a concentration of older people receiving home help and/or warden support, and Manor Park but resources were not sufficient to meet the financing of these parts of the project.

As it turned out, delays to the building programme meant that the Manor Centre was not completed until 1986, two years after the date originally proposed. Operationalization of the support worker service was set back further as a result of protracted trade union discussions over the local grading of support worker staff, most of whom were being redeployed from positions within the existing home care service, the pay award system of which was based on national gradings. The description of duties relevant to the grading offered to nursery nurses likewise failed to recognize the full range of activities expected of them in their new posts within the unit and a local agreement had to be reached. Team leaders were brought into post whilst talks were still ongoing but they refused, meanwhile, to manage home care workers along traditional lines. A compromise was finally reached regarding the funding of the support worker jobs when it was agreed to freeze a number of hours allocated to support worker, clerical and domestic posts. There is no need to spell out the research implications of these delays in the implementation of the

Manor NSU. The original plan to conduct a before and after experimental evaluation had to be abandoned and the project put on ice until it was certain that the NSU would actually start to provide services.

These hitches aside, the support service was brought into effect in October 1988 bearing the new title of Neighbourhood Centre to reflect its wider orientation. That is, while the main aim of the unit was still 'to care for elderly people in their own homes and prevent the need for them to go into residential care if they did not want to' (F&CS 1987), it also spelt out the need for and provision of facilities for young children and their families and the community in general.[1] A second explicit aim of the Manor NSU was to 'strengthen family, friendship and neighbourhood networks by supporting individual carers and developing voluntary and community services' (F&CS 1984) indicating the department's increasing recognition of and sensitivity towards the use of informal carers and informal care networks by the formal sector.

The scheme additionally differed from the Ecclesfield EPSU in that it developed into a jointly collaborative project with the health services. (The EPSU at Ecclesfield involved liaison with the health services but health worker input was minimal – approximately 18.75 hours per week according to the senior nurse on the Manor project.) Margaret Butler was appointed to the post of director of community nursing services in 1986, bringing with her enthusiasm and support for the idea of a locally-based community health team, especially in light of the Cumberlege report (1986), which criticized the general organization of the majority of practice-run teams. Joining forces, among others, with Jean Gregory and Mike Newton – officers from the service development section of F&CS[2] – and with Tony Nuttall from the health authority, she helped to draw up plans for a team of primary health care personnel based within a geographically defined location, the boundaries of which incorporated the area serviced by the Manor NSU.

The health project similarly faced delays while individual members of the team were recruited and discussions held over the levels of staffing and accommodation. Unfortunately the design of the centre did not allow enough space for the health team in its entirety and so the team operated from a base approximately half a mile away and separated from the NSU by a busy dual carriageway. However the scheme was up and running in more or less its completed form in the summer of 1988, before the opening of the centre.

The day-to-day operation of the Manor Support Unit

The aims of offering a more flexible and user-oriented social care service clearly had implications for the organization and running of the NSUs. A picture of the day to day operation of the units was built up through extensive observation of the work of staff at the Manor Neighbourhood Centre and in the homes of older people (Chapter 8), and through interviews with support workers

(Chapter 7). A handful of workers from Manor and from Southey Green also agreed to keep diaries of their daily activities over the course of two separate weeks, providing valuable detailed comparative data (appendix).

The core unit

The NSU itself was a building, Manor Neighbourhood Centre, with offices and a staffroom to house the clerical workers, team leaders, unit manager and other staff providing support services to people living within a specified radius (the project area included Lower Manor, Upper Manor and Manor Park council housing estates). It contained communal facilities comprising a large hall/activity area which doubled as a dining room, three lounges, an interview room, a craft/hobbies room, and a reception area with coffee bar. It also had a kitchen, a laundry, a hairdressing room and a bathroom equipped with a Parker bath designed for use by disabled people. The centre acted as a base for the transport facilities as well as being fully furnished to provide for the under-5s service. The building was thus available for use by a wide range of community groups, it being the intention of the service not only to assist a core of the most frail and severely disabled older people but also to promote activities that would bring together members of all age groups.

Staff

The key figures involved in the organization and provision of care to older people comprised the unit manager, three team leaders, support workers, two clerks and two cooks. Support workers were divided into three teams – covering each of the three estates within the Manor area – and replaced the wardens and home helps of the traditional service. (Before our evaluation commenced, the traditional service was retitled 'home care' hence its use throughout this book.) On average, each team employed 14 workers, the equivalent to 435 hours per week.

The teams were managed by team leaders whose duties included regular supervisory sessions with individual support workers, assistance with the drawing up of weekly team rotas and the overseeing of unit-based activities, in addition to being responsible for the assessment and review of service users. Given the increased remit of the team leader role, their average caseloads of 80 to 90 service users were smaller than those typically held by home help organizers managing more traditionally organized services (as many as 300 – see Allen *et al.* 1992). Team leaders were directly accountable to the unit manager who oversaw the running of the NSU as a whole.

Joint collaboration

Singling it out from the other NSUs was the fact the Manor initiative additionally involved joint collaboration between the health and social

Figure 3.1 A classification of support worker activities within users' homes

Personal care: personal/private/intimate tasks relating directly to older people themselves.
E.g. help with rising and retiring, dressing and undressing, washing, bathing and hair, going to the toilet; administering medication (including morphine and heroin-based drugs to terminally ill users), incontinence management and carrying out basic verbal and physical health checks; arranging visits to and/or from other professionals, e.g. doctors, district nurses, dentists, chiropodists, occupational and physiotherapists.

Emotional care: 'stroking' (Bernard 1971).
E.g. being concerned/friendly/sympathetic; being an advisor/confidante/friend.

Domestic care: housework/domestic chores.
E.g. 'light' and 'heavy' housework including respectively washing-up, dusting and tidying; cleaning floors and inside windows, hanging curtains, making and changing beds, washing and ironing laundry; supervision of heating/fire-lighting and of locking up; emptying commodes; changing lightbulbs etc.; looking after pets. Also, 'mass clean-ups'.

Errand care: tasks performed from older people's homes.
E.g. fetching shopping, pensions and prescriptions and paying bills.

Meals: tasks relating to the nutritional needs of older people.
E.g. the provision of drinks, snacks and cooked meals.

Supervision: 'pop-in' calls.
E.g. monitoring the circumstances of older people, checking on their well-being and needs, or supervising the eating of meals and the taking of medication.

Non-routine/one-off tasks: 'anything that keeps them going'.
E.g. purchasing items of furniture or household equipment; making arrangements/putting users in touch with (council and private) services such as decorators, gardeners and plumbers; letter reading and writing; filling in tax and benefit forms; burying dead pets.

services. Working alongside the F&CS support workers were a team of community health personnel. The team comprised a senior nurse, three district nursing sisters, one district enrolled and three enrolled nurses, a community psychiatric nurse, two health visitors, an occupational therapist and a physiotherapist all working full-time, and two nurse auxiliaries, two school nursing sisters, three health visitors, a speech therapist and a dietician working part-time.[3] In respect of older people, a key directive for the health team was the nationwide establishment of screening for the 75 to 85 age group, which effectively placed increased emphasis on prevention and on the social aspects of health care rather than concentrating on crisis intervention.

Figure 3.2 A classification of unit-centred support worker activities

Unit-based activities: day centres; bathing; laundry; administration.

Transport: conveyance to and from the day centres; bath runs; shopping trips; day trips and other social outings; meals on wheels; laundry runs.

Local resource panel referrals: referral of older people for respite, day and residential care.

Non-routine and one-off activities: including accompanying older people to hospital; Christmas show; holidays away.

Activities

Changes in the traditional organization of the social care services were most visible in the activities which frontline workers were called upon to perform. The bulk of their work still constituted the support given to service users within their own homes which encompassed domestic, errand, personal and emotional care, the preparation of meals and supervisory visits (see Figure 3.1). 'Mass clean-ups' involved a number of support workers operating as a small team to clear out houses which had been subject to neglect over a considerable period. Support workers also referred to an additional set of non-routine or one-off activities which fell under their remit. The influence of joint collaboration could be seen in the expansion of the very basic 'nursing' tasks carried out by support workers.

An entirely new set of activities, performed by workers outside older people's homes and centring on the unit (Figure 3.2), clearly demanded enhanced social and practical skills. A major new initiative was the involvement of workers in the running of three day centres at the unit. Held on a weekly basis, they included a session specifically for older people with mental illness which was led by the community psychiatric nurse. Other activities comprised driving/providing transport,[4] delivering meals on wheels, and organizing shopping trips, outings and other social events. Support workers were also able to bring referrals before the local resource panel, a group of professional representatives from various health and welfare bodies who met to discuss applications, amongst other things, for places in day, respite and residential care.

Weekly diaries: a comparison with traditional services

Figures 3.3 to 3.6 give some idea of the workloads and working patterns of NSU frontline workers in comparison with staff employed in the traditional home care services. The charts are based on the diaries of a support worker, a home carer and a home warden chosen, as far as possible, for their representativeness, and constitute a pictorial depiction of weekly activities (appendix). In

Figure 3.3 Weekly diary: home carer

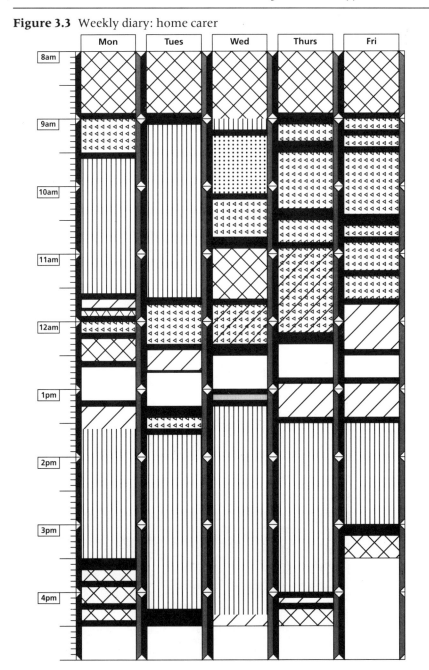

Figure 3.4 Weekly diary: home warden

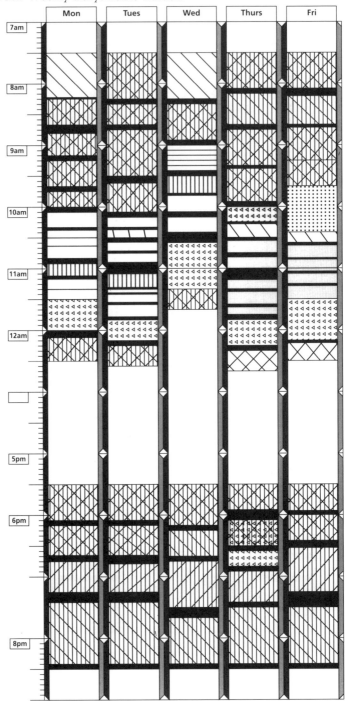

Figure 3.5 Weekly diary: support worker, week 1

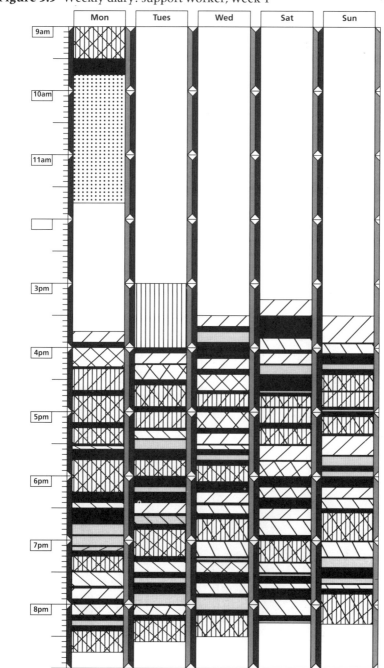

Figure 3.6 Weekly diary: support worker, week 2

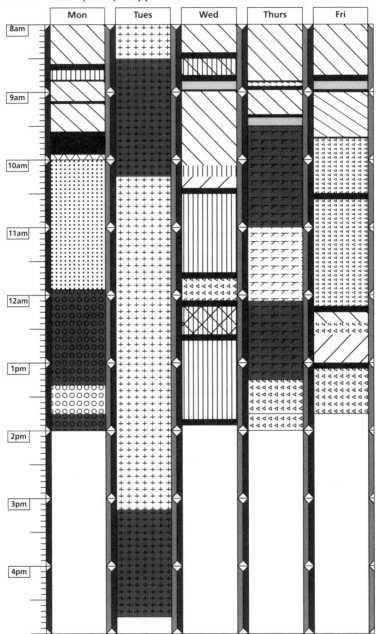

Key

 Light cleaning

 Heavy cleaning

 Errand care

 Drinks, snacks, meals

 Personal care

 Laundry

 Day centre

 Shopping trips

 Driving/transport

Lunch or gap between split shifts

Travel time

Supervision

 Administration

 Supervisory/team meeting

the case of the home warden, a more representative diary might have been one which illustrated a weekend shift. Unfortunately, none of the diaries submitted included such a shift. It is important to bear this point in mind when considering factors such as the amount of time spent by wardens on errand tasks, which is obviously considerably reduced on Sundays.

The days of the week are divided into clearly outlined activity slots. The slots commonly symbolize a visit to a user though, in the case of support workers, they also show the performance of unit-centred activities including laundry runs and day centre duties. They are typically separated by time spent travelling between locations – including users' homes, the shops, post office, doctors' surgeries, and the respective premises used for staff meetings – though also by lunch-breaks or gaps between shifts. Where slots are not separated by chunks of travelling time but immediately precede each other, it indicates that activities were being carried out consecutively within the same location. For example, home care staff might visit more than one older person living in the same sheltered housing unit where supervisory sessions with home care organizers were also held (Figure 3.4, Friday 8.43 a.m.–10.35 a.m.). Similarly, support workers might go straight from a team meeting into laundry tasks, both of which were unit-based activities (Figure 3.6, Monday 10.00 a.m.–2.00 p.m.).

Participants found it time-consuming, as well as very difficult, to produce accurate records of the time devoted to each of the separate tasks they undertook during any one slot, not least because many were performed simultaneously. For example, workers commonly collected pensions and prescriptions at the same time as fetching shopping, or cleaned the kitchen while a meal was cooking. For this reason, a number of slots depict an overlapping of activities though, where detailed information was provided, others have been broken down into their constitutive parts (e.g. Figure 3.3, Wednesday 8.00 a.m.–9.10 a.m. and 1.15 p.m.–4.30 p.m., and Figure 3.6, Friday 12.15 p.m.–1.00 p.m.). In Figure 3.5 (Monday 11.55 a.m.–2.10 p.m., Tuesday 8.30 a.m.–10.15 a.m. and 3.10 p.m.–4.45 p.m., and Thursday 9.30 a.m.–11.00 a.m. and 12.05 p.m.–1.15 p.m.), transport has been deliberately shown as an overlapping activity representing its integral status as part of laundry, day centre and shopping trip activities respectively.

Unless narrowly defined through actions such as sharing a cup of tea or taking a user to the pub, it proved virtually impossible for workers to measure or quantify the social, emotional and motivational support which they provided to older people. Support of this kind was largely a product of their visits in general or, again, given at the same time as another task was being performed; workers talked to users as they helped them to dress or while tidying up, for example. Table 3.1 therefore shows a breakdown of workloads in terms of the more concrete categories of care as well as time spent by staff in travelling and attending team meetings. Where activities overlapped, the total time of the slot has been shared in weighted amounts between the number of activities which it encompasses to arrive at an approximate figure.

Table 3.1 Comparison of workload distribution between support workers and home carers/wardens

	Home carer	Home warden	Support worker	
			Week 1	*Week 2*
Status	full-time	full-time	part-time	
Hours worked	39 hrs 10 mins	39 hrs 25 mins	28 hrs 7 mins	32 hrs 35 mins
Caseload				
Main users:				
daily	1	4	7	0
4 × week	1	1	1	1
3 × week	0	0	0	2
2 × week	1	0	0	3
1 × week	9	1	2	4
New users	2	0	0	0
Covering/				
supervision only	2	9	8	1
Total	14	15	18	11
Average number of individual users visited per day	4	12	13	4*
Activities				
Average number of activity slots per day	9	18	18	6
	% total weekly time			
Personal care	9.7	20.5	21	18
Domestic care	41.9	20	12	9
Errand care	15.9	8	1	13.5
Meals	17.7	23	21	2.5
Supervision	0.2	12.5	11	1
Unit-based care	–	–	0	15.5
Transport	–	–	0.3	30
Travel	12.2	14.5	25.7	4.5
Team meetings	2.4	1.5	8	6
Total	100	100	100	100

Note:
* This number is based on visits made to older people to assist them within their own homes. If calls made to people's homes for the purpose of collecting laundry, and taking users to the day centre or on shopping trips are included, this number rises to an average of eight individual users per day.

Both members of staff from the conventional services whose time diaries have been reproduced were employed full-time and worked standard shifts – more or less within the hours contracted to them – with little, if any, variation in their schedules from week to week.

The split-shift arrangement of hours which characterized the home warden's timetable contrasted with the 'nine to five' pattern of the home carer. As a consequence of the activities they performed, differences also existed between the two workers with respect to the number of daily activity slots each was allocated, the number of individual older people each visited in a day and the user categories into which these older people fell.

The home carer's day contained an average of nine activity slots, composed chiefly of visits and support given to a handful of older people requiring help with practical tasks on a weekly basis. Her workload focused on practical activities to which she devoted three-quarters of her time, primarily giving domestic support, followed by assistance with food and drink preparation and errand care. A tenth of total weekly time was spent on personal care tasks and only 0.2 per cent on supervisory visits.

The home warden recorded a mean of 18 activity slots, which comprised visits to an average of 12 older people, the majority of whom were classed as needing supervisory visits or daily help. Nearly a quarter of weekly time was given to food and drink preparation, one-fifth to personal care tasks and one-eighth to supervisory visits. Domestic and errand care featured in the home warden's schedule but, in each case, half as frequently as in that of the home carer. Thus, the home warden's timetable was composed entirely of small to medium sized activity slots, without the large blocks of often solid cleaning support which characterized the home carer's daily routine.

The analysis and subsequent presentation of two separate weekly workloads extracted from the diary of the chosen support worker showed that staff at the NSU worked a far more varied pattern of shifts in terms of their hours as well as the tasks which they performed. The worker in question was employed on a part-time basis, supposedly for 23 hours per week, though the system enabled workers to accumulate extra hours put in responding to users' needs and to take time off in lieu (Chapter 6).

The first diary week recorded a shift spent away from the NSU 'on the patch', and included weekend cover. The pattern of activities and categories of users visited were comparable to those of the home warden in terms of the focus on personal care, meal preparation and supervisory visits. Differences lay in the greater number of older people who required daily help. The subsequent increase in the overall number of service users visited in the week partly accounted for the extra time spent travelling. This was also a result of the necessity of covering the 'main clients' of other support workers, while they were carrying out unit-centred activities or taking time off work, or in an emergency; in other words, it was not always possible to organize timetables so that shifts were composed of visits to users living within the same area.[5] Less time was spent by support workers on domestic and errand care.

The second diary week represented a far more notable break with traditional domiciliary service organization. The proportion of time spent on domestic care (9 per cent) was the lowest recorded across the three workers, as was that given to meal preparation (2.5 per cent) and supervisory visits (1 per cent). The only category of care remaining more or less comparable was personal care. Otherwise, the support worker's week was dominated by activities which required transport (30 per cent) or which were unit-based (15.5 per cent), hence the drop in the average number of visits to older people (see Figure 3.4). Totally new tasks included a laundry run, shopping trip and day centre duties though, with the exception of transport, they all effectively augmented help given by support workers to older people under different activity headings. For example, shopping trips broadened the scope of errand care, while day centres offered extended supervisory and motivational activities, as well as offering alternative eating arrangements through the provision of a cooked meal in a communal setting.

Finally, over three times the proportion of time was spent by the support worker in team meetings as compared to staff from the traditional services, reflecting the space and energies required for the careful planning and coordination necessary to the achievement of a flexible service.

Staff attitudes towards the NSU innovation

As well as interviewing support workers for the purposes of the NSU evaluation and higher management staff to obtain details of the policy development process, we also spoke to management and other staff involved in the day to day operation of the NSU. The extent to which the NSU innovation was considered as a departure from traditional service organization and the nature of any perceived variations differed between the health and F&CS teams as well as among individuals according to their respective employment history, though there was consensus on certain issues such as collaboration between the services.

The NSU as innovation

In terms of the novelty of the NSU initiative, F&CS workers tended to emphasize the notion of 'community working'. For one of the managers, who had moved from a position as a home care organizer, the major change was in 'taking services local' so that 'everything was coming from under one roof'. That is, instead of having to contact a number of independent bases or departments across the city to arrange for the various services a user might need – meals on wheels at one place, laundry at another, transport at the central department within the town hall, different day centres – along with the home care or, in this case, support worker service, these facilities were organized at the local level. Frontline staff, who it was believed ideally should also be local people, were more in touch sympathetically with the needs of older people and communicatively with their families. Users and carers, in their turn, were judged to prefer the accessibility of a local service to a 'big decentralized social services department' as one informant described it.

A second key element of the innovation was seen to be the notion of flexibility, a term employed repeatedly by all of the F&CS employees. Its practical implications included making available the support worker service 24 hours a day, if necessary. The aim of responding in such a way as to meet the various and varied needs of users and their carers also had knock-on effects for the processes of assessment, allocation and review, especially if resources were to be managed efficiently (Chapter 8). One person defined the objective as 'concentrating on individual need and being creative and reviewing existing clients'. As the unit manager at the time of the opening of Manor Centre, she saw her primary task as being to prepare support workers who required 'a lot of training on understanding need and how to meet need and individual care plans' as well as encouragement to change the emphasis from cleaning to caring. Her words were echoed by the manager of the first unit to be opened, at Ecclesfield, who defined the 'main areas' as being:

> selecting your staff, training your staff, developing your staff, listening to them, cherishing them and actually making them aware of the things that we don't want to be as well. Working 'with' not 'for'.

Under this broad umbrella, it was also a mission of the unit to develop new services, such as shopping trips, which encouraged community involvement. The three team leaders, all of whom had come from home care organizer posts (in one case, from the post of acting senior home care organizer) thus found themselves directly responsible for managing a whole range of activities and not simply the services provided to people in their own homes. They were allocated a much smaller number of workers the supervision of whom, both individually and on a group basis, was a central part of their role. Since the job of support worker was much more autonomous and encompassed the reviewing of users' needs, it was particularly important that regular contact be maintained between frontline staff who might need guidance and backing and team leaders who required updating on their caseloads.

Within the health team, stress was placed on the concept of neighbourhood nursing and the system of generic management which it entailed. Thus the novel features of the project similarly included the provision of a service which was locally based and, in many respects, more informal in nature than traditional district nursing. For example, someone who first joined the project as a health visitor described her aims in that role as including the setting up of 'drop-in' sessions and liaising with the staff at the local advice centre as well as with other health workers working within the area (but not necessarily part of the actual project team). Another mentioned the scheme to set up a whole food shop on the estate. New initiatives also encompassed the team organization of workers which was of a multidisciplinary and much more closely collaborative nature. The notion of flexibility was used in this context to describe the working patterns of members of the project team who were 'willing to give and take [in] their role and to negotiate and compromise'.

Attitudes towards the social care of older people

Among staff on the F&CS side of the Manor project the need for a more flexible approach to social care was felt to be particularly important in regard to older people. The traditional service was seen to be failing to respond sensitively to need. This was partly the result of the lack of emphasis placed on the assessment and review of users. One person gave the example of a woman in her 60s who had initially been allocated home help while recovering from an operation on a broken arm. Her case had never been reviewed and, 10 years on, she was still receiving the same level of support – two hours cleaning help per week. This was the amount of help, coincidentally, being given to a woman in her 90s and living alone who was blind and had an amputated leg. This older service user had turned down the offer of extra help claiming there were others worse than herself. Indeed, a second informant pointed out the need of service providers to address the polar cultures surrounding service use which were characterized, on the one hand, by deference and gratitude and, on the other, by the belief in entitlement to help as a 'right': 'like you got your pension when you were a certain age, you got your home help when you were 75'.

Service providers themselves frequently did not explore beyond these attitudes with the result that organizers gave

> a service to people who didn't really justify it – that's an expensive service – while there were people going into care who could be supported at home, so the balance wasn't right at all.

Either way, users were not motivated to do things for themselves or with the support of others. Neither was input from relatives positively recognized but rather the implicit understanding of the domiciliary services was, in the words of one interviewee, 'if you've got a relative we don't give you anything, the relative can do it'.

Of course, limited resources and the ever-increasing dilution of services affected the extent to which formal carers could offer people choice but the 'fitting of people into what was available' was also seen as another negative feature of the social care culture. One of the members of staff we interviewed used the term 'Cinderella service' to indicate the low levels of training given to those working with older people as well as pointing out the absence of legislation to 'protect the right to choice of elderly people'. He also criticized the traditional organization of frontline staff who commonly worked in isolation, some with little or no contact with their colleagues and/or supervisors. Teams were too large to be run in a way which encouraged collaboration among individual workers or cooperation with users. Indeed, there was a belief among some staff that women were undervalued as workers, as were older people as 'an important facet of services which we, all of us, may one day become'.

Finally, in purely practical terms, the traditional services were found wanting in regard to the speed with which support could be allocated to older people. Under the new scheme team leaders were able to directly assess users for and inform them of the availability of a range of services provided, more or less, on their doorsteps while support workers were able to respond to changes in individual user's circumstances by using their own initiative.

In health terms, the screening programme for older people was regarded as very welcome given the generally poor health profile of the residents of Manor. One of the nursing staff noted that while there were no major differences in the type of complaints reported, people appeared to suffer the onset of 'typical' illnesses a good 10 to 15 years earlier than the average population. With early intervention, many of the conditions were highly treatable and hospitalization avoidable, though this necessitated a more intense health visiting service which was one of the aims of the project. Thus both health visitors and the district nurses (who carried out the screening process) took a greater health promotional approach in their work with older people, placing emphasis on their quality of life.

The objectives of the Manor NSU

The overall objective of the NSU was seen then as being primarily to meet the needs of older people in order to enable them to remain in their own homes as members of the community. All of those to whom we spoke emphasized this general aim though how they expanded on it differed. For example, some emphasized a proactive approach in the sense of working with older people to meet their self-defined needs within their homes/the community (see Chapter 8). Others defined the goal as being to keep people out of institutional care which was 'the last step'. This suggested a more reactive approach whereby staying at home and entering residential care were viewed as lying at opposite ends of a positive/negative continuum, but with little thought as to what might lie in between. Either way, appeals were made to the qualities of security and dignity. Health care managers added to the idea of maintaining older people in their own homes, the aim, in the words of one, 'to prevent the *preventable* admission to hospital'; that is, 'to be able to identify needs early on and to be able to respond to those needs to try and lessen the number of crises'.

The support of carers was also regarded as important though largely, it seemed, as a means of achieving the primary objective of keeping older people at home rather than as an end in itself. Thus our informants generally needed to be prompted about this area of assistance while they couched their responses in terms of working 'with' or 'alongside' carers but never 'for' them alone.

Again there were differences between F&CS and health staff in how they saw the objectives of the NSUs in relation to their specific employment backgrounds and, where relevant, how these objectives and their implications for practice differed from those of the traditional services. Starting with social services, one person described the basic social care aims of the two services as being 'very, very similar'. The main difference for her – as indicated earlier – lay in the provision of a much more comprehensive range of services for older people organized locally from one base which inevitably meant an increase in the number of activities for which all F&CS staff were responsible. So, for example, whereas under the traditional system home help organizers referred on candidates for day care to a social worker for placement, within the NSUs team leaders actually ran the centres themselves. Similarly, they organized the meals on wheels and luncheon club service – the food being prepared in the kitchens at the unit – and they managed the transport and bathing facilities.

As a result of these extra demands as well as the concomitant increased flexibility of support worker hours (see Chapter 7), the ratio of frontline staff and users to supervisors was much smaller than under the traditional services. The manager of the Manor Centre estimated that, as a home help organizer, she had been in charge of approximately 40 home helps/wardens providing services to 280 users. On her transfer to the position of team leader (the post she held before becoming manager), these numbers dropped to 13 and 90 respectively. The lower levels also reflected the expectation of increased – or in the words of one member of staff 'proper' – supervision with frontline staff given their enhanced role in the monitoring and assessment of users. Team leaders were regularly involved in weekly team meetings of the support workers and also arranged planned supervisory sessions with workers on a one-to-one basis (see Chapter 6):

> Really home care staff aren't supervised very good. It's a quick visit to the client and to the home help. 'Are you all right?' and that's like a supervision session.

The unit manager at the time the Manor Centre was opened had a background in the residential sector as well as having worked as a district nurse for some years. She shared the prime objective of achieving greater flexibility. For her, this involved effecting changes not just in the practical organization of services – particularly in the time span between referral and assessment for services, the hours within which support was provided and the difficulty for carers in obtaining special aids and equipment as well as recognition and support in general – but also, and relatedly, in F&CS management's rigid attitudes towards and the wider public's lack of awareness of older people's care needs. The former she criticized for not being at all 'consumer orientated', the latter for ignoring the 'people who don't shout', that is 'people who are disabled in their home and who don't get out into the community'.

The manager of the Ecclesfield Unit had attended a management course prior to taking up his post and saw the development of the teamwork component of services – in particular networking, training and induction – as important to the achievement of flexible support and therefore a key objective. Through such processes, he also hoped to operate a preventative or 'minimal intervention' – model of services based on the early identification of (potential) problems and user-defined needs:

> Don't make people into clients unless you have to and when you have to, try and respond to what they're asking for rather than what you are limited to giving.

Of the three team leaders, one had transferred to the unit initially as a support worker after the closure of the residential home where she was employed as an assistant principal. She too stressed the development of a close working relationship between frontline workers and their supervisors as an important ingredient of efficient service organization based on her experiences within both social and residential care. She was concerned about identifying instances of unmet need and saw support workers as playing a key role in this process through their regular contact with people at the local level. Other objectives which she held also included reducing the loneliness and isolation of older housebound people and offering greater support to carers but, in both cases, within the framework of people's self-defined needs.

The remaining two team leaders had both come to their posts from managerial positions – as a home help organizer and acting senior home help organizer – within the domiciliary services in Sheffield. Both spoke of being attracted to the 'forward looking' approach of the NSUs which dispensed with the traditional and very rigid division of workers into home helps and home wardens, offering instead a flexible, responsive support worker service which was far more concerned with the effective targeting of 'services that people actually needed that kept them in their own homes for as long as they wanted'. One stressed the particular aim of encouraging independence through helping to motivate older people while the second spoke of preserving people's dignity.

For the managers from the health team, coming from backgrounds in health visiting, district nursing and health education, a key objective was the achievement of a high standard of nursing and nursing care. To this end, the screening programme for the 75 to 85 age group was particularly important – in terms of monitoring quality of life for individuals as much as their activities of daily living. Standards of care also rested on close liaison and communication with F&CS staff ('that didn't finish at five o'clock in the afternoon'), GPs and other professionals and voluntary bodies working in the area, though bringing together a team of health workers with different skills and interests (as well as being accountable to different line managers) was as equally new an initiative which required coordination and cooperation. Indeed, the examination of a 'whole group of ideas all in one place and developing under several fronts at the same time' as well as in a 'proactive fashion' was the major factor distinguishing the project from traditional organization of health services.

Eligibility for services

The eligibility criteria used by F&CS staff were those drawn up by the manager of the unit at the time of its opening. On her own initiative, she had identified a very general set of principles for the allocation of support services which gave priority to:

1 people who would be unable to remain in their own homes if support services were not provided;
2 those whose physical conditions or handicap would seriously deteriorate if support services were not provided;
3 those without personal, social and emotional support who would be at risk without support services;
4 people who are so highly dependent that they would be at risk if their basic needs were not met; and
5 those people whose emotional state is going through crisis and who would deteriorate if support services were not allocated.

(F&CS 1989)

In terms of activities, personal care was thus placed at the top of the list, followed by emotional and social support through to cleaning help at the bottom.

The first manager of the unit had later begun work 'to establish a way to measure need' though she was not sure they had 'cracked it'. Looking at existing home help guidelines and work on dependency levels which had been carried out within the F&CS department, she had aimed to build up a picture of need which was 'task orientated'. Thus she had designed a 'dependency characteristics' form containing questions about mental and physical health, personal care and household tasks ('rather than whether or not a person smoked') which could be scored to produce a 'dependency rating'.

Written guidelines relating to the work of frontline staff had been drawn up as a result of discussions between the unit and the health team manager. However, these were 'codes of practice' concerned with spelling out individual medical tasks which lay outside the remit of the support worker post rather than with detailing the many activities which the role was expected to (or did) encompass.

With regard to the health needs of users, anyone requiring a nursing service (though exactly what constituted a 'nursing service' was not defined) automatically received support 'by hook or by crook'. Prioritization came into play at 'secondary levels' such as the need for assistance with bathing, especially since there were only two nursing auxiliaries. As in the case of F&CS services, however, there appeared to be no written policy to guide judgements which were made on the basis of district nurses' assessments of 'relatives and other care givers and support workers and everything else, all the other resources that are available'. The action of the district and enrolled nurses were subject to codes of practice but these were set outside the Manor project at the health unit and national levels.

Integration of the innovation within F&CS and the Health Authority

Despite feedback in the form of written reports and meetings, the general feeling among all those we spoke to was that the NSU initiative was not well integrated within either F&CS or the Health Authority. Given the long history of failed attempts at joint planning and operations between the health and social services in the UK (Sargeant 1979; Webb 1991) it might have been expected that the path for this joint initiative would have been prepared carefully at all levels. Yet the key figures from both services involved in the actual operationalization of the Manor scheme clearly believed that its success rested on their shoulders as individuals. Indeed, one person was head-hunted for the post while another was told that her reputation would go if the project failed. Both worked tremendously hard drawing up policies and organizing staffing and other practical matters relating to the delivery of services with very little support and guidance from their respective managers.

Within F&CS, attitudes to the NSU initiative varied across staff groups. Members of the higher management were accused by interviewees of remaining largely ignorant of, or disinterested in, the purpose and character of the NSUs. Many of the frontline staff within the traditional services perceived support workers to be of an 'elite' status. Other personnel from outside the units had expressed 'petty jealousies' and 'bitterness' in relation to, among other things, the location of the NSUs and elements of their organization such as the greater flexibility and the concomitant revised salary grades of the workforce. A number of social workers based in the area were clearly unhappy about the new capacity of support workers to refer people for assessment for residential and respite care, a duty previously restricted to the social work service alone.

The cumulative effect of these attitudes was the treatment of the units as separate entities from domiciliary and fieldwork services. Management attitudes were explained as resulting partly from the fact that key figures involved in the setting up of the initiative had since moved on to other projects or had left their posts and not been replaced. Thus the units had come to be treated as temporary 'hybrids' rather than as permanent units with the necessary coordination. Additionally, the political commitment to developing the project was not necessarily 'shared by senior officers in [the] department in a practical and operational sense', a belief attested to by the lack of evaluation of the NSUs:

> The department quite often . . . hasn't given us the level of support that this service deserves but I think that's largely due to the fact that, although it's changing, Sheffield has been, and still continues to be in some areas, a very traditional department. It's almost as if there's a 'don't rock the boat' mentality about it and there are those people who really think the boat deserves a good rocking because, in fact, nobody seems to know where it's going. There's a lot of disdain towards this service

because we have succeeded and we have achieved and I don't think it was expected.

These problems were compounded by the sense of resistance which typically follows any attempt at change, especially where the new set-up is seen to benefit only a section of the population and workforce.

Within the health team, it was the organization of service delivery more than the actual role of individual workers which changed as a result of the initiative (see above). Nevertheless, one person still spoke of feeling the threat of marginalization within the health services. This feeling lessened as the project progressed, as the team grew more confident and as a result of a number of well-received presentations to various key health service representatives, including the chairman of the district health authority. The promotion of the original project manager to a position where she came into contact with more senior managerial figures also helped to get the project known.

However, certain stereotypes about the Manor health team continued to persist among workers in equivalent positions but based in other districts. It was commonly thought, for example, that staff at Manor did their 'own thing'. They were envied for their collaboration with the support workers and for access to a wider range of services without thought being given to the hard work and planning which these aspects entailed. Members of a specific disciplinary background had found themselves the subject of debate over whether they should be allowed to attend meetings of a recently established peer support group while, on a number of occasions, information was circulated to the other 10 clinical nurse managers in Sheffield but not to the manager of Manor project.

Collaboration between social services and health personnel

Joint working was slow to get off the ground. This was due in part to the familiar obstacles to collaboration between health and social services (Sargeant 1979; Walker 1984; Hudson 1987; Webb 1991) and partly to a failure to prepare the way for effective joint working. Thus when the manager of the Manor Centre first arrived in her post, her line manager was off sick and no one bothered to inform her that the initiative involved joint collaboration with a health team. She was not even aware of where the district nurses were based. Despite this unfortunate start however, collaboration appeared to be more successful than that of integration, at least within the day to day running of the initiative. Managers from health and F&CS services reported meeting regularly on an informal as well as a formal two to three month basis. They were also involved in the meetings of the local resource panel held every three weeks. Joint meetings – or 'two team liaison meetings' – took place quarterly and involved the respective managers, team leaders and members of the health team though not, it appeared, support workers (at least not one support worker attended any of the joint meetings at which a researcher was present during the course of the evaluation).

Although they shared an open invitation to attend one another's meetings, in practice it was the district nurses who were more likely to drop in on support workers' weekly team sessions (Chapter 7). This may have been partly a result of the distance between the two bases and the fact that the nurses were mobile, though it was also thought to reflect differences in the cultures of the respective professions. Support workers continued to see the nurses 'as a bit elite' or as 'experts' and were inhibited about calling in at the project base. However, they did readily phone the nursing team to request their help or refer individuals for assessment. Indeed, the ease and extent of communication across the two services had increased considerably as a result of the initiative. A number of activities were run on a joint basis by staff while individual members of the health team had participated in training sessions for support workers.

Conclusion

This chapter is intended as an introduction to the detailed findings of the evaluation contained in the next five chapters. Thus we have explored the main philosophy behind the NSU innovation and sketched the processes of policy development and critical service implementation.

Key features of the NSU concept were flexibility, user involvement and community-orientation and community support workers were charged with putting them into practice. The main activities of the unit were then described and compared with traditional home help and warden services. Finally in this chapter we have included the first feedback from the extensive evaluation of the NSU initiative in the form of a commentary from the operational managers on the objectives of support units and the assumptions of the social services planners responsible for introducing them. On the whole both health and social services staff acknowledged the innovatory elements of the Manor NSU and were committed to them. However there was concern about the sense of marginalization felt by staff within both health and social services. There was also a perception of a general drift away from the original ideals of NSUs – a phenomenon that appears to be inherent in the process of service innovation though, in this case, it was compounded by the lack of preparation, guidance and a lack of ongoing departmental support felt by staff.

In the following chapters we will report on the extent to which the NSU achieved its objectives.

Notes

1 The Manor Centre offered 20 full-time nursery places with flexible half or full-day contracts, facilities for parents and childminders, a toy library and a parent and toddler

group. In terms of general community use, it provided a reception lounge with a coffee bar, hairdressing amenities and a library service with books and cassettes on loan. The main hall and lounges acted as a base for user groups to hold various clubs including homecraft, keep fit, indoor games and bingo. These facilities were also used on a sessional basis to offer a psychiatric nurse, health visitor and a local NSPCC (National Society for the Prevention of Cruelty to Children) service as well as welfare benefits advice and work with young women. Day centre, bathing, laundry, meals on wheels and domiciliary services were provided for elderly people and a number of younger disabled people living in the community, and the two minibuses owned by the unit were hired out to various community groups and organizations.

2 Mike Newton later moved to the job of liaison officer with health services. The other core members of the Manor planning group comprised Dorothy Robinson (research officer, F&CS), Jack Day (day care officer, F&CS), Tricia Farley (residential officer, F&CS), John Cadman (divisional officer), Jean Geddes (senior home care organizer) and Ann Stricklen from division 5, Keith Dainty (community nursing services), Janet Weinmann (manager of Carbrook day nursery) as well as local representatives from the Upper Manor Tenants Association (including Tom Dyson, Betty Holden, Frank Ridge, Sam Sylvester and Jessie Taylor) and from the housing (D. Paine and P. Swain) and library services (Richard Proctor, Cath Pyle and Ivor Vincent).

3 Joint collaboration as a built-in feature of the Manor NSU initiative was effectively ended in December 1991 when the recommendations of the Sheffield Health Care Services' report (1991) for practice-based primary health care teams were enforced city wide. However, support workers from the unit and health personnel still based within the Manor area expressed a clear commitment to pursuing and developing their collaborative activities.

4 Not all support workers could drive or had taken the mandatory test demanded of F&CS workers, but a number of more recent recruits to the service had been required to possess driving skills in an attempt to relieve the pressure of what was considered a very onerous task on the existing drivers.

5 Despite these features, during the course of the evaluation, one team leader attempted to minimize the amount of time spent travelling between homes through the review of caseloads and the subsequent reallocation of support workers to users living within the same area. The exercise succeeded in reducing routine travelling time with implications for the organization of schedules within the remaining two teams.

4

Older people: attitudes towards services

The main focus of any service evaluation should be the users themselves. Accordingly older people were the starting point for our evaluation of the effectiveness of NSUs and represented the most extensive fieldwork component of the research. Our investigation into the impact of the Manor NSU on the older people it was designed primarily to serve comprised the main quantitative element of the evaluation, with two rounds of interviews separated by a year to 16 months, though there were also some qualitative approaches adopted during the interviews (see appendix). Two chapters are devoted to the older persons' perspective on the NSU innovation. The first part of this chapter provides a profile of older people in the two geographical areas of Sheffield and the sort of assistance they required. Then we turn to older people's views on the services they received, covering the aims of the support unit, changes in service provision, relationships with their formal carers and the tasks performed for them by these carers. In Chapter 5 we examine the actual impact of the new service on older people in terms of their ability to remain interdependent in the community.

Older people in Manor and Southey Green

As indicated in the methodological appendix, first round interviews were conducted with a total of 96 older people in Manor and 84 in Southey Green. Both samples displayed a high average age – 79.2 in Manor and 80.4 in Southey Green – which was a reflection of the service source of their referral. There were no statistically significant differences between the age and sex distributions of the two samples. Predictably, women far outnumbered men in

Table 4.1 Reported disabling conditions of older people

	Manor		Southey Green	
	Number of older people reporting condition	Percentage of older people reporting condition	Number of older people reporting condition	Percentage of older people reporting condition
	(Number of respondents = 96)		(Number of respondents = 84)	
Arthritis	67	70	61	73
Eyesight	51	53	39	46
Minor nervous complaints	38	40	34	40
Hearing	38	40	27	32
Chest condition	33	34	36	43
Heart trouble	31	32	32	38
Stomach problems	27	28	19	23
Bladder control	27	28	19	23
Falls	24	25	26	31
Blood pressure	23	24	21	25
Effects of stroke	19	20	16	19
Bowel control	11	11	9	11

both places: 72 to 24 in Manor and 67 to 17 in Southey Green. It was equally unsurprising, therefore, that the majority in both samples were widowed: 77 per cent in Manor and 76 per cent in Southey Green.

The trend towards living alone in old age is well documented (see for example Ermisch 1983; Willmott 1986; Grundy 1989; Warnes and Ford 1995) though this is sometimes mistakenly portrayed as part of a long term trend stretching back into the last century (Wall 1984). In our samples, 77 per cent of those in Manor and 86 per cent in Southey Green lived alone (among those aged 75 and over the proportions were 80 per cent and 88 per cent respectively). The two areas consist mainly of council estates and, therefore, it was to be expected that the vast majority (95 plus per cent) lived in such accommodation.

Physical and mental health and the need for care

There were no significant differences between the two communities in their subjective assessment of health or of disabilities (Table 4.1). Approximately one-fifth of respondents from both areas judged their health to be good, while the remaining 80 per cent judged it to be fair to poor.

The majority of older people recorded multiple disabilities. The most

Table 4.2 Potential need for care among older people

	Manor		Southey Green	
	Number of older people with different needs	*Percentage of older people with different needs*	*Number of older people with different needs*	*Percentage of older people with different needs*
Critical interval disability	17	18	8	9.5
Short interval disability	31	32	30	36
Long interval disability	47	49	43	51
Moderate disability	1	1	3	3.5
	96	100	84	100

common limiting factor was arthritis, affecting 70 per cent of those interviewees in Manor and 73 per cent of those in Southey Green.

As for mobility, equal proportions of older people were chair or bed bound (4 per cent), but more people in Manor (36 per cent) than in Southey Green (30 per cent) were housebound and fewer were able to go out even with assistance. The fact that only a minority of people in both samples – 18 per cent in Manor and 19 per cent in Southey Green – were able to go out without assistance indicates the substantial need for support on a regular basis.

A composite measure of the potential need for care, based on the work of Isaacs and Neville (1976), was used to categorize older people into groups with 'critical interval', 'short interval' and 'long interval' needs. An additional category of 'moderate disability' was drawn from the work of Davies and Challis (1986).

'Critical interval' disability was associated with people for whom needs arose at short and unpredictable intervals, necessitating immediate attention and thus constant availability of help. Respondents with such needs were commonly unable to rise from a bed or chair unassisted and to get to and use the toilet without risk of falling. Alternatively, they experienced frequent incontinence of urine or faeces, or were suffering from a mental abnormality of such severity as to create a potential hazard to themselves or their environment. 'Short interval' disability was characterized by the inability to carry out regular daily tasks, such as the preparation of food and drink. Such tasks, although essential, are not regarded as critical since they do not have to be performed at an exact time. 'Long interval' disability was defined as being present when assistance was needed with certain basic care tasks such as shopping, cleaning, or laundry once every 24 hours or less often. While unquestionably necessary, such activities are non-critical in the sense that they

Table 4.3 Help required by older people with activities of daily living

	Manor		Southey Green	
	Number of older people requiring assistance (Number of respondents = 96)	*Percentage of older people requiring assistance*	*Number of older people requiring assistance (Number of respondents = 84)*	*Percentage of older people requiring assistance*
Getting up/going to bed				
Getting into/out of bed	17	18	14	17
Washing self	13	14	11	13
Dressing	24	25	16	19
Any of the above	28	29	17	20
Looking after self during day				
Getting around indoors/Using toilet	14	15	8	10
Feeding self	6	6	1	1
Getting around outdoors	62	65	54	64
Any of the above	70	73	55	65
Daily household chores				
Light housework	42	44	36	43
Cooking hot meal	47	49	45	54
Either of the above	52	54	52	62
Weekly household tasks				
Heavy housework	85	89	79	94
shopping	91	95	80	95
Laundry	72	75	64	76
Any of the above	95	99	82	98

can be performed by any available person at any convenient time. People suffering from moderate disability fell into none of the above categories but required help with certain basic care tasks because of low morale, apathy and a tendency to neglect themselves.

As Table 4.2 shows, levels of need were comparable between the two groups, though the difference in critical interval disability between the two groups suggests a greater need for care in Manor.

In order to identify more specific areas of need among older people, information was also collected about help required with 11 separate activities of daily living (Table 4.3). Clearly, the most common problems for both groups were presented by tasks requiring considerable mobility and major physical effort such as weekly household chores; it is interesting to note, for example,

Table 4.4 Frequency of assistance required by older people

	Manor		Southey Green	
	Number of older people needing assistance	Percentage of older people needing assistance	Number of older people needing assistance	Percentage of older people needing assistance
Help at least every few hours or constant supervision	25	26	15	18
Help at least once a day	20	21	25	30
Help at least once a week	37	39	35	41
Less	6	6	4	5
No answer	8	8	5	6
	96	100	84	100

that in both samples, all but four older people required help with shopping. The difference is small but, on the whole, older people in Manor were more likely to need help with personal care tasks compared to people in Southey Green who required more support with household tasks. This difference may have reflected the aim of the NSU to place the emphasis of services on caring rather than cleaning.

The overall implication of the findings relating to mobility, potential need and help required with activities of daily living is that a greater number of more severely disabled older people were being supported in Manor than in Southey Green. This difference is borne out by Table 4.4 which, in line with Table 4.2, shows the greater frequency of the assistance required by older people in Manor.

Further evidence suggesting that higher levels of dependency and need were to be found among older people using services in Manor as compared to their counterparts in Southey Green comes from the data on mental impairment. The Survey Psychiatric Assessment Schedule (SPAS) showed that while the majority of older people (just under two-thirds of respondents in Manor and Southey Green) suffered no impairment, there were differences between the two groups relating to levels of severe impairment. Although the total number who were found to be severely mentally impaired was small (12 in Manor compared to three in Southey Green), older people in Manor were still three times more likely to be suffering severe mental impairment compared to those living in Southey Green.

The pattern of difference between the two groups with regard to mental impairment was reversed with respect to morale. The overall level of morale across both groups was low, but older people in Manor appeared to suffer less from low morale than did those in Southey Green. Nineteen per cent of service

Table 4.5 Frequency of support received by older people

	Manor		Southey Green	
	Number of older people receiving support	Percentage of older people receiving support	Number of older people receiving support	Percentage of older people receiving support
<weekly	3	3	5	6
1 × week	24	25	40	48
2 × week	6	6	11	13
3 × week	2	2	2	2
4 × week	2	2	–	–
5 × week	14	15	12	14
6 × week	–	–	2	2
7 × week	35	36	5	6
No answer/don't know	10	11	7	9
	96	100	84	100

users enjoyed high morale in Manor, 10 per cent experienced only moderate morale and 40 per cent low morale. The equivalent percentages in Southey Green were 17 per cent, 6 per cent and 52 per cent respectively.

Receipt of formal care

We also collected extensive information about the frequency (Table 4.5) and amount (Table 4.6) of support required by older people in both areas (as assessed by older people themselves).

In both Manor and Southey Green, only a small proportion of older service users received help less than once a week, it usually being the case that they required only occasional assistance with heavy household tasks such as cleaning or laundry. Otherwise, the frequency of help received by older people varied from once-a-week to daily care.

As can be seen from this summary of the data, there were higher levels of disability and care needs in Manor than Southey Green and, concomitantly, formal support was provided on a more frequent basis in the former than the latter area.

Older people's opinions about services

Next we turn to the attitudes of older people towards the services they received, including the aims of the NSU innovation, changes in service levels

Table 4.6 Amount of support received by older people

	Manor		Southey Green	
	Number of older people receiving support	Percentage of older people receiving support	Number of older people receiving support	Percentage of older people receiving support
<weekly	3	3	5	6
0–30 min	7	7	3	4
31–60 min	18	19	14	17
61–90 min	6	6	7	8
Up to 2 hrs	7	7	14	17
Up to 3 hrs	6	6	10	12
Up to 5 hrs	11	12	13	15
Up to 10 hrs	10	10	5	6
>10 hours	10	10	4	5
No answer/don't know	18	19	9	11
	96	100	84	100

and/or frequency, relationships with formal carers and the sorts of tasks carried out by these carers.

Community care policy

Respondents in Southey Green had not, of course, experienced NSU services. Only 11 per cent said that they had heard of the scheme. Nevertheless, when asked for their views on the prime aim of the NSU to assist older people to remain in their own homes as members of the local community, there was quite a close correspondence between Southey Green and Manor respondents in terms of their response. A handful of people stressed the notion of individual choice – 'It's up to them, they're all different' (M) and 'Some like to go in a home. That's all right' (SG) – but by far the majority of respondents from both groups endorsed the aim in most cases by simply indicating their general or personal support for the idea.

There was widespread agreement that people wished to remain in familiar surroundings, especially if the alternative was entry to a hospital, an old persons' home or, as in the past, a workhouse: 'Well, they look after old people better. It was workhouse in my mother's day. They do keep you in your home – much better now' (M).

Living at home was perceived as a source of independence or autonomy: 'If you can do for yourself as much as possible and if you're in your right mind, there's nowt like independence' (M). 'You can please yourself. You can't never sit where you want in them homes' (M). 'Yes, I think they're better off in their own homes with their own furniture. They can do what they want in their own way' (SG). 'People in their right minds don't want to go into a home. It takes away their dignity' (M).

The threat which residential homes were felt to impose extended beyond freedom of action. For some older people identity was intimately bound up with where they lived, so that removing them from their homes was robbing them of their history: 'no one wants to give up a home they've struggled to keep together' (M).

A couple of older people claimed that, as a consequence of such losses, people in residential accommodation lacked motivation and became lazy. One woman drew on personal experience to illustrate this:

> It's better for people to stay in their own homes, if possible, in their own surroundings. I've seen it happen to so many people: my sister-in-law, they put her in a home. She could get around marvellous. Next time I saw her, she was in a wheelchair, next she couldn't move. It was awful. (M)

A handful of people felt that the feasibility of the community care aim was conditional on a person's physical or mental well-being. One argued, for example, that it was not the role of the domiciliary services to support severely mentally ill people at home:

> Well, if they're mentally ill or confused I don't think it's a good idea. They're thrown out onto the community and there's not a lot of help for them. If they're fit, I think it's what most of them want – to be independent – but you have to be careful. Old people are funny – they sometimes resent help. (SG)

> I presume they want to stop in their own home, but these people who're cabbages should be in homes. It's not home helps' job. It should be an intermediate service, nursing them if they're incontinent and that. (M)

Community care in practice

A similar pattern of responses was generated when we asked what the aim of the service meant to the older people themselves. Only three respondents, all of whom accepted the community care goal in principle, were equivocal about the idea for themselves. One was a blind man who lived in Manor with his doubly incontinent wife and who was persistently depressed and troubled by the fact that he could not see to do anything, including making up the fire. Two older women from Southey Green felt extremely vulnerable living on their own. One was scared to be alone at night while the other – a very frail woman who found activities such as dressing laborious and time-consuming – felt at risk without someone at hand to give assistance if she needed it. In the latter case, the person had previously spent some time in residential accommodation where she had been very happy and wanted to return there to live permanently. A fourth respondent, an older woman from Manor, had been living in her flat for only a few weeks when her husband died and consequently it held bad memories for her. Her ideal was to be able to return to her old address.

Of those older people who wished to remain in their homes, a number expressed the desire very strongly: 'I want to be taken out of here in a box and not before' (SG). 'I won't go in [a home]. I will have to be dragged there' (SG). Some people said they could not explain why, though a couple indicated the length of time they had lived at their addresses (42 and 50 years respectively). One went on to observe that she liked the area and knew people round about. A number referred to features of their surroundings which were important to them, such as their garden. Others spoke of not wishing to become a 'burden' or to 'put on anyone'. Indeed for most that ventured a direct opinion, remaining in their own home was an assurance of privacy and autonomy – 'I am my own boss' (SG) – which residential care threatened to undermine:

> That is important to me. I can get up and go to bed when I want, have meals when I want, do things in my own way, in my own time. In a home you have to do what they say, when they want it. It's overpowering. They make the decisions for you. Here you have the best of both worlds. (SG)

> I've worked too hard to get it together. My mother brought me up to be independent and I've no wish to rely on other people unless absolutely necessary. (M)

Older people were surrounded by their personal effects and were familiar with the layout of their homes. These features were a source of comfort and security, especially for individuals whose eyesight was failing. One couple stated that remaining in their own home was their major aim. In this case, the husband's eyesight was 'very bad' but as his wife explained, 'He knows where everything is and can get around without any bother' (SG). Similarly, a woman living in Manor said that although she got lonely, her home was her 'life', while another described being in her own home as '*the* most important thing' to her: 'I love my home and all I want is to stay here' (M). As long as they remained in their own homes, it seems that older people were motivated to remain active, to 'carry on going': 'Until I can't carry on I want to stay here. I need to keep doing whatever I can to keep me going' (M).

A number of older people qualified their agreement with the NSU aim by pointing out the importance of adequate levels of support. For some, help took the form of necessary aids and adaptations to their homes. With the exception of hospital check-ups, one wheelchair-bound woman in Manor never left her second floor flat as there was no lift to the ground floor. Another woman with severe arthritis in the joints of her hands had been waiting several months to have her taps fitted with special handles. During this time she had made do with strip washes only, preferring this arrangement to the services of a bath nurse. Likewise, a third woman living in Southey Green was unable to have a bath since she could no longer climb the stairs to reach the bathroom while a fourth older woman wanted a ramp from her door so she could get outside.

However, the qualification which was most commonly made in Manor was that, while wanting to live in their own homes, people still needed help of a domestic kind, chiefly to keep the house clean: 'I do want to stay in my own place, but must have help to keep it clean. It's so upsetting to see it go downhill' (M). 'We want to be having the best sort of life – retirement – and we can't do that if we can't be clean' (M). Nine older people (9 per cent) in Manor made such a qualification. This compares to only two (2 per cent) in Southey Green, though it is interesting to note the comments of one of these latter interviewees which were made in response to the news of impending changes to services in the area:

> I'm better off here. There's always someone about, they do my shopping and my cleaning. But I heard that the home helps are going to stop cleaning. My blind friend who I telephone told me. They don't clean any more for her. She's blind so she can't see the dirt but it's necessary isn't it? They tell us about having to be clean and then they stop the cleaning. People never used to get poisoned like they do now. We scrubbed things. You have to be clean, don't you? (SG)

Changes in services

It is significant that seven out of the nine individuals in Manor who stressed the importance of domestic help for older people living in their own homes had been receiving home help prior to the setting up of the NSU in Manor and all believed the service to have declined as a consequence. Overall, just under two-thirds of older people (61) had used the home help service before support workers were introduced. Of these, roughly one-fifth (13) felt there to have been no change to the quality of services, but over half (31) thought that there had been a change for the worse. Individual complaints included, among other things, poorer laundry facilities, the replacement of (some) staff and a less reliable service. But by far the biggest cause of dissatisfaction was a perceived reduction in the amount of help given with domestic chores – 'You just don't get the sort of help you need such as cleaning' (M) – which was noted by close to 50 per cent (28) of this group.

Taken in isolation, these responses may appear to suggest that services in Manor were in general being spread more thinly. However, other evidence challenged this assumption. Everyone was asked if, as individuals, they had ever had their help cut down or withdrawn. Only a fifth of all older people in Manor receiving a support worker said that their help had been cut down or withdrawn. Over two-fifths said that there had been no change in the amount of help received. In Southey Green, just under two-thirds of respondents reported no change while just over a quarter reported having services cut down or withdrawn. In sum, those people reporting individual reductions in service were, overall, in a minority and, across the two groups, more likely to live in Southey Green than in Manor.

All older people (seven in total) who reported having had services withdrawn were receiving help at the time of interview. Explanations were given by four people for the withdrawal of services. They included admission to hospital (one) and general cuts in services (one). Support for one older man was taken away due to a misunderstanding: a neighbour reported him for having two workers when one visitor was actually his daughter – 'It was soon cleared up though. I couldn't manage without help' (M). The fourth respondent explained:

> They said they'd seen me in the shops and that my daughter called so I couldn't have help. I was disgusted because it wasn't true. It's put a very heavy burden on my daughter. (M)

Of those older people in Southey Green that had experienced a (temporary) withdrawal of services (three in total and in each case temporary), two said the explanation was due to shortages in staff, while the third – like the respondent above – had been seen out shopping:

> I had to go and fetch a loaf and some dog food and a fish for my dinner and they saw me and reported it. [I was] very upset, but they came the week after. I'd had to go to the post office because they didn't come and I collapsed and my insurance man saw me and brought me home in his van . . . I can't do it myself, I was helpless. (SG)

These instances of service withdrawal were too few for any discernible patterns to emerge. However, there did seem to be differences between the two sample groups in their understandings of the reasons for reductions in services. In Manor, only two people out of a total of 14 who said their help had been cut down could not offer an explanation for the reduction. Three said help was reduced because they were judged as no longer being in need of it. One person felt 'down' because of this decision; she was struggling to cook her own dinners because she '[couldn't] eat the dinners they sent' (meals on wheels). The other two were happy to manage with less since help had been reduced due to improvements in their health. Two more people said that help was reduced 'on odd occasions' when workers were very busy or were on holiday. Neither minded, though one pointed out that while she could manage for the 'odd day', she needed to be able to rely on regular help with shopping.

The remaining older people explained reductions as being due to the changes in the service. This is not necessarily to suggest that people fully appreciated those changes, however. Only one person talked of a shift in emphasis of the service from 'home help to caring' and he rejected the idea as a bad one:

> They've put too much burden on home helps to make them care for

people. I think medical side should look after the people who're not capable of looking after themselves. Now it's care instead of help. (M)

Otherwise, changes were commonly perceived to be the result of a general cutting down of services and/or the fact that support workers were overstretched:

There's a lot less attention given to cleaning. When she came as a home help – it was Thursday for four hours – and she kept the place very clean, but that's what we need. She's got so many to see she has to fit them all in. They have to attend a lot of meetings, which is ridiculous and unnecessary. They have a bit of paperwork, too much. (M)

Most older people affected by it reported being given no individual explanation for the decrease in support and (along with the two respondents who could give no explanation at all) were disgruntled with the situation:

They stopped doing cleaning, they only came for shopping. I wanted cleaning doing so I paid for it . . . I was very displeased. I wondered if it was just me or everyone had been cut . . . It got very untidy and I don't like that. After three weeks I couldn't stand it and I got paid help. (M)

Some older people in Manor said that rather than having had their service reduced, the nature of support received had changed: 'I don't get any cleaning done now. It's been replaced with two weekend (bed) washes. It seems a funny idea to me' (M).

A handful of people, all of whom were receiving regular supervisory visits, thought the service had improved since the NSU had been in operation. Two indicated an increase in the frequency of calls yet they too felt that it had been at the cost of a reduction in (cleaning) help: 'They come more regularly even though they don't do as much each time' (M).

In Southey Green, only one older person said her help had been reduced because she no longer needed it; she had recovered from a broken hip but missed 'the company as well as the help' of the workers. Seven people said they had no explanation for individual reductions, while the remaining 11 people reported reductions as being due variously to cuts, short-staffing or an increase in the numbers of very dependent older people. In some cases the reason was communicated directly to the older person but, in others, it was not.

In general then, where the amount of support received had changed, older people in Manor were more likely than those in Southey Green to have been given explanations for this change. What is unclear is the extent to which service users understood the aims of the move to the new system. With the exception of two older people, all those in Manor who spoke negatively of reductions compared the new system unfavourably with the old. There was little evidence to suggest that these older people were aware of the 'rechannelling of

Table 4.7 Services received by older people

Service	Manor		Southey Green	
	Number of older people receiving different services	Percentage of older people receiving different services	Number of older people receiving different services	Percentage of older people receiving different services
Support worker/home carer/ warden	50	52.1	52	62
Day centre	5	5.2	–	–
Meals on wheels	1	1	–	–
Shopping trips	1	1	–	–
Support worker/home carers/ warden and day centre	24	25	17	20
Support worker/home carer/ warden and meals on wheels	10	10.5	6	7
Support worker/home carer/ warden, day centre and meals on wheels	5	5.2	9	11
Total	96	100	84	100
District nurse	8	8	10	12
Bath nurse	8	8	9	11
District nurse and bath nurse	2	2	8	10

help'; like Southey Green respondents, they largely saw changes in terms of shortages and cuts.

Services received

Table 4.7 shows the services received by older people across the two samples. It should be noted at this point that not all older people interviewed in Manor were visited by a support worker. The aim of the unit was to provide a range of support to meet a variety of needs. This being so, a number of older people were included in the group who used one of the other facilities available (appendix). Eighty-nine (93 per cent) of Manor respondents were visited by a support worker and five (5 per cent) attended a day centre. One person received meals on wheels while another one went on shopping trips only. Fifty (52 per cent) of the Manor sample used only the support worker service. Twenty-four (28 per cent) were visited by a support worker and attended a day centre. Ten (10 per cent) received meals on wheels as well as visits from a support worker. Five (5 per cent) older people used all three services – support worker, day centre and meals on wheels. In terms of the health team input, eight (8 per cent) were being visited by a district nurse, eight (8 per cent) by an auxiliary nurse and two (2 per cent) by both.

In contrast, since the control group of older people living in Southey Green were drawn from the files of the home care services (appendix), everyone in this sample received a home carer and/or warden. A number of people also used day centre and meals on wheels services but, given that these sources of support were not under the direct management of the home care organizers, none of the comparison group made use of meals on wheels or day centre services alone. Fifty-two (62 per cent) of older people used only the home carer/warden service. Seventeen (20 per cent) were visited by a home carer/warden and attended a day centre. Six (7 per cent) received meals on wheels as well as visits from a home carer/warden. Nine (11 per cent) people used all three services. Additionally 10 (12 per cent) of older people were visited by a district nurse, nine (11 per cent) by a bath nurse and eight (10 per cent) were visited by both.

Relationships with formal carers

In addition to recording the services they received we also asked older people about their attitudes towards service providers. Their responses revealed that the discontent expressed over the nature and quality of services outlined earlier did not necessarily extend to the frontline workers themselves.

Of the 89 people in Manor who were visited by a support worker, nearly four-fifths (70) said that they were visited regularly by one particular worker; that is, either the same support worker visited them on every occasion or, if different workers called, they were able to identify a key figure. Eleven people (12 per cent) said that they were visited by a number of different workers. Their responses may be explained by the amount of help they received. Nine of the 11 were given help on a daily basis, weekends included; three received regular supervisory visits, six were given 'full care', that is, daily help with getting up and going to bed, medication, drinks and snacks, as well as help with cooking, shopping and cleaning. One person received full care on weekdays while her son took over at the weekends. In these instances, it was simply not feasible for the same support worker to call every time. A key figure may not have stood out since, in a sense, all the support workers became key figures. At the other extreme, one older person used the services only once a fortnight when she was escorted to the local shops by a support worker. In this case, the older person would be accompanied by whoever was available.

Clearly not all older people being visited were able to comment on the nature of their relationship with their support worker(s). As one relative speaking of his mother pointed out: 'She gets confused and doesn't know who [the support worker] is, she doesn't know us sometimes' (M).

Two people said they did not know how to describe the relationship, one because she had not known the support worker for long enough. However, over two-fifths (39) of service users visited at home believed that they had a friendly relationship with the staff who assisted them. One older woman claimed that her support worker treated her as though she was her mother, and that she reciprocated: 'I bought her a gift for her birthday' (M). A large number detailed specific traits which they liked in members of staff. These commonly included a caring nature, kindliness and goodness: 'There's that sort of charisma between us when she comes and I'm always greeted with a kiss' (M). Some people thought it important that they could talk with the support worker: 'She is a friend, I can tell her owt and tells me owt' (M). Others felt close because they had known the support workers for a long time (not necessarily as users, but in two cases as 'neighbours') and felt they could trust them and/or because they were willing to do small favours for respondents.

Slightly fewer than a third of older people in Manor (28) described themselves as having a working relationship with staff, although a significant proportion qualified this description by pointing out personal qualities of workers: 'It's just a job to do and as far as I can see they come and do and they go, but always as helpful as they might be' (M).

Those who reported being visited by a number of different support workers were more likely to describe their relationship as a working one while users who were visited by the same worker or who could identify a key figure were more likely to say that they knew their worker(s) on a personal level. However, a significant number of this latter category did describe their relationship as of a working nature. Where comment was offered, the reason for this was typically attributed to the hectic schedule of support workers:

> She's not in the house long enough to be friendly, she's in a hurry. They've too much to do. She just picks up my book and shopping list and goes. (M)

Only three older people said they disliked support workers as individuals. One woman described her support worker as having a 'bad attitude'. On one occasion, for example, the member of staff in question had tossed a newspaper to her to read despite the fact that she was almost totally blind. Another respondent criticized her support worker for not washing up properly and for being sarcastic, while a third complained that the support worker could not distinguish between or cook different cuts of meat: 'She'd bring us chips every day from the chip shop if she could' (M). Other criticisms tended to be directed at support workers in general rather than towards individual helpers.

In comparison to Manor, an equal proportion of older people in Southey Green (four-fifths) who received home care said that they were visited by the same member(s) of staff on each occasion or by a key figure. A greater percentage (just under one-fifth) said they were visited by a number of different people. A quarter of these (four) received full care every day – weekends included – while one received regular weekday assistance with getting her breakfast. Seven had help only once a week – five with cleaning, two with shopping. However, three people from this group fell between the two extremes; all were given assistance twice a week with tasks that included shopping, cleaning and bathing. One user was too confused to be able to say how she was helped but she did say that different people called.

As with the sample in Manor, responses can be linked to the amount of help received by older people; the intensive input required by some inevitably necessitated assistance from more than one carer while those receiving a minimal amount of weekly support with just one task were often visited by whoever was available. The picture was more complex in Southey Green, however, due to the division of staff into home carers and home wardens. In general, this division made it more likely that people receiving full care would report having different helpers. It may also account for the response of those people having help only two days per week, since all three received help with a mixture of personal and practical tasks (the former provided by home wardens, the latter by home carers).

The division also appeared to have some influence on older people's relationships with staff. Only one service user actually distinguished between home carers and home wardens, while two other people said their relationship with the staff who visited shared both a working and a personal level. In general, the comments of older service users in Southey Green followed a similar pattern to those in Manor. A slightly greater percentage of older people (52 per cent) said they knew their helper(s) on a personal basis. A similar proportion of service recipients in Southey Green as in Manor (one-third) described theirs as a working relationship. For the majority of this group this was precisely because they saw staff simply as 'workers': 'It just is [a working relationship]. She comes and does and that's that' (SG). These older people commonly received help only once or twice a week – sometimes less – with practical tasks, predominantly cleaning, followed by shopping and the collection of pensions. There were some exceptions (six) where older people were visited more often but still said they shared a working relationship. However, in three cases only the minimum amount of help was given, respectively with the management of medication at night, supervisory checks and the preparation of breakfast. Comments made by the remaining three users appeared to suggest that they actively chose to keep their relationship at that level. For example: 'You try to keep it on a working relationship but you get to know them – it should be half and half' (SG).

In sum, Southey Green and Manor service users alike were more likely to see their relationship as of a working nature if visited by a number of different helpers and of a personal one if visited by the same or by a key figure. If there existed a difference between the two groups, it was in their attitudes to staff as 'workers'. In Southey Green, the division between home carers and home wardens and the two-tier system it affected (albeit unintentionally) tended to legitimate people's views of home carers as being simply 'workers' or 'cleaners' as opposed to 'carers'.

In Manor, such a division no longer existed, nor did support workers provide weekly blocks of cleaning help but, instead, gave priority to personal care. Nevertheless, a considerable proportion of older people (still) saw the relationship as being of a working nature. The lower priority given to practical activities such as cleaning led some less disabled older people to observe that staff were 'too busy' to get to know them as people. It should be pointed out, however, that this was a comment most commonly made by those who had formerly been users of the home help service and who had seen their help reduced as a result of the move to the support worker system. Grievances expressed at such reductions suggest that there were a number of service users in Manor unable to understand and/or unwilling to accept the aim of the new system. In other words, the residual affects of change on service users' attitudes to workers should not be overlooked.

Replacement of formal helpers

The comments of the two groups on their relationships with their formal carers were borne out by their responses to the question of what they would feel if their regular helpers were to be replaced. In Manor, just under a third of older people said they would not mind replacements as long as the work was done. Two-fifths disliked the idea or were, at best, resigned to the possibility. Changes in staff were felt to be disrupting, especially when older people and helpers got on well, or had known each other for a time and had established a routine (a fact which was stressed by a number of informal carers in proxy interviews). Only the three older people who disliked their support workers said they would not mind or would be pleased with a change.

In Southey Green, a greater proportion of older service users – just over half – said they would not mind replacements. Most qualified their response, for example by emphasizing the importance of seeing the job done, rather than the specific person doing it. Just over a quarter of Southey Green users said they would dislike or would resign themselves to the idea of the replacement of staff, offering the same explanations as those in Manor, that is, the length of time for which they had known their helper(s) and/or the subsequent disruption it would bring to their lives.

Tasks performed by formal helpers

Older people were asked about the things done for them in their own homes by statutory carers. In both areas people were helped with an average of two to three tasks, though assistance with as many as 12 activities was given to one older woman in Manor who lived alone and had severe dementia; they included rising and retiring, washing and dressing, heavy and light housework, the preparation of hot drinks and all meals, the management of medication, shopping, pension collection and the payment of bills.

Table 4.8 shows the number of older people assisted with individual tasks. As noted above, the vast majority of service users reported needing help with shopping which is reflected in the high level of support received across

Table 4.8 Tasks performed by support workers and home carers/wardens

Task	Manor		Southey Green	
	Number of support workers performing tasks	*Percentage of support workers performing tasks*	*Number of home carers/ wardens performing tasks*	*Percentage of home carers/ wardens performing tasks*
	(Number of respondents = 89)		*(Number of respondents = 84)*	
Shopping	48	50	40	48
Heavy housework	37	39	60	71
Dressing	22	23	7	8
Collecting pension	20	21	22	26
Washing hands and face	20	21	4	4
Cooking meal	18	19	23	27
Making hot drink/snack	17	18	27	32
Getting up	16	17	10	12
Going to bed	14	15	10	12
Supervision	14	15	13	14
Medication	12	13	10	12
Light housework	11	11	10	12
Laundry	4	4	5	6
Getting to/using toilet	2	2	3	4
Managing coal fire/fuel heater	2	2	2	2
Feeding self	1	1	–	–
Bathing	2	2	1	1
Finances/bills	2	2	3	4
Accompanying out/trips	2	2	1	1
Shaving	1	1	–	–
Rising from chair	–	–	2	2

both areas with this job. Cleaning also constituted a core activity but there were substantial differences between the two communities of service users in the extent and nature of support received with domestic tasks. Heavy housework (cleaning floors, washing windows, making beds) was the category of activities most commonly listed by respondents in Southey Green which by far eclipses the prominence of any other task performed in either area (see Chapter 3). In Manor, it was the second most commonly received category of help, but the figure represents only three-fifths the number of those receiving cleaning help in Southey Green. Moreover, there were also differences in the regularity with which such help was provided. Although not prompted, almost one-third (12) of those in Manor who were helped with heavy housework pointed out this was not on a regular basis, but only two people in Southey Green made a similar observation. In contrast, support workers and home care workers appeared to give assistance with light housework tasks (dusting, washing dishes, tidying beds) on an equal basis.

Patterns of support relating to the area of personal care seemed to bear out the finding of the various measures of disability and need for care outlined earlier in the chapter. They suggested the existence of more intense levels of need in Manor and, indeed, tasks associated with rising and retiring were listed far more commonly by older people from this area than by those in Southey Green. The differences were not great but became more accentuated when we looked at assistance provided with the washing of hands and face and with dressing: in Manor 22 per cent (20) of older people reported receiving help with the former and 25 per cent (22) with the latter compared to only 5 per cent (four) and 8 per cent(seven) respectively in Southey Green.

In addition to heavy housework, the activities more frequently received by older people in Southey Green compared to respondents in Manor were those associated with the preparation of food and drink. Considering the higher levels of need recorded for the Manor users, this finding seems surprising. The explanation may lie partly in the fact that, since the package of care organized by the NSU includes meals on wheels, referrals to this service are made more easily and routinely in Manor compared to Southey Green. Indeed, a greater proportion of older people in the Manor area were using this service. Likewise, more older people were also visiting day centres run by the unit where hot meals and snacks were provided.

It is important to note the information used to construct Table 4.8 which was obtained from the response to the question 'What does the support worker or home carer/warden do for you when s/he calls?' The item did not contain a checklist of possible activities. This raises several issues. First, as noted above, a number of respondents reported without prompting that cleaning help was given but not on a regular basis. This suggests that there may have been other instances where help was provided 'when judged necessary' by support workers but which – because of irregularity or infrequency of provision – was not mentioned by older people. Similarly, supervisory checks may not have been included by older people in both areas because they are not seen as a 'thing done' in the same way that a task such as cleaning is. On the other hand, certain activities may not have been separately listed but subsumed with others: for example, some service users may have implicitly understood help with getting up to include assistance with the washing of their hands and face. Shopping and pension collection were often linked together while other people spoke of housework in general and did not distinguish between 'heavy' and 'light' tasks. In all cases, the outcome is the same: namely, the underrecording of activities. That there were discrepancies in tasks listed by older people and the help they received from workers showed up where checks were made between responses to different items on the questionnaire.

Service users' prioritization of assistance

Having detailed the help which they received, older people were asked to say what they considered to be the most important thing done for them by their support worker/home carer/warden. While nearly three-quarters of older people in Manor who gave an answer referred to only one task, some mentioned two and even three activities. Shopping headed the list of essential support nominated in 28 per cent (25) cases: 'If they didn't shop I might as well pack up my bags and go' (M). Nine per cent (eight) included the fetching of their pension with this task. Three per cent (three) mentioned it separately. Nineteen per cent (17) of users listed heavy housework: 'The windows is the best thing, we can't stretch, and then the vaccing. It is very heavy and I can't carry it' (M).

Two per cent (two) mentioned light housework. Ten per cent of older people (nine) felt that having a hot meal prepared for them was important and 8 per cent (seven) appreciated the supervisory visits: '[We] talk things over, you worry about things, letters, bills and things' (M).

Other activities listed as important included assistance with washing (five), getting a hot drink/snack (three), help with getting up (two), light housework (two), laundry (two), medication (one), getting to the toilet, and, in one case, chatting. Only two older people replied negatively.

Service users in Southey Green also listed an average of only one activity, though two people named as many as five while two more failed to single out any one task, stressing instead that all activities carried out by their home carers/wardens were of equal importance.

The task most frequently nominated in Southey Green as being of greatest importance was heavy housework, which was so designated by as many as 48 per cent (35) of older people. Shopping was the next most common, chosen by 19 per cent (16) of respondents, closely followed by the cooking of a hot meal, selected by 18 per cent (15). Two per cent (two) interviewees linked shopping and the collection of their pension together. Five per cent (four) felt help with medication to be essential, while another 5 per cent chose supervisory calls. Light housework, in contrast to heavy, was listed by only 4 per cent of people (three). Two per cent (two) nominated help with getting up, 2 per cent more with making a hot drink or snack.

Other individually named activities included getting to and using the toilet, going to bed, washing, dressing, the payment of bills and chatting. For one couple, the most important element of support provided by the home carer was given at an informal level. The worker in question had agreed to give her telephone number to the couple. They called her at least once a day for reassurance which included checking the date of her next visit. Another older person simply said that her carers were 'good to [her]' (SG).

In sum, heavy housework and shopping were ranked by older service users in both communities as being the most important tasks carried out for them by their formal carers. In light of the discontent expressed by a number of

Manor users regarding reductions in the amount of cleaning help provided it is perhaps surprising to find that substantially more people in Southey Green rated this activity as being of prime importance. However, it is probable that the reversal of the relative positions of shopping and cleaning was a reflection of service priorities in the respective areas. That is, if only two-thirds the number of people in Manor than in Southey Green were receiving heavy cleaning assistance then considerably fewer were likely to nominate it as the most important task performed (and vice versa in respect of help with shopping).

Need for additional assistance

Finally, in this section, older people who were receiving help were asked if there were things they wanted doing that their formal carer(s) did not do. Over two-fifths of users in Manor said that they desired no support with additional tasks (seven proxies indicated likewise) compared to over half the group in Southey Green. In general, where people expressed a desire for 'additional' assistance it was with jobs traditionally provided by the respective services (and often already received by the user). Typically, requests were for help with one activity only and by far the most commonly listed activity was heavy cleaning. In both areas, over a quarter of older people said they would like workers to do more housework: 'spring-cleaning' chores were mentioned by several: 'Like paintwork/doors washing down once a year. Clean windows' (M). 'Cleaning the oven, my help won't do that' (M).

Four older people in total (one in Manor, three in Southey Green) expressed a desire for additional help without specifying the exact nature of that help; their comments suggested that what they wanted was extra time rather than tasks: 'I would just like them a bit longer' (SG).

Three people in Manor and one in Southey Green desired additional help with laundry, while two each in Manor wanted someone to chat to, to be taken out (on trips) and to be helped to bath. Only one older person from each community wanted extra shopping assistance. All other tasks – light housework, preparing a hot drink/snack, cooking a hot meal, supervision, dealing with finance/bills – were individually nominated. Only two people – both from Southey Green – desired assistance with tasks not already provided by the respective support worker and home carer services; one wanted help with decorating, the other with gardening.

The consistency of desire for additional cleaning help across the two groups lays to rest the possibility suggested by the findings of the preceding section that less importance is attached to heavy cleaning by older people in Manor. The degree of desire illustrates the core role that these duties are (still) seen to play.

Conclusion

In this, the first half of our discussion of the service innovation from the perspective of older people, the two geographical groups of service users have been seen to share broadly similar socio-demographic characteristics. The two main exceptions were the higher levels of disability and need for services in Manor compared to Southey Green.

As to users' views of the services, across both groups there was widespread endorsement of the basic community care aim of the services – to support people in their own homes for as long as they want to stay there – but not at the expense of cleaning help. Users received help with a variety of tasks, from shopping to shaving, and were generally very satisfied with individual workers. The ranking of tasks according to their importance tended to reflect existing differences in the priorities and organization of the two services so that shopping was chosen as the most important task by a majority in Manor in contrast to cleaning in Southey Green. However, an equal – and significant – proportion of people from both communities said they would like more assistance with heavy cleaning tasks.

Service users in Manor were no more likely to talk of reductions in support than were older people in Southey Green. Of the former, those whose help had been reduced were conscious of the fact that changes had been made to the service. Nevertheless, like their counterparts, many used the language of 'cuts' to explain reductions and they expressed frustration at the fact that support workers were 'too busy' to provide (cleaning) assistance. Such views suggest that older people were not necessarily fully aware or appreciative of the shift in emphasis of the service from cleaning to caring, which needed to be explained more carefully to users.

On the other hand, evidence of reductions in the amount of cleaning given may have been easier to perceive than the positive input of help in the form of supervisory checks, for example. The views of the carers of older people living in Manor lend weight to this argument (Chapter 6). Before examining the carers' perspective however we turn to the second part of the analysis of the impact of services on older people.

5

Older people: impact of services

The crucial question with regard to a service innovation is the extent to which it achieves its stated aims. In the case of the NSUs this is primarily a matter of their impact on older people and, particularly, the outcome in terms of a sustained interdependent presence in the community. Thus this second chapter on older people focuses on a longitudinal comparison of the two groups of older people to assess the impact of services over time, and reports the main results of a special analysis of outcomes based on a pair-wise sample matching exercise. Then we discuss the fluctuations in the need for care caused, for example, by short term crises and alterations in the levels of services. Finally we assess the extent to which the two forms of service succeeded in meeting the care needs of older users. We start with the impact of 12 months on the two samples of older people.

One year older

The longitudinal element of the evaluation was crucial to understanding the impact of the NSU services on older people. Ideally an extended period of, say, three years would have provided a firm scientific base on which to draw conclusions concerning effectiveness. Though, in any similar research among very elderly people, such an aspiration would have to be tempered by the need to limit sample attrition. Moreover, as usual in social research, we were constrained by resources and had to cut our methodology to fit the available budget. The minimum period between interviews was set at 12 months and the project was sufficiently well funded to allow us to achieve this goal. Thus, as detailed in the appendix, follow-up interviews were conducted with older people (as well as their carers – see Chapter 6) 12 to 16 months after the first round.

Predictably there was some loss of sample numbers between interviews. The high average age of the 96 people originally interviewed in Manor meant that 14 (15 per cent) had died before follow-up interviews were attempted. Declining health also meant that one older person was unable to be reinterviewed because she felt too ill to take part, and two additional older people were in hospital waiting for a place in residential care. A move into residential care accounted for three of those older people unable to be reinterviewed. It is actually surprising that so *few* older people were unable to be reinterviewed for reasons of ill-health or entry into hospital or residential care. A further three older people had moved out of the service area and could not be traced.

Of the 73 older people remaining available for reinterview only five refused to speak to us for a second time, and a further one was unable to be contacted. Sixty-seven older people were finally reinterviewed, amounting to 70 per cent of the original sample. Fifty-six of these older people were interviewed face to face, the remaining 11 interviews being conducted by proxy.

The number of older people available for reinterview was similarly depleted in Southey Green. Twelve of the 84 older people originally inter-viewed had subsequently died, and a further three were in hospital at the time that follow-up interviews were attempted. Most noticeably in comparison to the Manor sample, 12 (13 per cent) of those interviewed on the previous occasion had now entered residential care. One older person had moved out of the service area and could not be traced. Of the 56 people still available to participate seven refused to be reinterviewed and one could not be contacted. Forty-seven older people were successfully reinterviewed in Southey Green, representing 56 per cent of those 84 people who had agreed to take part a year earlier. Of these, 44 were interviewed face to face and the remaining three interviews were conducted with a proxy.

The lower follow-up rate in Southey Green (56 per cent) compared with Manor (70 per cent) is largely accounted for by the greater number of people entering residential care from the former area. Considering the inevitable difficulties in reinterviewing a sample of older people after one year the follow-up rates were very satisfactory. Indeed when we look at the response rates for those older people actually available for reinterview we find that 92 per cent of those in Manor and 84 per cent of those in Southey Green were successfully followed up.

Care needs and outcomes after one year

Important influences on successful maintenance of life in the community are the older person's levels of disability and care needs. The ability of domiciliary services to meet these needs provides the acid test of the effectiveness of the NSU innovation. With this in mind we looked at the outcomes after one year for older people with varying degrees of need in the two communities.

It is clear that, in both communities, those with the lowest levels of need were the most likely to have remained in their own or relatives' homes after one year. Those older people with intermediate or short interval needs were slightly less likely, in Manor, to remain in the community but in Southey Green the difference in outcomes was much larger. In both groups those with critical interval needs were the least likely to still be living in the community after one year but, again, the difference between the two areas was large (though the sample numbers are small).

Sample matching

The question of how far this difference in outcome between older service users in Manor and Southey Green was a product of the services themselves or a result of other factors was the most important and the most difficult one to answer. We knew that the two geographical areas in Sheffield were very similar in terms of social class and housing, as well as in the numbers of older people and levels of need for social care (appendix).

To evaluate the effectiveness of the NSU compared with the traditional service in maintaining older people in their own homes it was also important to ensure that the two groups of people chosen for inclusion in the study were as similar as possible across a range of health and social factors. Any differences in the circumstances of the two groups when reinterviewed would then be more likely to be the result of the type and style of service offered in the respective communities.

We enhanced comparability by matching groups of older people from Manor and Southey Green, though it must be acknowledged that we were able only to match on the basis of a limited number of variables, as detailed in the appendix. Many factors may affect the ability of an older person to live independently in the community. These include the availability and extent of informal care, income and social support. Ideally we would have liked to have included such factors in the matching procedure. The limited number of older people available to participate in the research meant that it was impossible to use a more rigorous matching procedure without the number of pairs declining into single figures. (A comparison of the two matched groups on a range of health and social factors is presented in the appendix.)

Community versus residential care

What was the distribution of outcomes after one year between the matched sample groups? Table 5.2 shows the pattern across the three main outcomes, achieved by amalgamating the categories used in Table 5.1. As can be seen from the table the most striking difference was in the proportions entering

Table 5.1 Care needs and outcomes after one year

		Need for care					
		Long/moderate interval		Short interval		Critical interval	
		N	%	N	%	N	%
Community	M	43	90	25	80.5	9	53
	SG	38	83	17	57	2	25
Hospital	M	–	–	1	3	1	6
	SG	2	4	1	3	–	–
Residential care	M	1	2	–	–	2	12
	SG	1	2	7	23	4	50
Deceased	M	4	8	5	16.5	5	29
	SG	5	11	5	17	2	25
Total	M	48	100	31	100	17	100
	SG	46	100	30	100	8	100

Note:
M = Manor
SG = Southey Green

Table 5.2 Location after one year: Matched pair sample

	Manor		Southey Green	
	N	%	N	%
Community	44	83	37	70
Residential care/Hospital	2	4	8	15
Deceased	7	13	8	15
Total	53	100	53	100

residential care or hospital, which suggests that the NSU was more successful than the more traditional home care service in preventing admissions to homes in particular.

It was critical to examine how the intensity of need affects the ability of older people to remain in their own homes. Two questions had to be addressed. Did the NSU assist those older people with the greatest needs to survive in the community for longer than their counterparts receiving traditional services? Were those most frail and confused older people still less likely to remain living in the community than older people with less intensive needs, irrespective of the style of service delivery? When we compared what happened to older people with different needs across the two communities the results represented an endorsement of the NSU, but by no means an unconditional one.

Older people were grouped according to whether they had minimal requirements for help (moderate/long interval needs) or if they made more intensive demands on services (short/critical interval needs). The most important result of the comparison was that older people from Manor were more likely to remain living in their own home and less prone to institutionalization than their counterparts in Southey Green. This trend was particularly striking among those older people with the greatest need for support. Not only did those people from Manor with the most intensive needs have a much greater chance of continuing to live in the community than their counterparts in Southey Green, their chances of remaining in the community also approached those of older people in Manor with only minimal needs.

In Manor 89 per cent of those older people with only moderate or long interval needs were still living in the community after one year (the remaining 11 per cent had died). Among those with the most intensive need for care, 11 per cent had entered residential care but 72 per cent were still living in ordinary housing (17 per cent had died). In Southey Green the proportion of those with moderate care needs remaining in the community (83 per cent) was similar to that in Manor. A further 6 per cent had moved into a residential setting and 11 per cent had died. However, among those with the greatest need for care, only just over two-fifths (44 per cent) were still living in the community after one year, while 33 per cent had entered residential care and 22 per cent had died. Thus the differences in service outcomes discovered for the whole sample (Table 5.1) were repeated among the matched samples. In the Manor sample the differences between those with moderate and those with intensive care needs, in terms of their chances of remaining in the community, were not statistically significant, but in the case of Southey Green this difference was significant.

Informal care and ageing in place

The extent and nature of informal support is a critical factor in enabling an older person to remain living in the community for as long as possible. The contribution of informal carers may make up for deficits in the provision of formal services and, in practice, exaggerate the latter's actual contribution to the maintenance of older people in the community. The intention of the Manor NSU was to assist older people to live in their own homes for as long as possible, but also to support informal carers, the objective being to implement the idea of care *in* the community, rather than simply care *by* the community (Bayley 1973; Walker 1982, 1993a). Given this, we decided to compare the survival rates of those people receiving intensive informal care with those receiving informal help on a less frequent basis in order to get a better idea of the relative contribution of the NSU to supporting people at home.

Older people were classed as receiving minimal or intensive informal

Table 5.3 Informal care and outcomes after one year: Matched pair sample

		Receipt of informal care			
		None/long/moderate		Short/critical	
		N	%	N	%
Community	M	37	84	7	78
	SG	36	78	1	14
Residential care/Hospital	M	1	2	1	11
	SG	6	13	2	29
Deceased	M	6	14	1	11
	SG	4	9	4	57
Total	M	44	100	9	100
	SG	46	100	7	100

Note:
M = Manor
SG = Southey Green

support, depending on the intervals – long to moderate, and short to critical respectively – at which such help was provided. Help included support from all informal sources, and not just that of the main carer, though the category of minimal informal care included a number of older people receiving no informal help. Table 5.3 shows how levels of informal care affected the likelihood of older people remaining in their own homes.

Because of the small numbers caution must be exercised in interpreting the results of the analysis shown in Table 5.3 but there are some inferences that can be made. Among older people in Manor the presence of either intensive or minimal informal support appeared to make very little difference to whether an individual survived in the community or entered residential care. The situation in Southey Green, however, was noticeably different; a very much smaller proportion of those receiving intensive informal care were able to remain in the community for an extended period. Thus there is some, albeit tentative, suggestion that the NSU was better able to support *both* older people and their informal helpers than the home care services.

Entering residential care: case studies

We have seen that older people in Manor receiving services from the NSU were less likely to enter permanent hospital or residential care and were more likely to remain in their own homes. It was essential, nonetheless, to look at the circumstances under which independent living in the community is no longer possible. Some brief biographies are presented below to illustrate the conditions under which living at home may no longer be possible. These are drawn from the interviews with the five people who entered hospital or residential care from the total sample of 96 in Manor.

Mrs Kingman

Mrs Kingman (aged 66) suffered from Alzheimer's disease and showed definite signs of confusion when first interviewed. She also reported the presence of arthritis, heart trouble, a chest condition, stomach problems and headaches. She had recently fallen and broken her wrist, although her mobility was good and she could get around unassisted. She had moved into her present flat two years ago with her husband, but he had died shortly afterwards of cancer. These events had obviously affected her attitude towards her life in the new flat. Her son remarked: 'She associated moving and his death, blames it on moving, so she's not got pleasant memories here.'

Her son, Phillip aged 34, was the family member providing her with most care. Her daughter had moved out of the Sheffield area some time ago and only visited a few times each year. Phillip visited his mother twice a week for about an hour on each occasion. This was becoming increasingly difficult because of his other family commitments (he had a six month old son) and his full-time job as a computer project leader: 'I'm under a lot of pressure – being torn between responsibilities earning a living, looking after family, caring for mother, and guilt.' His wife had expressed worry about both his emotional and physical health during the interview.

The main practical assistance with which Phillip provided his mother was shopping. The twice-weekly visits to her flat were to check on her well-being and to chat. A neighbour popped in four times a day to keep an eye on Mrs Kingman and to assist with her medication. Mrs Kingman also attended a day centre for Alzheimer's sufferers twice a week which Phillip claimed helped 'to keep her occupied'. Although she was fully mobile, this was the only time that she was able to get out because of her confused condition.

Originally the support workers had called once a day at lunch-times to help Mrs Kingman with her medication. Following her fall, she had also been given assistance with getting up and going to bed and dressing. Her increased confusion and concomitant inability to look after herself led to support workers popping in more regularly – three times a day. However, her son explained, 'She was losing keys, leaving the cooker on. . . She was dangerous to herself and everyone else.' Mrs Kingman had gone into respite care for a while and Phillip began to view permanent residential care as inevitable. He thought that the services were doing what they could but his mother really needed constant supervision: 'they came to realize I couldn't cope'.

Phillip met with the team leader and social worker and they agreed to try and find Mrs Kingman a place in permanent residential care, despite her ambivalence. Mrs Kingman had said when interviewed, 'I don't want to go into a home, I've got my family', though Phillip explained that she sometimes felt that she'd be better in a home because she was lonely in the flat.

At the time of the second interview, Mrs Kingman had moved into residential care and her son was visiting her once a week. The move, which was permanent, had not solved all of Phillip's problems but rather had created different tensions:

> She's not happy with life generally and when you leave she gets upset. She doesn't relate well to the people there. I get upset when I go to see her there.

A new dilemma now presented itself: 'I find it difficult to visit because it's traumatic but if I have to miss going I feel guilty.'

In sum, the main reasons for Mrs Kingman's entry into residential care were Alzheimer's disease and her need for constant supervision, coupled with the inability of her informal carer to cope with these demands. The severity of her confusion meant a need for constant supervision which neither formal nor informal sources of care could satisfy.

Mr Mansfield

Mr Mansfield (aged 86) had suffered a severe stroke which had left him unable to talk or look after any of his own needs without assistance. He was doubly incontinent, had a chest condition and required constant care from his wife. His degree of disability entitled him to receive attendance allowance.

A support worker called twice a day to assist Mr Mansfield with getting up and going to bed, dressing and washing. Mrs Mansfield did not feel confident about managing these activities alone. Indeed, her own health problems restricted Mrs Mansfield's ability to perform heavier domestic duties, and she felt help with washing the linen soiled as a result of Mr Mansfield's incontinence to be inadequate. None of Mr and Mrs Mansfields' four children contributed to the day to day care of their father, despite the fact that, at the time of the interview, Mrs Mansfield helped to look after her grandchildren. She had suggested to her children that they care for their father in their own homes for a while, but this proposal had never been taken up.

Mrs Mansfield's caring responsibilities obviously imposed a great strain on her. Given the chance, she would have liked a night out though by 8.30 in the evening she was usually exhausted, especially since she did not sleep well. Mrs Mansfield seemed to accept that her husband would have to go into residential care at some point, but felt that she would be worn out before this was 'allowed' to happen. She expressed the view at one point that the whole family would be better off if her husband were no longer alive. Mr Mansfield did eventually move into residential care and died shortly afterwards. (Mrs Mansfield was not interviewed for a second time in her bereaved status.)

It was clear that Mr Mansfield's extreme physical dependency made intensive demands on Mrs Mansfield who found it very difficult to cope with the stress of providing constant care, especially when her contribution to the care of other family members was not reciprocated.

Mrs Wilkinson

Mrs Wilkinson (aged 89) was unable to be interviewed personally because of her severe confusion caused by Alzheimer's disease. It was this condition rather than physical infirmity which led her to require intensive support. Her confusion was coupled with a restlessness which meant that she never sat still and she wandered without knowing where she was. Mrs Wilkinson had been widowed for 17 years and continued to live alone in her own house where, according to her proxy, she was happy to stay: 'She'd be very upset if she thought she'd have to leave home. She worries that she might have to be put away.'

The bulk of care was given to Mrs Wilkinson by her two nieces, one of whom visited three or four times a week, the other twice a week. Between them they cooked for their aunt, saw to her housework, and assisted her with personal care such as bathing. They also helped with tasks outside the home including shopping and paying bills. Mrs Wilkinson had one sister who was still alive but they did not see each other.

Support workers called on Mrs Wilkinson twice a day. They helped to get her up in the morning, prepared her breakfast and, when necessary, her lunch, and made sandwiches for her to eat later in the day. They also assisted Mrs Wilkinson with her medication and helped her to wash and change if she were incontinent. The niece providing the majority of care described herself as grateful for the regular visits by the support workers: 'They visit her every day and you know there is someone popping in.' She claimed that her aunt got on well with her regular support worker, though she sometimes refused to let the relief workers into her house. Mrs Wilkinson was also visited by a social worker on a regular basis and attended a day centre once a week, which her niece judged to be particularly important as Mrs Wilkinson's social contacts were very limited.

Mrs Wilkinson eventually entered hospital for assessment of her condition and subsequently moved into permanent residential care, where she died soon after. In this case also, it was the need for constant supervision because of severe confusion which ultimately necessitated a move into residential care. The ability of the NSU to provide adequate supervision in this context must therefore be called into question. Pop-in visits offered some degree of cover for older people at risk and helped to mitigate the anxiety of carers, but they could not take the place of the constant presence of another person.

Short term crises

Although the majority of older people were still living in their own homes after one year this does not tell the whole story about their capacity to live independently. Illness, accidents or shortfalls in care may all temporarily affect the older person's capacity to look after themselves. If the older person's needs are very severe it may necessitate moving out of their own home for a short time into hospital, residential care or to stay with friends or relatives. The frequency and length of such moves out of the community may give some insight into the capacity of domiciliary services to respond to such crises in older people's lives and also to rehabilitate the person after a spell in hospital.

Of the 67 older people reinterviewed in Manor 33 per cent (22 people) reported that they had stayed in hospital for some period of time since we last spoke to them. Among the over 75s nationally it has been reported that 20 per cent of men and 16 per cent of women had stayed in hospital as an in-patient during the previous year (Victor 1991). Bearing in mind the high levels of need among our sample of older people this high rate of hospital admissions would be expected (and we have to remember that these admissions relate only to those older people continuing to live in their own homes). A similarly high proportion (30 per cent) of older people in Southey Green had been admitted to hospital. Those 22 people having stayed in hospital had experienced 33 admissions between them. Fifteen people had experienced only one ad-mission, four people had been admitted twice, two people three times, and a single individual had been into hospital on four occasions.

The length of stay was very variable, ranging from a single night for a bad cut on the leg after a fall, to over three months for a skin graft operation. The majority of admissions (19) were for between one and three weeks, although a significant number (seven) had been for more than a month. The reasons given by the older people for admission into hospital were very diverse. No single condition predominated and those listed included pneumonia, cataract removal, diabetes, urinal infection, anaemia and a bypass operation. Strokes were the most frequently cited reason for hospital admission, accounting for six of the 33 incidents reported.

Admission to hospital could follow traumatic experiences. As one woman aged 80 recounted:

> I collapsed on the floor [fell out of my wheelchair]. Blacked out while watching TV. I managed to crawl to the phone to dial 999. I was taken to the Northern General – my blood sugar was too high. I stayed in for just over a fortnight [17 to 18 days] while they controlled the sugar. The district nurse is now calling daily to give me an insulin injection every morning.

Another woman required an urgent artery bypass operation. Her left foot felt cold and dead and there was a danger that it might eventually require amputating. Other people experienced a series of admissions in rapid succession – one woman had been hospitalized on three occasions in the previous year, each time following a stroke. The reasons for readmission could also be the result of completely separate illnesses – one man, discharged following a heart valve operation, was readmitted soon after when he started passing diarrhoea and blood.

Support workers were directly involved with admissions to hospital on two occasions. One incident involved a man who had told his support worker that he had experienced a 'turn' on Saturday night. The support worker had contacted the doctor and the man concerned was subsequently admitted to hospital for two weeks. On the other occasion a woman complained that she was just too poorly and the support worker arranged for her to be admitted into hospital.

Six people had stayed for a short time in residential care in the year since we last spoke to them. Five of these had received respite care, either to give the older person themselves or their carer a break from living at home. Of these, four older people received such care on a regular basis, three reporting staying in for two weeks out of four and the remaining one for two weeks out of six. The fifth had been into respite care on two isolated occasions to give her informal carer a rest. The remaining person reporting staying in residential care had done so only for a day just to see what it was like, reaching very negative conclusions:

> I couldn't wait to come home. I saw an old neighbour of mine who's been there three years and she didn't remember me. It put me right off.

No one in Southey Green reported regular respite care, though three people had stayed in a residential home once in the last 12 months.

Older people in Manor, if they were unable to look after themselves, rarely stayed with friends or relatives for a period of time. Only two older people reported having done this in the previous year. The first case was a woman who, following the death of her son, had stayed with her daughter-in-law for a while. The other instance was of a woman who went into hospital for a cataract removal and stayed with her daughter-in-law for three days after being discharged. She was unable to return to her own flat as the daughter who normally cared for her was ill herself, and so unable to visit on a regular basis. Only two people in Southey Green reported staying with friends or relatives for the provision of care.

It was equally rare for friends or relatives to go and stay with an older person unable to look after themselves. This had happened in the case of only three older people in Manor and none in Southey Green. One woman, who had been admitted to hospital four times during the previous year, explained that her son had stayed with her on odd occasions when she had not been well. The two daughters of another woman had taken it in turns to stay with her at night when she was experiencing hallucinations and had taken to wandering outside. The medication their mother was prescribed greatly reduced the need for these supervisory visits. In the third case, a husband's back trouble meant that he was unable to care for his wife temporarily. Their son and daughter-in-law stayed with them for six weeks until the husband was able to resume his caring role.

Service responses to changes in need

Levels of need are not constant. Many of those older people with critical interval needs at the time of the first interview subsequently died or moved into residential care. A significant number of older people remaining in the community (18 per cent in Manor and 6 per cent in Southey Green) reported decreases in their levels of need, either because they had been only temporarily incapacitated at the time of the first interview or a change in circumstances, like a move into a bungalow or ground floor flat, meant a renewal of their ability to perform certain activities of daily living like getting to the toilet or going to bed. Both of these trends are useful in emphasizing that old age is not a static condition but a fluctuating status. It also demonstrates that need and disability can be imposed by external circumstances, such as access to buildings and public places, as well as being a permanent attribute of an individual because of injury, accident or disease.

Having made these qualifications, the fact is that the majority of those experiencing changes in the need for care (just over a quarter in both areas) had seen an increase in their needs. Most of these increases were from long interval to short interval needs and mainly associated with the older person's declining ability to prepare and cook meals.

Mrs Althorpe

Perhaps the most striking example of an increase in the need for help was Mrs Althorpe who had entered hospital on three separate occasions since first being interviewed, the total stay amounting to eleven and a half weeks. On the first occasion, Mrs Althorpe had suffered a heart attack and was hospitalized for two and a half weeks. This was followed by a six week admission after a stroke and a further three weeks when her condition had generally deteriorated. Previously, Mrs Althorpe had required help with cooking her meals, carrying out housework and laundry, and doing her shopping. Following her period of prolonged ill-health her needs were considerably more intensive. She was now chair-bound, as well as completely deaf and very confused. Out of 11 activities of daily living she was only able to feed herself without assistance.

Before the deterioration in Mrs Althorpe's health, a support worker had called every day to prepare dinner for her. Now she was visited twice daily by workers who helped her to get in and out of bed, assisted her to wash and dress, prepared her breakfast and a snack in the afternoon, as well as supervising her medicine. Mrs Althorpe's two daughters took it in turns to visit her every day to prepare lunch and assist with household chores like cleaning and washing, as well as collecting shopping and prescriptions. Although one of the daughters said that they coped between them she recognized the important role of the support worker in enabling their mother to remain in her own home:

> If they were to ever stop getting her up and putting her to bed I dread to think what would happen. It's essential. It wouldn't be humanly possible to go there twice a day, seven days a week.

How well did the services respond to such increases in need? Twelve people from Manor reported increases in the amount of help that they received from support workers compared to a year earlier. This included one person effectively classed as receiving services for the first time, and another person whose help had been reintroduced after being temporarily stopped.

Mrs Treacher

Mrs Treacher had recently been bereaved. She was now living alone and was reliant on the use of a walking frame to get about the flat. Her sister-in-law visited twice daily and described Mrs Treacher as getting very lonely and frightened on her own. She claimed that, although Mr Treacher had been the ostensible recipient of support worker visits, Mrs Treacher herself required practical help on a daily basis.

Indeed, since the death of her husband, support workers had called twice a day to help Mrs Treacher to get out of bed in the morning and dress and prepare her breakfast, and to assist her to get into bed in the evening. Her sister-in-law continued to clean the flat and do the laundry as before, for which she received Mrs Treacher's attendance allowance. A neighbour popped in daily and fetched her shopping for her once a week. Mrs Treacher was very determined to stay in her own home as long as she could, and had applied for a bungalow so that she would be able to get around more outdoors.

Eight users in Manor reporting increases in the level of services said that this was in response to ill health or disability. The circumstances were varied and included four cases of temporary illness or disability comprising a badly cut leg, a recent fall, an unspecified hospital discharge, and influenza, and four cases of a more chronic nature involving increasing confusion, worsening eyesight, declining mobility and terminal illness. Half of the eight cases were given extra help in the form of check-up visits to ensure that the older person was all right. The remaining half received assistance of a more directly practical nature. The type of extra help provided did not follow any obvious pattern, but seemed to vary according to the needs and circumstances of each individual.

Mr Jenkins

In one instance, extra help was provided to an older person who was terminally ill. Previously Mr Jenkins had been visited twice a week by a support worker, who carried out housework and occasional laundry. Three weeks before he eventually moved in with his son and daughter-in-law, supervisory checks were provided twice a day. This was to ease the worry that Mr Jenkins' daughter-in-law experienced at leaving him on his own. The support workers had her telephone number in case there were any problems.

Ten older users in Manor indicated that the amount of help that they received from support workers had been reduced since we spoke to them a year previously. Included in these were three people whose help had been completely withdrawn and one woman who had cancelled the service herself. None of those people whose service had been withdrawn were able to provide a reason. The woman who cancelled the service herself had been told that the support workers would, from that point onwards, only be able to do her shopping, not her cleaning as they had done in the past. Her neighbour now fetched her shopping and she paid for a private cleaner. Of the remaining six people whose service had been reduced, all but one said that this had primarily involved a reduction in the amount of cleaning performed. The remaining older person no longer received assistance with shopping. Most people were unhappy about the reduction in their services, although some showed magnanimity: 'Well, we're not too bad, we can manage. There's many worse off than us.'

In Southey Green, only one older person reported an increase in the level of services provided since the last interview. This woman had suffered a heart attack and the home care input had been boosted from two to seven days. The home care service had been withdrawn completely from one person, with no explanation. An additional three service users in Southey Green reported reductions in the level of the service provided.

Meeting needs

The final part of this assessment of the impact of services from the perspective of older people consists of an analysis of the extent to which services succeeded in meeting the different care needs of this group. This is not to suggest that the provision of formal services will always coincide with an older person's need for help. Need will obviously be a major influence on the allocation of services, but will be mediated by the availability of informal sources of help and the relative severity of a user's disability compared with other applicants (James and Saunders 1988) as well as the supply of formal care. At the same time, it is rare for the ideal and actual levels of service provision to equal each other. One study in the late 1970s reported that levels of provision may be as much as 25 per cent below actual levels of need (Howell and Boldy 1977). In the mid-1980s the term 'care gap' was coined to describe the growing distance between the need for home care on the part of older people and the supply of formal care services (Walker 1985a). In a previous Sheffield-based study a significant care gap was found within the informal sector, with, for example, one in six older people in substantial need of care not receiving any help (Qureshi and Walker 1989: 261). Therefore we expected to find that some older people were not receiving all of the help that they required, despite receiving assistance from a variety of sources. The extent and size of this care gap is an important indicator of the degree to which older people are being successfully maintained in their own homes.

Older people participating in the study often found it difficult to assess how much time each help source spent assisting them with each activity associated with daily living. We should not simply assume that this is because of an inability to remember such information on the part of older people. Research has demonstrated that older people are as reliable at recalling factual

Table 5.4   Sources of help and support for older people: Manor

	Need for care					
	Some (N = 71)		Substantial (N = 173)		All* (N = 244)	
	N	%	N	%	N	%
No help	16	23	12	7	28	11
Help from:						
Spouse	7	10	25	14	32	13
Other resident	1	1	21	12	22	9
Relative outside	10	14	62	36	72	30
Friend/neighbour	6	8	19	11	25	10
F&CS	41	58	102	59	143	59
NHS	–	–	3	2	3	1
Private	1	1	5	3	6	2
Other	–	–	3	2	3	1
More than one source	12	17	74	43	86	35
Total no. of help sources	66		240		306	
Average no. of help sources	0.9		1.3		1.3	

Note:
* The totals in this table exceed the actual numbers because they represent items of need rather than individuals.

information as their younger counterparts (Herzog and Dielman 1985). The amorphous nature of care, particularly that which is provided informally, makes it very difficult to estimate the amount of time spent performing different activities. Time spent cooking a meal may also be used to clean and tidy the kitchen. Supervisory visits may be carried out in conjunction with other chores such as managing medication (see Chapter 7). At the same time, the existence of help does not imply that it is adequate, efficient or reliable and as such can only act as a crude indicator of whether needs are being met.

Because of these difficulties it proved impractical to gather reliable subjective information concerning the amount of time devoted to different tasks by the various sources of care. Instead, we settled for approaching the extent of need in terms of the ability to perform tasks in the four broad areas of daily living at the same time as examining the sources of help providing assistance in response to these needs. This follows closely the approach adopted in the Sheffield study of the Family Care of Older People (Qureshi and Walker 1989) and addresses two questions. First, did 'care gaps' exist in the two communities and, if so, around what activities was the shortfall in help concentrated and how serious was it? Second, what was the relative contribution of formal and informal sources of help and how, if at all, did the emphasis differ between the two communities?

Table 5.5 Sources of help and support for older people: Southey Green

	Need for care					
	Some (N = 58)		Substantial (N = 148)		All* (N = 206)	
	N	%	N	%	N	%
No help	21	36	24	16	45	22
Help from:						
Spouse	3	5	12	8	15	7
Other resident	–	–	5	3	5	2
Relative outside	8	14	48	32	56	27
Friend/neighbour	2	3	7	5	9	4
F&CS	30	52	105	71	135	66
NHS	–	–	3	2	3	1
Private	–	–	12	8	12	6
Other	–	–	2	1	2	1
More than one source	6	10	62	42	68	33
Total no. of help sources	43		194		237	
Average no. of help sources	0.7		1.3		1.2	

Note:
* The totals in this table exceed the actual numbers because they represent items of need rather than individuals.

An index of the extent to which care needs were being met in both areas was constructed on the basis of analyses of the data on the four broad groups of activities of daily living which covered rising and retiring, daytime assistance and supervision, daily household chores and weekly household tasks (see Chapter 4). The addition of these items resulted in a total consisting of all of the functional items with which older people required help (244 in Manor and 206 in Southey Green). Thus we were able to assess the extent to which both moderate and substantial care needs were being met in both places. The results are shown in Tables 5.4 and 5.5.

What conclusions can be drawn from these two tables? We can say, with confidence, that if help was required in any of the four sets of activities of daily living it was usually available and, as the severity of disability increased, so did the amount of support provided. In Manor we found that in 77 per cent of instances where some help was required in any of the items of daily living on our index, assistance was received, rising to 93 per cent among those highly dependent on such help. The pattern in Southey Green was the same although the frequency of available assistance was less among both groups of older people. Sixty-four per cent of those requiring some help received assistance from at least one source, rising to 84 per cent among those highly dependent on help. In each of the four groups of care needs, assistance came primarily from the formal sector and F&CS was the main supplier of care. The two tables show that, despite the overall responsiveness of the care system to need, there were significant minorities in both places receiving no help. Most worrying were the 7 per cent in Manor and 16 per cent in Southey Green with substantial need for care but not receiving any.

If we compare the care gaps in the two communities across the four broad areas of daily living important differences emerge. With those activities associated with rising and retiring there was no significant care gap in either community; only one person in Manor and none in Southey Green were without assistance if they required it. The most visible differences emerged with respect to the activities associated with older people looking after themselves during the day. Thirty-six per cent of older people in Manor requiring assistance were unable to call on any help, which is very unsatisfactory. In Southey Green, however, the proportion of older people who found themselves in this vulnerable position was very nearly double the Manor level at 71 per cent. With daily household chores there was only a relatively small care gap in both communities, although three times as many people in Southey Green (six) requiring help were unable to rely on any support than in Manor (two). Nobody in either Manor or Southey Green requiring assistance with weekly household chores was unable to gain assistance from at least one source. Overall, across the four areas of daily living, twice as many people in Southey Green (22 per cent) as in Manor (11 per cent) found themselves with no available help if they needed it.

In other words a care gap existed in both communities of older people, but the shortfall in assistance was much smaller among NSU service users in Manor than for home care recipients in Southey Green. This difference was more pronounced among older people most dependent on assistance, which suggests that the NSU had some success in targeting the most frail and confused older people.

Turning to specific sources of care, the major role of F&CS has been noted already, but there were significant differences in the sorts of assistance provided by F&CS on the two geographical areas. The support worker's role in Manor was intended to emphasize care tasks of a more personal and intensive nature than those of the traditional home carer (Chapter 3). In practice the accounts of older people in the two communities concerning the nature of the help received from F&CS did seem to reflect this different emphasis. Seventy-eight per cent of people in Manor reported receiving help with rising and retiring compared with 71 per cent in Southey Green. The most profound difference though was with the help older people received from F&CS in looking after themselves during the day; 31 per cent of those individuals in Manor requiring assistance with these functions received help compared with only 18 per cent in Southey Green.

The focus of domiciliary assistance in Southey Green was more on the traditional areas of help such as cleaning and shopping. So 75 per cent of service users in that area reported receiving help with daily household tasks compared with 67 per cent in Manor. The same pattern emerged regarding weekly household tasks, with 66 per cent of people requiring help in Southey Green receiving it from F&CS compared with 59 per cent in Manor. Although older people in Manor needing help with these activities were less likely to be given assistance by F&CS they did not seem to lose out by much and this care gap is bridged by informal sources. Furthermore they are actually *less* likely to find themselves with no source of assistance at all. Thus the theoretical role of the support worker does appear to have been translated into practice.

Conclusion

This chapter has demonstrated the success of the support unit in enabling a high proportion of those with substantial care needs to remain in their own or relatives' homes. There were significant differences between the support units and the home care services in this most critical of outcomes. Also there was some indication that the NSU was more successful than the home care service in supporting the informal carers of older people with the greatest care needs. Our evidence shows, too, that the NSU was responsive to changes in individuals' needs.

Overall the need for care among the majority of older people, in both Manor and Southey Green, was being met and there was a clear positive relationship between need and the amount of support provided. However, in both areas, there was a significant care gap among those requiring moderate levels of support and a smaller but, nonetheless important shortfall among those needing substantial support. In both cases the care gap was greater under the home care service than the NSU. On the negative side, the Manor Support Unit failed to meet the daytime assistance and supervisory needs of more than one-third of older people, though the home care service's failure rate in this respect was nearly double that of the NSU.

6

The carers' perspective

Introduction

In addition to enabling older people to retain their independence by remaining in their own homes, a major aim of the NSUs was to strengthen informal networks by supporting individual carers. Therefore the evaluation sought to ascertain to what extent and in what ways the initiative had achieved this second goal by interviewing the informal carers of older people involved in the study.

Initial interviews were conducted with a total of 55 carers from Manor and 37 from Southey Green.[1] The idea of matching carers was not viable because of the small sample sizes. It was rendered even less feasible when efforts to set up the second round of interviews revealed carers to be grouped according to a number of different criteria, which made the use of a common questionnaire impossible (see appendix). This being so, what follows is a brief profile of carers based on data gathered during the initial survey. The bulk of the analysis concentrates on the comments of respondents made in reply to open-ended questions contained in first and second round interviews. Though this approach cannot claim to offer a systematic comparison of carers, it does highlight important issues, chiefly to do with the response of services to changes in the circumstances of older people and/or their carers, which lay at the heart of the NSU appraisal.

A profile of carers

Not surprisingly the typical carer of the service users in our samples proved to be a married daughter, in her mid-to-late 50s and in reasonable physical

Table 6.1 Carer's relationship to older person

	Manor		Southey Green	
	N	%	N	%
Spouse	8	15	3	8
Child	25	45	21	57
Daughter/son-in-law	2	4	1	3
Grandchild	3	5	1	3
Sibling	2	4	3	8
Sister/brother-in-law	3	5	1	3
Niece/nephew	4	7	2	5
Neighbour	6	11	2	5
Friend	2	4	3	8
Total	55	100	37	100

Table 6.2 Carers' activities

	Manor						Southey Green					
	Daily		Weekly		Less often		Daily		Weekly		Less often	
	N	%	N	%	N	%	N	%	N	%	N	%
Personal care:												
Rising and retiring	10	18	1	2	2	4	2	5	3	8	–	–
Personal care tasks	8	15	8	15	2	4	1	3	7	9	2	5
Night-time care	4	7	3	5	3	5	1	3	1	3	5	14
Domestic care:												
Light housework	10	18	22	40	9	16	3	8	13	35	6	16
Heavy housework	9	16	18	33	8	15	1	3	11	30	8	22
Soiled linen	5	9	11	20	4	7	1	3	7	19	–	–
Errand care	7	13	35	64	2	4	1	3	27	73	3	8
Meals	17	31	20	36	5	9	4	11	13	35	3	8
Visits:												
Pop-in	20	36	24	44	1	2	10	27	19	51	2	5
Supervision	18	33	6	11	1	2	3	8	6	16	5	14
Companionship	23	42	26	47	1	2	10	27	23	62	2	5
Less regular activities:												
Outings	–	–	5	9	27	49	–	–	5	14	15	41
Accompany on visits	–	–	1	35	16	29	–	–	10	27	18	49
Spring cleaning	–	–	–	–	32	58	–	–	–	–	17	46
Gardening	–	–	2	4	7	13	–	–	–	–	8	22
Decorating	–	–	–	–	25	45	–	–	–	–	17	46

health. She lived separately from the older person to whom she had been providing support for more than two years. The activities with which she most commonly gave help were shopping, meal preparation and light housework.

This typical picture hides some interesting demographic features, however. These include the wide age range that existed among carers, from the youngest in Manor at 19 years to the oldest in Southey Green at 86 years, and which, to an extent, was linked to the diversity of relationships between carers and older people (Table 6.1). It also conceals the wide spectrum of caring activities carried out by interviewees from intense personal care and night sitting to occasional outings (Table 6.2).

As far as differences between the two samples were concerned, in Southey Green there was a higher percentage of men, 35 per cent (13) compared to 27 per cent (15), in the role of primary carer. A greater number of Manor carers, 25 per cent (14) compared to 8 per cent (3), lived with the older person. Nine of the Manor and all of the Southey Green carers in this position were the spouse of the older person. The remaining carers in Manor comprised two daughters, one granddaughter, one grandson and a brother-in-law.

In view of the fact that physical labour is often emphasized in studies of caring (Nissel and Bonnerjea 1982; Levin *et al.* 1983; Baldwin 1985) it is important to note the comparatively high levels of emotional care or tending (such as companionship) being provided in both places, though with a higher frequency in Manor. Only a third of Southey Green carers, compared to nearly half of all Manor carers, said the older person had stayed with them though, in both places, visits were generally reserved for specific occasions, such as Christmas. Similarly, of respondents in Southey Green, 32 (86 per cent) were more likely to reject the idea of the older person living with them in the longer term than were those in Manor, 39 (70 per cent), but their reasons for this were comparable. Impracticability was one of the chief explanations; on the one hand, carers' houses had stairs, no spare room or bed, or could not accommodate a wheelchair; on the other, carers worked full-time, had families to look after or were ill and in need of support themselves. A second common reason given was that the older person themselves would not like the idea; they did not want to be a 'nuisance' or they wanted to remain independent. A few carers said that they or their families were against the idea – they could not cope or would clash – that they were not close enough or related by blood to the older person, or that they lived nearby anyway.

A slightly smaller proportion of carers in Manor, 56 per cent (31) compared to Southey Green, 62 per cent (23), expressed objection to the idea of institutional care on the grounds that it was unacceptable to the older person, to themselves or to both of them. Just under a third of carers from both samples acknowledged the possibility of the future use of residential care, but commonly as a last resort only or in the form of respite visits. Two carers from Manor had, in fact, just secured respite care on a regular basis. Two more carers, one from each group, were in the process of applying for places in residential care for the older person.

It is likely that some of the above patterns were linked to the higher level of physical disability among older people in Manor than Southey Green. This disability factor helped to explain the smaller percentage of carers from Manor who were in paid employment, either full-time, 12 (22 per cent), or part-time, eight (15 per cent), compared to those in Southey Green, 11 (30 per cent) and nine (24 per cent) respectively. Of those not earning a wage in Manor, 10 (18 per cent) said that they would like to undertake paid employment of whom five (9 per cent) attributed their employment status to the responsibilities of caring. Only one person in Southey Green (3 per cent) said they would have liked a paid job and none regarded caring duties as the cause of her or his unemployment. Difficulties at work were experienced by three carers (5 per cent) in Manor and two (5 per cent) in Southey Green. The difficulties were linked to their caring role by two people from each sample (4 per cent and 5 per cent respectively) though not all – two (4 per cent) and one (3 per cent) – had taken time off as a result.

These negative trends were reversed when the question of health and well-being was raised, however. While the majority – over four-fifths – of all carers reported their health as being fair to good, a greater percentage of respondents from Southey Green, 57 per cent (21) compared to Manor, 36 per cent (20), said they had suffered some ill health recently, which was linked to their caring role by 14 per cent (five) and 9 per cent (five) of interviewees respectively. A similar pattern was found in relation to emotional health: 43 per cent (16) carers in Southey Green and 27 per cent (15) in Manor reported suffering recent emotional problems which were related to their caring role by 22 per cent (eight) and 15 per cent (eight) of respondents.

Notable similarities between the two samples lay in the respective percentages of carers who feared a shortfall in support should they be unable to perform their duties for any reason. While most felt confident that there would be a stand-in available, roughly a quarter of carers from both areas said that if they were unexpectedly ill for a few days, the older person would not be able to manage alone and there would be no one available – either formal or informal – to provide support. Just under one-fifth of carers from both samples stated that a similar situation would occur if they wished to go on holiday. Four people (7 per cent) in Manor and three (8 per cent) in Southey Green thought their leisure time to be limited by their caring activities, while four respondents from each area, 7 per cent and 11 per cent, claimed that their social life was impaired, though the majority of interviewees – 48 (87 per cent) and 28 (76 per cent) respectively were left with some spare time every day.

Severe financial problems among carers were extremely rare – a single carer from Manor reported such circumstances. Roughly one in seven respondents from each sample said that they were on a low or reduced income, though only two carers from Manor made a definite association between their financial difficulties and their caring role.

Table 6.3 Hardest aspects of caring role for informal carers

	Manor	*Southey Green*
Nothing	14	7
Practical activities (inc. travel)	12	7
Well-being of older person	8	5
Carer's personal circumstances	6	8
Behaviour/attitude of older person	6	4
Personal care tasks	7	1
Carer's feelings	0	3
Don't know	3	0
Everything	0	1
Not answered	1	1

The caring role

Initial analysis of quantitative data from the first round survey suggested, then, a general picture of two groups of carers with largely moderate needs, though a not insignificant number of people appeared to be performing their caring roles without potential back-up and with only limited financial support. Qualitative items on our questionnaire were designed to put flesh on the bones of this profile. Their specific aim was to examine the role of services in providing support to informal carers, though they also asked in greater depth about the context of care and it is to this issue that we turn first.

Demands of caring

The aim of NSUs to strengthen informal networks of support, was, in part, a reflection of increasing public awareness of the sometimes extremely heavy demands placed upon carers looking after older people living at home. Interviewees were therefore asked what, if anything, they found it hardest to cope with in their role.

A significant number of carers denied finding any aspect of caring difficult. However, with the exception of one person in Southey Green who said that everything was stressful, a majority of carers spoke of at least one feature as being troublesome. When their responses were grouped (Table 6.3), practical activities turned out to constitute the largest category included, among which were cleaning, cooking, (incontinence) laundry, bedmaking, management of finances and above all travelling to and from the home of the older person. Some of these tasks were found demanding and unpleasant but they were unpopular chiefly because they were highly focused and took away from the time which carers were able to spend with the older person.

The concrete issue of travel distance, and the concomitant inability to be 'on hand' or to just 'pop in', was related to the fear expressed by some of leaving older people on their own. This, in turn, tied in with specific aspects of older people's physical and emotional well-being highlighted as a source of concern by carers and including the effects of confusion, dementia and a stroke, deafness, one man's obsessive fear of death when ill and another's drinking patterns.

Carers' personal circumstances also posed difficulties. Visiting time was limited for some by their jobs and/or responsibilities to their partners and children; carers spoke of having to 'find' or 'make time' to care. This made it all the more frustrating for the carer whose aunt resisted help from outside the family. Others spoke of the older person being unappreciative or expectant of more of their support, or simply irritable and even nasty.

In terms of personal care, the main issue concerned the intimacy required for some of these tasks. One man did not like to undress his mother, perhaps because of the incest taboo associated with such intimacy between mature children and their parents (Ungerson 1983a, 1987). Another woman was 'bothered' by her inability to dress her sister without assistance from workers and therefore to guard her privacy. Some carers found matters of hygiene problematic, particularly coping with the smell of urine and/or faeces. More general feelings of impotence, responsibility, resentment and a lack of sympathy, and the loss of privacy were raised by a number of carers.

Reasons for continuing to care

While carers nominated certain tasks as 'hard', this was not to suggest that caring was an entirely negative experience or that they were on the point of giving up. Carers gained reward most commonly from the happiness and appreciation of the older person. Others were motivated by a strong sense of duty, 'closeness' or, in one case, purpose, by the desire to reciprocate the care given to them by the older person in the past, or by feelings of 'satisfaction', 'warmth' and 'goodness'. These elements were not always easy to disentangle. A number of carers said that caring was good because they were able to draw from experience (three, as paid carers) or because it taught tolerance and gave an insight into old age.

There were differences between the two geographical groups of carers. More of those in Southey Green nominated spending time in the company of the older person as rewarding, while a number of carers in Manor listed practical activities including cooking and keeping the house or, in one case, the older person looking clean and tidy. This may have been due, once again, to the higher levels of need among older people in Manor, with obvious knock-on consequences for carers; that is, respondents spent more time carrying out practical activities and had less time to spend simply chatting, or confusion on the part of the older person reduced the quality of their relationship. Indeed, a notably greater number of carers in Manor (eight) than in Southey Green (one) said that they found no aspect of caring rewarding. The reorganization of support services in Manor, which gave such work a high local profile, may also have contributed to the instrumentalization of informal care in that area.

Nevertheless, it is of great significance that more than three-quarters of carers from both samples said there was nothing they would like to hand over to someone else, even if the older person agreed. Of those who did nominate tasks – 12 (22 per cent) in Manor and seven (19 per cent) in Southey Green – their comments suggested that they wished for help not necessarily to relieve themselves of the responsibility of caring but to augment what was already being given; for example, two carers in Southey Green wished to be assisted with bathing the older person since they found this task difficult to manage on their own. Indeed, most aspects put forward, and predominantly by Manor carers, tended to be practical in nature, though a handful of people mentioned supervisory checks and holiday cover.

This reflected the findings of Table 6.2. It was also confirmed by carers' responses to the question of whether there were any tasks which they were particularly anxious to carry on doing; roughly four-fifths of all respondents indicated that they wished to carry on caring. It should be stressed that not every person was able or willing to single out any one aspect – 'I want to carry on with everything'; 'I don't do much, just visit' – or offered a positive explanation – 'I'm all right as I am'; 'I just plod on'. But among those who did distinguish activities, visiting was cited most commonly, especially by carers in Southey Green, followed by personal care tasks and assistance with financial affairs. Of the handful of carers who nominated practical tasks, some gave specific reasons. For example, one carer wanted to shop for her mother since she was on a special diet and the local shops charged too much for the foodstuffs that she wanted, while another explained that she would continue to clean upstairs since her mother had recently been burgled and became very anxious if a stranger went upstairs.

Assistance with caring

Echoing the sentiments that they did very little or were able to manage alone, that they did not believe extra help would be available or forthcoming, or that they saw caring as their duty, a significant proportion of carers – 25 (46 per cent) in Manor and 15 (41 per cent) in Southey Green – had not sought help from formal sources in looking after the older person. A small number of respondents claimed the older person would object, or they did not have knowledge of what was available or the time to find out.

Only a few carers had requested help – nine (16 per cent) in Manor and eight (22 per cent) in Southey Green – though some had sought assistance from more than one source. Two people in Manor and three in Southey Green had asked for help from the health services, while another two carers in Manor and one in Southey Green had approached the council for help with gardening and decorating. The majority – seven in each sample – had applied for domiciliary support but the outcome was not always successful. In Manor, one carer's request for meals on wheels was turned down on the basis that she cooked for her father every day (despite the fact that she worked part-time and had her own family to care for). Another respondent was granted extra domiciliary assistance only to have it turned down by the older person, while a third described increased visits as 'tailing off' after a while. Two carers from Southey Green asked for assistance with bathing the older person. In the first instance the older person was given a shower which she was too confused to operate safely, in the second the subsequent order for a chair lift was so long in coming that the older person had been admitted to hospital by the time it arrived.

In sum, the comments of carers suggested that emotional care, such as spending time with the older person, was an important part of the caring relationship, though it was not always easy when the person in question was confused or suffering from dementia. In the latter case, practical tasks could be a source of satisfaction where conversation or intimacy were hard to achieve. On the other hand they could be an added burden. Practical tasks were vital but time-consuming and hence were resented in situations where they limited the social contact which the two parties desired or judged to be the norm. For this reason, more than any other, these were the tasks with which carers, when under pressure, required assistance or were desirous of handing over to others. However, it is obvious that a strong moral code existed alongside people's beliefs about the limited availability of services, which tended to prevent respondents from requesting support to assist them in their caring role (Qureshi and Walker 1989). Before exploring the extent to which the formal services recognized their needs, it is important to examine the relationship that carers enjoyed with the statutory services.

Carers and formal services

Carer involvement in service organization

As indicated in Chapter 3 a key feature of the Support Units initiative was to involve older people in determining their own care needs and service packages. What role did informal carers play in this process? As Table 6.4 shows, few carers said that they were involved in the organization of support to the older person. Only a minority – 36 per cent in Manor and 27 per cent in Southey Green – reported having dealings with either the support unit or the home care service respectively. However, this did not automatically guarantee participation in service organization or review, as seven of the 20 carers in Manor and two of the 10 in Southey Green suggested. In the few instances where explanations were given for this lack of general involvement, carers said they were satisfied with, or happy to leave it to the older person to make arrangements. Some expressed a sense of powerlessness to effect changes to provision; one spoke of limited opportunity for contact with service providers or organizers.

Table 6.4 Carers' involvement in the organization of the older person's services

	Manor		Southey Green	
	N	%	N	%
No involvement	34	62	24	65
Some involvement	12	22	4	11
Close involvement	5	9	6	16
No response	4	7	3	8
Total	55	100	37	100

A number of people who did claim some involvement explained that they had initially referred the older person to the services. '[I was] initially involved in getting her social services but have no involvement now unless anything goes wrong' (SG). Contacts with formal services did not appear to be sustained outside of these initial ones. The main exception was where needs had to be constantly reviewed as, for example, in the case of the carer whose mother had become incontinent and required regular toileting visits when she was unable to call. Otherwise, contact with formal services typically came about through changes to the older person's circumstances – as a result of hospitalization or increased frailty, for example – or was specific to certain occasions, such as those times when the sister of one carer went away on holiday and the respondent needed help with washing her mother, or the incident when an older woman was assigned a male support worker to help her to dress but revealed her subsequent distress only to her daughter.

This lack of carer involvement could not be traced exclusively to any one reason. The comments of carers suggested a general stance of passivity in relation to participation in service organization:

> We don't have control over what gets done, but we don't want it really. As long as they're giving satisfactory help and they're doing what needs to be done, we're satisfied. We know they're constrained with financial constraints. (M)

Contact with service managers

In terms of contact with middle managers – that is, team leaders and home help organizers – the NSU seemed to open the door wider than the home care service to the possibility of involvement. Three carers in Manor said they had actually met with the team leader to discuss support for the older person, another was present at his wife's assessment and two more lived close to the team leader and the Manor Centre respectively and often saw staff 'on the street'. No carers in Southey Green reported face to face meetings with home help organizers. However, contact of any kind was still the exception: 69 per cent (38) of carers in Manor and 65 per cent (24) in Southey Green said they had no contact with service organizers, a surprisingly small difference given the community orientation of the NSU. Excluding the two respondents, one from each sample, who were themselves frontline workers, most carers who established communication did so by telephone, either to update middle managers on the circumstances of the older person or, more typically and generally more formally, to make arrangements in specific circumstances, for example where respite care was required or workers had failed to call, for example.

Interesting observations were made by a small number of interviewees who responded ambiguously or negatively to the question of contact. A couple of carers in Manor felt that although they had no regular contact, it would be easily available if needed. In contrast, three carers in Southey Green claimed that they lived too far away to see anybody, that nobody ever came 'to see what's what' and that they were not supposed to be there when staff called. A single carer from each of the two samples said that arrangements for support had been made when the older person was in hospital and by hospital personnel, suggesting that middle mangers in general needed to do more to follow up such referrals if carers were to become involved.

Contact with service providers

It was anticipated that carers would be more likely to have contact with frontline workers than with middle managers. They were asked to describe their relationship with staff who supported the older person. Slightly fewer respondents in Southey Green (five) than in Manor (nine) had never met frontline workers. A number of Manor respondents (six (or 11 per cent)) said the question was 'not applicable'. It was likely that the formal support received by the older person for whom they cared was limited to centre-based activities, including shopping trips. A higher percentage of carers in Southey Green, 70 per cent (26), than in Manor, 62 per cent (34), stated that they had met workers but a greater proportion of the latter, 53 per cent (18), compared to the former, 46 per cent (12), described knowing staff 'as people'.

Explanations for the nature of contact were uniform across the two samples. Personal qualities of 'niceness', 'friendliness' and 'helpfulness' were the chief ingredients of closeness, though a couple of carers in Manor mentioned pop-in visits and, in Southey Green, emergency telephone contact as being conducive to more personal relationships with formal carers. 'Working relationships' arose where there was infrequent and unsustained contact between carers and frontline workers: 'It's always a different one – we don't see much of them' (M).

Five carers in Manor described their relationship as 'other'; one thought it to be borderline formal/informal, while another said simply that the social

Table 6.5 Extent to which services understood the position of carers and their needs

	Manor		Southey Green	
	N	%	N	%
Understanding*	20	36.5	7	19
Some understanding	10	18	6	16
No understanding	15	27	16	43
Don't know	6	11	8	22
Not answered	4	7.5	0	0
Total	55	100	37	100

Note:
* Includes the two carers, one from each sample, who were frontline workers

worker left her notes. Six respondents in Southey Green explained that the older person was visited by both a warden and a home carer, though they were more likely to have a closer relationship with the former.

Understanding of carers' needs

In light of their comments on contact and involvement, did carers think that service providers understood their position and needs? Table 6.5 shows that only roughly one in six people from both samples thought that services had some understanding of their position and needs. Carers in Manor were more likely to agree conditionally with the question and carers in Southey Green to disagree.

Their comments suggested that understanding was linked to their relationship with middle managers. A lack of communication, at one extreme, was put down to the fact that team leaders and home help organizers were 'not bothered':

> I don't think they think about us, actually. I don't think they care. I think they just accept us. They don't need to do the things if you're there. (SG)

Others thought that services were too stretched. Even where carers – or the older person – had been able to explain their needs, expectations concerning the ability of middle managers to help remained low.

This being so, most carers still offered a response to the question of which aspects of the services they found to be of most support (Table 6.6). Overall, monitoring/supervisory visits, especially when on a daily basis and/or at antisocial times such as first thing in the morning, were most helpful to carers. The fact that Southey Green carers listed cleaning more frequently than did the Manor carers who, in turn, placed greater stress on personal tasks (including

Table 6.6 Most helpful aspects of formal support for carers

	Manor	*Southey Green*
Monitoring/supervisory role	18	13
Cleaning	4	10
Meals	8	4
Rising and retiring	6	3
Shopping	6	2
None	2	6
Cover	4	3
All	2	3
Friendliness/company	1	2
Pension	1	1
Medication	0	2
Prescriptions	1	0
Day centre	1	0
Daily requirements	1	0
Acceptability to older person	1	0
Taking older person out in wheelchair	0	1
Not answered	10	0
Not applicable	1	0

meals) probably reflected the relative priority given to these tasks in the respective areas. The 'none' response had to be treated with caution since some of the accompanying comments revealed the ambiguity of the question: 'It doesn't really help *me*' (SG). The 'everything' response indicated an appreciation of the general lightening of loads. In fact, a majority of carers were reluctant to say that services were of no help at all.

Roughly equal proportions of carers in Manor and Southey Green were frustrated by the limited amount of support offered and the hours during which it was available. Otherwise, the deficiencies highlighted by carers again reflected the respective priorities of services in the two areas, so that Manor carers more commonly experienced limitation with cleaning support, Southey Green respondents with meals, shopping and laundry. Staff in Southey Green proved more likely to be criticized for the irregularity of their visits, suggesting that, to an extent, older people and their carers in Manor had adapted to the increased flexibility and autonomy enjoyed by support workers and perhaps saw the benefits of it, while those in the former area still expected a timetabled system.

Of course, domiciliary services were not the sole source of support for carers. Roughly a quarter of carers from each sample listed other services as being helpful. Health services (district nurse, auxiliary/'bath' nurse, chiropodist, health visitor, occupational therapist, physiotherapist) were mentioned more often by Manor respondents and day centre and luncheon club activities by Southey Green respondents. Numbers were small but, once again, these differences may have reflected the higher levels of need among older people in Manor and, perhaps also, the effectiveness of the Manor health care team.

The concept of community care

Given carers' general lack of contact with or direct support from formal services, what were their views on the concept of community care as the main approach to caring for older people? Only one carer failed to endorse the primary aims of community care, to keep older people in their own homes for as long as possible, with the comment that 'older people should be allowed to please themselves' (M). A majority simply said they were in favour. Just over a third observed that living in their own homes was what (older) people wanted; it was a source of independence in contrast to institutional care which robbed them of their dignity. An equal number sanctioned the idea, as long as the older person was able to cope physically and emotionally, and with adequate and efficient support.

Carers were not quite as ready to endorse the idea of giving support to family, friends and neighbours who cared for older people at home though this is not to suggest that the idea was unpopular. Again, in some cases it was supported without comment. A number of carers said it should be an integral part of the work of frontline staff. Others noted how carers became too tied to, or isolated by, their role, were taken for granted or struggled to cope with jobs and other family responsibilities. Support from the services helped to raise the morale of such individuals and to encourage and assist them to continue with their activities in a way that significant others in their lives were not always able to do.

However, a fifth of all carers expressed reservations about the idea. Some suggested that individuals could take advantage of services and that carer assessments were necessary. Others pointed out the limitations of staff time and the potential difficulties of 'fitting [formal support] into the family circle'. The idea was put forward that sufficient support to older people would 'automatically relieve carers right across the board', while one carer's personal experiences made her doubt the promises made by staff: 'They change arrangements without consultation' (M).

Just under a fifth of all carers rejected the proposal. One woman – a neighbour to the older person – said she was not family and therefore 'not involved'. Most, including the former respondent, said that they did not need support. As in the case of a number of other items, it may have been that some carers were taking the question too literally to mean practical assistance within *their* own homes. This possibility is strengthened by the fact that more than one went on to stress that all help should go direct to older people who 'come first' and who would 'lose out'.

It was interesting to ask, then, if changes to the services in Manor had made any notable differences to the lives of carers. Just over half the Manor

Table 6.7 Carers' suggestions for improvement to services for older people

	Manor	*Southey Green*
Increase in help:		
Overall amount	17	9
Regularity/frequency	10	10
Specific areas of help:		
Cleaning	5	9
Supervisory visits	6	3
Financial support	5	2
Emotional support/company	0	7
Meals	4	2
Housing	2	4
Day centre	3	2
Aids and adaptations	3	1
Personal care	3	0
Decorating	0	2
Shopping	1	1
Outings	1	0
Respite care	1	0
Transport	0	1
Medical care	0	1
Gardening	0	1
Organization of services	7	4
No suggestions	5	7
Don't know	7	2

carers, 28 (51 per cent), said the older person had been receiving home help before the establishment of the NSU initiative. Of these, a little under a fifth (six) said that services had not been affected. Eleven (39 per cent) said that the domiciliary services were less helpful, without exception due to the reduction in support with domestic tasks, primarily cleaning and, in two cases, also shopping and laundry.

Of the eight carers (29 per cent) who saw it as being more helpful, two appreciated the extra supervisory visits, and two more the fact that workers were more closely involved with the older person than home helps had been. Other individually nominated benefits included the increased involvement of the carer in the organization of services, greater frequency and reliability of help and a round-the-clock service, if necessary, and the availability of a laundry service. One carer welcomed additional help with errand tasks though she bemoaned the concomitant decrease in cleaning support. Indeed, two additional carers expressed mixed feelings about the changes: 'More helpful – more visits. Less helpful – no cleaning' (M). Other comments suggested a degree of ambiguity: 'I didn't think you could get any help. They say they don't do cleaning any more, they're carers' (M).

Bearing in mind the experiences of these latter respondents, carers were asked what they thought was necessary to make community care work effectively and how they could best be supported by formal services. Most carers listed more than one feature essential to the success of community care (Table 6.7). Above all, carers were concerned that sufficient help was available on a regular and flexible basis, especially in the absence of family support. Where respondents singled out specific areas of help – generally within existing service provision – it was typically to call for greater assistance. Differences between the two groups in the areas chosen were small but, once again, tended to reflect service priorities, so that Manor carers favoured supervisory visits and personal care, while Southey Green carers favoured cleaning. On the other hand, the desire among Southey Green carers for more emotional support – including motivation – for older people living alone or feeling lonely probably indicated the inadequacy of provision in this domain.

Carers' suggestions went further than domiciliary support. A number said they would welcome financial provision for older people (though whether in the form of pensions and benefits or through the increased funding of services was not made clear). Others noted the lack of choice and comfort in the types of housing on offer calling, on the one hand, for sheltered accommodation and, on the other, for integrated estates which might encourage neighbourly support. Aids and adaptations within the home were also referred to. Only one person mentioned medical cover, suggesting that community care translated principally as social care, that care gaps existed chiefly in the social care field, that they felt less able to challenge the medical world, or a combination of the three.

A final set of responses related to the organization of services. One carer from each sample called for a key figure to oversee and review the delivery of care in general and, in the words of one interviewee, to involve the family more – a role with the basic characteristics of the recently introduced care manager post. Another carer called for the greater participation – or 'cooperation' – of the older person. Two carers from Manor specifically stated that they wished for a return to the traditional home help system which, according to one, allocated more time to giving 'help', that is to shopping and cleaning. On the other hand, a woman in Southey Green called for the introduction of a team system – which very much reflected the patterning of service delivery in Manor – as well as for more training for workers to increase their sensitivity to users' and carers' needs. Another interviewee similarly spoke of the need for compassion which she felt was better provided by 'middle-aged' people.

As for their own need for support, after reiterating a general increase in the amount and frequency of assistance to older people, carers in both areas listed specific areas of help to the older person by which they believed they would also benefit, albeit indirectly. These included extended transport facilities (suggestions were for more trips out and the use of voluntary drivers), more supervisory checks and increased respite and day care provision.

Individual carers desired respectively a telephone for the older person, access to the laundry service and, in the case of one man, relief from undressing his mother. There was also a significant desire on the part of carers in both areas for increased contact with service providers.

Service response to changes in carers' circumstances

At the second stage of interviews with carers, the evaluation focused on investigating whether and in what way services had responded to changes in carers' circumstances. It was clearly not possible to administer a standard questionnaire – and consequently to achieve a rigorous and detailed longitudinal perspective on carers' lives – since four distinct subgroups of carers had emerged between the two surveys (see appendix). Here we examine each of the subgroups with regard to the services' responsiveness to their needs and respect of their right to be consulted.

Continuous carers

Not all carers had experienced any significant changes in their lives. Continuous carers, by definition, comprised those individuals who were still, at the second round, looking after older people living at home with no alterations to their previous living arrangements. In this case, 25 carers lived separately from and five with the older person in Manor, compared to 21 and one respectively in Southey Green. As few as three respondents, two from Manor and one from Southey Green, had stayed with the older person because they were feeling poorly or needed assistance, and no visit was longer than a couple of nights. Two older people had moved in with their carers in Manor while they recovered, one from a gastric bug and the other from an eye operation, but both had since returned to their own homes.

Two other cases were cited of older people receiving hospital treatment. In Southey Green, an older woman had been admitted to hospital on three separate occasions with chest and intestinal conditions, and for attention to superficial burns. In Manor, a woman who suffered from severe depression and regularly required psychiatric help, had passed most of the intervening period between interviews in hospital. Both were discharged to their own homes, however. Respite care was set up for an older woman with Alzheimer's disease, while an older man had twice spent two weeks in residential care to give his wife a break. Nevertheless, just as the possibility of the older person staying with them in the longer term was rejected by a majority of carers, so too was the idea of residential care.

Changes in service provision

Continuous carers had thus experienced a relatively low incidence of major changes in older peoples' circumstances. Revisions in help provided by the support worker and home care services were reported, though it was difficult to ascertain their exact nature and extent. Seventeen (57 per cent) carers in Manor spoke of change; four (13 per cent) said that the amount of help had been increased, three (10 per cent) that there had been a change to 'more intensive care'. On the other hand, five (17 per cent) stated that help had been reduced and/or, in the case of cleaning, was received less regularly. Another observed that both the amount and nature of help had altered:

> Support seems to have disappeared. It's gone from twice a week when they would clean, shop, pay rent etc., to popping in once or twice a week to ask if he wants any shopping. (M)

One woman replied ambiguously, denying an increase in the amount of support given to her mother, but commenting on the changes to the 'system' – from a weekly cleaning to a daily call-in service – which she thought to be 'much better'. In two instances (7 per cent) carers said that help had actually been withdrawn. In the case of a third, it was her husband's choice to stop attending the NSU day centre.

A smaller proportion of carers in Southey Green – 10 (45 per cent) – reported changes to services for the older person. Two (9 per cent) said that the amount had increased; in one case, help was now being put in at the weekend due to the illness of the carer who was waiting to be admitted to hospital for a heart operation. Another carer stated that the nature of help had changed; workers were 'popping in' to make sure that her brother-in-law had his meals. Five respondents (23 per cent) said that both the amount and nature of help had altered. Three (14 per cent) reported increased support with cleaning, cooking and meals on wheels respectively, but the fourth spoke of a reduction in cleaning help and the withdrawal of the laundry service from the older person, while the fifth answered ambiguously, saying the length of the home carer's visit had shortened but that her mother was given 'more thorough housework'. Two carers stated that help had been withdrawn.

Involvement in service organization

It continued to be the general case that formal arrangements were made without reference to carers. Few carers made direct requests for help. Even in situations where changes had occurred, there was a sense that the practical aspect of organization was a professional matter:

> They know how to work out how much help she needs and they know what they have got to offer – it's not necessary to involve me. (M)

Some carers who had sought involvement reported meeting with a very negative reception; for example, one carer and his wife in Manor had found the 'organizer' unhelpful and rude resulting in a 'lack of confidence in the service'. A daughter looking after her mother observed:

> I have to keep phoning them to complain. They haven't involved me. I have had to make a nuisance of myself to get something done and it's still not enough. (M)

Table 6.8 Continuous carers' judgement of the success of services in enabling the older person to live in the community

	Manor		Southey Green	
	N	%	N	%
Successful	16	53	18	82
Unsuccessful	13	43.5	4	18
No response	1	3.5	0	0
Total	30	100	22	100

A second carer and his wife had begun to speak with the team leader on a regular basis by telephone which, alongside contact with frontline workers, appeared the most common channel of communication used by respondents who expressed some degree of participation. Ideally, the carer would have liked regular meetings to discuss help for his mother, whose dementia was increasing steadily, but he recognized the 'problems incurred by wider restrictions', i.e. a lack of resources. Other carers likewise noted the limitations to their input into arrangements:

> I was involved when they had meetings in the beginning. There was no consultation over cut down − support worker just told us she wasn't coming as often. (M)

Five carers in Manor, compared to only one in Southey Green, said that frontline workers had asked about their needs; one support worker had 'made suggestions' about respite care to a carer planning to go on holiday, for example. However, inquiries tended to be made at a very general level and, in the main, carers from both areas still viewed workers as having little autonomy to effect changes directly.

Implications for service change
There was little deviation among continuous carers from the feelings expressed by the original carers sample with regard to positive and negative aspects of caring, and the desire to relinquish tasks to others. Where there was a difference, it lay in their response to questions which asked about the success of services in enabling older people to live at home as members of the community (Table 6.8) and in helping themselves in their caring roles (Table 6.9). While a majority in both samples judged services to have achieved these goals, it is highly significant that a greater number of continuous carers from Southey Green than from Manor expressed agreement. Despite the differences in the severity of disability between the two samples of older people this finding represents an indictment against the NSU.

Table 6.9 Continuous carers' judgement of the success of services in supporting them in their caring role

	Manor		Southey Green	
	N	*%*	*N*	*%*
Successful	13	43	15	68
Unsuccessful	9	30	2	9
Mixed	4	13.5	0	0
Not applicable	3	10	5	23
No response	1	3.5	0	0
Total	30	100	22	100

It was not easy to identify specific features that carers had found particularly helpful; respondents commonly spoke simply of the provision of support in general, including the relief from stress and worry and, in one case, the willingness of workers to do things 'above and beyond what [was] expected of them' (M). Monitoring/supervisory visits, especially those paid in antisocial hours, were the next most frequently listed aspect of care, otherwise numbers were too small to be of significance.

Likewise, carers couched the reasons for judging the services to have failed in achieving their aims in very general terms. Mixed responses were given by a handful of carers, including one woman in Manor who explained that her sister-in-law regularly refused the support workers' help when they visited, and a second woman, whose husband had stopped attending the day centre, who stated that it was not social but economic support that, as a couple, they required. But typically, it was the amount of help which workers were able to provide that was found to be inadequate. Of particular note was the reported failure of services in Manor to increase their assistance in order to support a carer whose husband had recently suffered a stroke, and to give extra care to an older person who had a bad fall the previous week. In the opinion of one carer, support workers had been given 'too much authority with regard to decisions on whether people get [help] or not'; 'It needs someone thoroughly trained to assess it. They tend to decide on whether they like a person or not, rather than on their needs' (M).

Bereaved carers

It was anticipated that carers of older people who had died or were in hospital or residential care were more likely to have experienced changes in their own circumstances as well as in services, given that death and institutionalization are commonly preceded by a period of declining health and increased dependency.

Interviews were conducted with nine bereaved carers in Manor[2] and three in Southey Green. Changes in living arrangements were experienced by only two of the 12 carers, both from Manor; one carer took her terminally ill father-in-law to live with her, the second had secured respite care for her mother who had become confused and 'nasty' and was wandering at night. Four respondents in Manor continued to share their home with the older person. The remaining carers – three in Manor and three in Southey Green – looked after older people who remained in their own homes up until their deaths.

In only one case, that of the terminally ill man, had a carer stayed with the older person (though unbeknown to the latter). However, one woman said that a night sitter had attended her neighbour in the week before she died, while she herself had stayed most of the day. Another carer worked a kind of shift system with her brother and sister, whereby she looked after her mother throughout the day and they took over in the evening. A third carer had taken her father home with her on the 'very odd occasion' when he was feeling unwell (though her brother was still living at home with him).

In total, five carers, all from Manor, were providing full care; three from Manor and two from Southey Green visited the older person daily and engaged in personal as well as practical care tasks. One respondent from Manor and two from Southey Green called two to five times per week providing help of a practical nature, although one woman occasionally cooked for her father.

All respondents reported changes to the health and/or behaviour of the older person prior to her or his death. In Manor, four carers spoke of significant mental and physical decline, two of chest problems which left one older person so dispirited that he 'let himself go in every way', and three of a general increase in frailty as the result of cancer, diabetes and gangrene respectively. In Southey Green, two carers likewise spoke of frailty, in one case as the result of a heart attack. The third respondent from this group had not known that her friend had cancer and she simply saw him as 'more cantankerous than usual'. Two carers from Manor and one from Southey Green specifically mentioned that the older person had also become incontinent.

The decline in the older person's health had mixed implications for respondents' caring loads. Four carers in Manor said they had not provided any extra support as such because they lived with the older person and were already doing everything. One daughter caring for her mother observed: 'The only time I had off was three hours on Thursday afternoon when a sitter would come in while I went shopping' (M). The carer in Manor looking after her terminally ill father-in-law stepped into a full-time caring role. Previously, she had simply paid him social calls, occasionally doing some cooking or cleaning. Two carers in Manor and one in Southey Green increased the frequency of their visits and, where possible, their practical activities so that one woman took on her neighbour's washing, for example, while another prepared the older person's dinner and tea. Only one carer in Manor and two in Southey Green said that the overall amount of support which they provided had not increased. In two more cases – one from each area – the older person was described as being too independent to let carers give more help.

With one exception, all respondents experienced stress as a result of changes in the older person's well-being. Most talked of being generally worried or upset. One woman said she was 'ashamed' of her father who, after spending time in hospital where he was treated for a chest infection, became 'more cantankerous than usual, rowed with everybody, got filthy dirty' (M). When an older man with cancer was given too high a dosage of drugs and 'turned nasty', his daughter-in-law 'broke down' and threatened to leave home:

> It was like me body was here but me mind had gone . . . It's like your mind is floating. You can't get hold of your mind and pull it back into your body. (M)

The stress they experienced had implications for carers' own health. Two women providing round-the-clock care spoke of an inability ever to relax and of a constant physical and emotional strain. Others described feelings of extreme tiredness which carried additional consequences. For example, one man who suffered from Paget's disease and asthma became quite ill with chest problems. Another carer, who could not sleep because her mother shouted out at night, lost weight and became a 'bag of nerves' (M); a third spoke of living 'automatically' and of going to work 'like a robot' (M).

Other members of the family were affected too. One carer, who herself suffered from depression, said that her son had broken out in a rash of boils while her daughter refused to be touched. A second said that she and her husband had no time for each other. A woman, who provided daily help to her mother who was confused and incontinent, was also caring for two young children and her husband who was seriously ill with a chest condition, as well as holding down a part-time job. She had no transport and described it as a 'terrible time': 'I didn't know where to turn' (M). Fortunately, none of the six respondents – four in Manor and two in Southey Green – who were in paid employment had been forced to take any time off from work as a result of caring for the older person, though two spoke of having very understanding employers.

Given their intensive input, carers found it difficult to identify single causes of stress, but blamed it on 'the situation in general'. Only one respondent actually named a task; she said that the shopping was heavy to carry on the 30-minute walk to her father's house. This being the case, had services helped to support carers in any way? Had there been any changes to services prior to the older person's death which had helped carers?

Changes in service provision
In one instance an older man, who had been included in the original sample as a user of one of the NSU day centres, had since become too ill to attend and therefore was reported as being no longer in receipt of services. His wife

continued to manage caring for him at home with the help of their daughter. In another case, assistance was provided but not on a regular basis. That is, support workers helped one carer to bath her mother on those occasions when the respondent's sister, who lived next door and normally assisted, was away on holiday.

These two people excepted, carers reported older people in Manor as receiving regular support from two or three sources prior to them dying. This compares to an average of one source in Southey Green. The figures are clearly too small to enable any firm conclusions to be drawn. However, they do appear to suggest that in Manor there was some movement in relation to users with high(er) levels of need, towards providing 'packages of care'.

One carer actually worked as a support worker in the team which covered the area of the Manor estate where her father lived and it had been agreed by her team leader and the manager of the unit that she be allowed to 'take him on regularly' as one of her main clients. Consequently, she was able to adjust her caring input as necessary. Otherwise, only two carers reported changes in formal support prior to the older person's death. One older man started to receive twice daily monitoring/supervisory visits during those hours when his son and daughter-in-law were unable to be with him. He was also assessed by an occupational therapist who made recommendations for certain aids and adaptations. A second older man, discharged from hospital following a chest infection, was similarly given daily visits as well as assistance with getting out of bed and extra domestic help.

Involvement in service organization
Four carers identified services which they felt would have helped them in their caring role. A carer from each sample listed an auxiliary nurse. The Manor respondent also said she would have liked help with cleaning and laundry – the laundry service had been withdrawn, even though the older person was incontinent – as well as physiotherapy for her husband who suffered with fluid on his lungs. A woman in Southey Green felt that a day centre would have benefited her friend who had no other informal carers, though she suspected that he would have refused to go if it had been suggested. The final respondent, from Manor, whose mother received respite care, said that she would have liked her to move into the residential unit on a permanent basis. The carer did not agree that her mother was fit enough to live at home on her own, though she had not been involved in the consultations between her brothers and the doctors responsible for her assessment.

This is not to say that the carer felt totally powerless in terms of service organization; she had been the one to initiate respite care arrangements. Likewise, a second woman in Manor whose request for a 'bath nurse' had been turned down (chiefly on the basis that her sister was available to help), had nevertheless been responsible for arranging visits from both the occupational therapist and physiotherapist. Of the remaining carers, another woman from Manor said she involved herself 'indirectly' by encouraging her neighbour to request help himself. An interviewee from Southey Green reported telephoning the home care organizer on a number of occasions to discuss the situation of her friend, though she had not requested any extra support because he was 'a difficult person to help'. A third carer, from Manor, revealed her worry at leaving her terminally ill father-in-law on his own to the support worker who responded by giving her the telephone number of the unit, recommending that she talk things over with the team leader. This she did and extra monitoring/ supervisory visits were the result.

The carer in question felt herself fortunate in the support worker allocated to the older person with whom she shared a 'really friendly relationship': 'She was the sort of person as if she wanted to care, like she wanted to do it off her own back. It was like she weren't getting paid for it.' A second carer from Manor praised staff who were 'wonderful' to her father. Although workers had not asked her directly what she wanted doing, she still felt supported and understood since, in her own words, 'They just seemed to know and do what wanted doing' (M). Only one other interviewee, from Manor, said that workers had asked him what he wanted doing. Although they always carried out his requests, he complained about their 'attitude': 'they were always saying they'd got people far worse than us'. On the other hand, neither did any other respondents report asking workers for extra or different kinds of help. In three cases, carers said that this was against the older person's wishes, two did not need it, one felt it was *her* duty to do everything, while another felt that, as a neighbour, it was not her place to ask.

Implications for service change

As to the achievement of the core aims of the service, five carers in Manor and two in Southey Green agreed that services had been of support to the older person, though the carers from the latter group both qualified their responses by saying that help had only been minimal. A single carer from each area, who said that the services had not enabled the older person to live as part of the community, attributed the reason for this to the older person themselves; one older woman had Alzheimer's disease and was, in the words of her carer, 'too far gone' (M), while the other older person was 'set in his solitary ways' (SG). Two more carers simply stated that it was they who had done the most.

Nevertheless, except in the case of one respondent who deemed the question inapplicable and the carer who was also employed as a support worker, all bereaved interviewees in Manor – even those who would have liked more practical assistance – agreed that the services had helped them to look after the older person in the community. None of the carers in Southey Green responded positively to the item, though it should be noted that they all qualified their answers. In one case, the respondent said that, as far as she knew, the services did not know about her since she was only a friend and had therefore never spoken with them. A second carer thought that more help could have been given to his aunt but added that he understood that they were 'short staffed all the time' (SG). The third carer saw the explanation as lying with the older person who 'didn't really want to know about social services' (SG).

The carer who had moved her terminally ill father-in-law into her home outside the Manor estate had subsequently been forced to switch from the NSU to the traditional services, and was able to make a direct comparison between the two. Commenting on the support workers, she stated that 'for the older ones themselves, you can't fault them . . . they were fighting to get in at the front door'. In general, she did not think that there was enough support for carers but she observed that:

> This area, it seemed as though they were going to take over and nobody mattered, but down there [Manor] they asked you what you wanted.

The carer was especially appreciative of the help which she had received from the district nurses in Manor who had just promised to start coming in every two days to monitor the condition of her father-in-law when he was admitted to hospital. They saw to it that the appropriate person was notified when he was discharged to live with the carer. Thereafter she felt lucky if the nurses called once a week.

Carers of older people who had entered hospital or residential care

In addition to bereaved carers there were carers of older people who had been admitted to (and were still in) hospital – two in Southey Green – and to residential care – two in Manor and one in Southey Green. In these cases, there had been no changes in the living arrangements of older people; in all but one instance, the older person lived alone in their own home. The one exception was a woman living with her spouse who was her main carer (SG).

None of the former older people had stayed with their carers for any period of time because they were unable to look after themselves, though one respondent from Manor had stayed with his mother for a couple of nights on four occasions because her sight was failing and she needed help being guided to the toilet. He was not able to do a lot for her, practically at least, since he himself was in his late 60s and had hip and circulatory problems. A carer from Southey Green had increased the frequency of her visits to her mother, who had not been well for a number of weeks, while another described the amount of help he was giving to his wife as having increased steadily in relation to her gradual deterioration.

His wife was, in fact, one of two older women – one from each area – who had spent time in hospital due to ill health before being admitted to residential care. She had severe bronchitis and 'stiffness all over her body' which prevented her from being able to do anything. She was doubly incontinent and confined to a wheelchair, and her husband, who was 83 and suffered from bronchitis and angina, was no longer able to care for her. He claimed to have ruptured all the muscles in his body through trying to lift his wife, and had to wear a truss because of a hernia. He described the situation as having got to 'saturation point' where even the two assistants who had been helping him to look after his wife could no longer manage. The second older person, in her carer's words, 'just could not care for herself'.

Increased mental and physical deterioration were the explanation for the third older person, from Manor, moving into residential care. Her son, who worked full-time, sometimes away from home, and had two preschool age children, was unable to provide the degree of help necessary to support his considerably confused and occasionally incontinent mother at home.

The two hospital residents had both been admitted after falling, spending the night on the floor and being discovered by their respective wardens. For one, it was the third time she had been in hospital in the past year. On this occasion, she had broken her humerus and collar bone, and dislocated her shoulder. Her carer insisted that, this time, she was going into a private home 'even if she change[d] her mind'. The carer herself had ME, the effects of which had forced her to retire three years earlier, her husband was off work due to ill health, and she still had a teenage child living at home, so she did not realistically feel in a position to offer increased practical help.

The second older woman was found to have pneumonia and diabetes. A home assessment demonstrated how little she was able to do for herself, and her carer, with the demands of her job and home weighing on her, felt overwhelmed at the thought of how much more again she would have to do for her mother, even if intensive home care and a full range of aids and adaptations were to be obtained: 'I felt like I was fighting for a life of my own' (SG). The older person finally suggested the move to residential care herself, having enjoyed the time she spent there while her daughter was away on holiday. At the time of the interview, she was awaiting the availability of a permanent place.

In sum, in every situation the older person had moved out of their home primarily because a crisis point had been reached in terms of their physical and/or mental health which was compounded by limits on the amount of support which carers were able (and, to some extent, willing) to provide.

All carers in this group reported changes in the health and/or behaviour of the older person, including forgetfulness, aggressive outbursts and depression, loss of self-will, decisiveness and motivation, frailty and incontinence, which were clearly a source of stress. Two carers were particularly distressed by their physical inability to carry on caring. One man, who had done 'everything' for his wife, stated that 'caring was life' (SG). Others spoke of suffering moods, tiredness, anxiety, nerves, tension and irritability. One woman from Southey Green described her social life as being restricted because she got 'too tired to bother'. Another struggled with the lack of obligation she felt towards her 'aunt', who was, in fact, a very distant, non-blood relative on her husband's side of the family, resisting the possibility that time spent looking after her might intrude into time devoted to her own parents.

Changes in service provision

In every case carers spoke of an increase in the number of visits and amount of help provided prior to the older person's entry into hospital or residential care. Both carers in Manor reported additional supervisory calls; in one case, the carer had also arranged regular visits from the district nurses and an assessment by the occupational therapist who supplied his mother(the older person) with a raised toilet seat and raised height chair. In Southey Green, satisfaction with caring arrangements varied. One carer described her 'aunt' as getting 'all she could'. An extra call had been put in at lunch-time to make sure the older person ate something, though she had started to refuse to let the nurse bath her, which was a source of concern to the carer. A second carer was grateful for the extra pop-in visits, but described her mother as a 'loner' who did not like people 'running in and out'. The third said that wardens were now calling in pairs twice daily to help him wash and dress his wife. He noted that he received no practical support, but would not ask for any more help having been turned down once before.

Involvement in service organization

The latter two respondents were clearly quite protective of their caring roles. The woman looking after her mother suggested that she found it difficult to hand things over to others to do: 'I felt that I couldn't leave her. I sort of knew best what she wanted and what she didn't' (SG). Consequently, unless she bumped into staff in passing or they phoned to say her mother was ill, the carer only had contact with the home care services to request extra support when she went away on holiday. Otherwise workers 'pleased themselves'. The second carer was a very proud man who dismissed the idea of workers understanding his position, saying that he had 'got stuck into [his] job, knew what to do and didn't need anyone else' (SG). Approached by the home care organizer, the carer's response was to query whether she had the staff to provide additional help and to conclude that there was 'no use in talking about it'.

The remaining carers were far more involved in service organization. The third carer from Southey Green had taken pains to explain to workers the nature of her relationship to her 'aunt', since she felt that they had assumed they were related and subsequently expected her to do more. After this, the main warden had become far more responsive to requests for support with, for example, the supervision of the older person's medication, and, when the older person had suffered a number of falls, she began telephoning the carer every other day with progress reports. Of the two carers in Manor, one described the key worker as being 'like a friend' who understood his needs; they 'worked together' to look after the older person. The second did not see a lot of the support workers but felt able to ask for small favours, such as the fetching of prescriptions or items of shopping, and said that staff came to realize when he could no longer cope.

Implications for service change

Four out of the five carers said that services had succeeded in the goal of supporting them in their caring role by visiting daily; one carer from each area was thus relieved of the pressure of having to call every day, while a third, from Southey Green, felt secure knowing that somebody would be in touch if something happened to the older person. One man from Southey Green claimed both he and his wife could have been better assisted through increased help of a practical nature. A second carer from this sample similarly spoke of the benefits to older people and carers alike of cleaning assistance. However, she later pointed out that she had actually worked as both a care assistant and a home help, and was therefore aware of the complexities of the caring context and the constraints on resources, given which she was generally satisfied with the services provided. The remaining three carers – one from Southey Green and two from Manor – all judged the services to have been more than adequate in looking after the older person, stressing that the ultimate reason for the older person's entry into residential care was the severity of their physical and mental deterioration rather than a deficiency of help.

New carers

The fourth group of respondents interviewed at the second stage of the evaluation were referred to as 'new carers', although only one of the six people involved had begun caring since the first round of interviews with the older person. The remaining five had been caring for between 18 months and six years, though not always as the older person's *main* carer; that is, one respondent had recently taken over as the named successor to a carer who had died between rounds. The transition meant that, in addition to cooking for the older person twice a week, she also undertook his shopping as well as checking daily on his well-being.

None of the respondents showed support for the idea of the older person moving in with them in the longer term, or for the idea of residential care. No incidences had occurred resulting in the carer having to stay with the older person or vice versa since the older person had first been interviewed. However, two carers in Manor and one in Southey Green reported a decline in the older person's mental and physical health over this period. The two Manor carers had increased their input as a consequence, though in one instance, it was on a temporary basis only; the carer's mother had begun to suffer heart pains and, for six to seven weeks, the respondent and her sister visited whenever they were able. The second carer suggested that the decline was irreversible – amongst other things, the older person suffered from arthritis, heart trouble and a chest condition – and had increased the number of meals she cooked for her neighbour as well as the daily pop-in visits she paid.

Changes in service provision

All three carers had attempted to get additional support from services but only one had been successful. The carer in question – herself 80 years old and caring for three elderly sisters – went to the NSU in person to request extra supervisory checks for her neighbour after support workers had failed to call for three days. Since this time, workers had increased the number of calls they paid from three to four a week to regular daily visits. A second carer spoke to the support worker when a prescription for the older person was not collected, but she claimed that this had not subsequently led to discussions about the amount of help being provided. More than anything, the carer wished for a 'warden' to check on her father at night while she was working shifts. The respondent in Southey Green had made enquiries about a chair-lift for his mother, who suffered from rheumatism and angina and was finding it increasingly difficult to climb the stairs. However, his request was turned down with the explanation that the lift could only be operated under supervision. The carer had also made an unsuccessful request for extra cleaning help.

In addition to the services outlined above, both the Manor carers spoke of their desire for help with bathing but pointed out the blocks to such assistance which, in this instance, were put up by the respective older persons rather than resulting from a lack of involvement in organization or limited resources. For example, one carer stated that her neighbour refused the services of an auxiliary nurse because of pride and embarrassment. The second carer said that her father had used the bathing facilities at the NSU only twice despite being registered for the service. He would not let the carer or her sister bath him: 'he tends not to bother'.

Involvement in service organization

The actions of the carer who had visited the NSU led her to feel she had played a part in service organization. She also saw the support workers, both in the older person's home as well as outside, since she lived close to the unit, and they usually had 'a little chat'. The other two carers claimed that they felt some involvement if not, in the words of one, 'any say' (M). That is, workers in Manor were thought to be aware of and to understand the position of carers, but the services were 'overloaded' so that families were often left to do what they could. On the other hand, the respondent from Southey Green claimed that workers in the traditional home care service were governed to too great an extent by rules and regulations shaping their tasks to make it worthwhile asking what the carer wanted.

Of the remaining three new carers, one said that she had talked with the unit manageress at the point of assessment of the older person only, the second that, as a neighbour, arrangements were not her business, the third, similarly, that it was his mother who had applied for assistance. None of the latter five carers had enough contact with workers to produce a meaningful relationship. Given these responses, it was not surprising that four of the new carers said that they were not asked by workers about the help that they desired. An additional carer did not think it necessary: 'They know what they're going for'. Even the carer who met regularly with support workers felt her contribution was 'taken for granted' at times.

Implications for service change

Three new carers, all from Manor, felt that services had achieved the goals of enabling the older person to remain in the community and of supporting themselves as carers. They had done this, in two cases through supervisory visits, in the third through helping the older person with rising and retiring since the carer was unable to get to her mother's house on a daily basis. One commented that the combination of visits from herself and the support workers provided essential company for her neighbour. She was helped by knowing there was someone for her to fall back on. Another said that her mother in fact resisted early morning supervisory checks from workers but that it gave her 'peace of mind'.

Of the three carers who did not respond positively to these items, one woman from Manor said she found it difficult to answer the first question because she did not see staff at work, and regarded the second question not applicable since she was 'only' a neighbour and did very little. The two remaining carers, one from each area, indicated an insufficiency of help provided by the respective services. The carer from Southey Green wanted more help of a personal kind for his mother, over and above the cleaning help and early morning warden call which she received. The carer in Manor said that she was happy continuing to see to both the practical and personal needs of her father, but wished for somebody to pay a supervisory visit at night when she worked shifts since he was very vulnerable living on his own.

Conclusion

This chapter has revealed that, despite the major investment represented by the Manor Support Unit, informal carers are still the mainstay of care for older people. Although, in common with all previous studies, we approached the issue of 'care' primarily through the performance of practical tending tasks, the research revealed a range of intrinsic rewards, such as satisfaction, warmth and goodness, associated with the caring relationship. Also, important in policy terms, we found no desire on the part of carers to off-load their tasks onto the formal services. Surprisingly, in view of the user-oriented aspirations of the NUS initiative, there was very little indication of carers being involved in decisions about the organization of services for the older person they were caring for, and actually less close involvement than under the Southey Green home care system. Moreover, while the majority verdict of those informal carers with continuous responsibilities for the support of older people in both areas was that the social services had enabled older people to remain in the community and had supported their own caring activities, the majority was larger in Southey Green than in Manor.

Notes

1 Given that carers were accessed via elderly respondents, they are identified accordingly as being from Manor (M) or Southey Green (SG) even if this does not reflect where they actually lived.

2 One of the nine bereaved carers from Manor was, in fact, the wife of the original respondent who was still too upset over his father's death to take part. She had been present at the first interview and had played a major role in caring for her father-in-law. She volunteered to take the place of her husband, having a number of comments about services that she wished to make.

7

Support workers

Introduction

This chapter focuses on the role of support workers and their participation, as frontline providers of care, in the translation of the NSU philosophy into practice. Surprisingly there has been relatively little research about the experiences of the personal social services workforce, despite their central role in the organization and delivery of care, and this evaluation specifically set out to place the key actors – users, carers and workers – at its core.

The organization of frontline staff, in fact, constituted the key departure of the NSU initiative from traditional practice. Home wardens and home helps – now known as home carers – were replaced by three teams of support workers fulfilling an expanded range of activities within people's homes, as well as day centre duties and a number of tasks undertaken by social work assistants (see Chapter 3). The expectation was that teams would respond flexibly to the fluctuating support requirements of individuals, based on overall assessments of their needs and resources. They would evolve their own ways of working according to local conditions, demands upon them, and the skills and experience of particular members. An additional goal was to establish close collaborative practices between support workers and community health personnel.

Support workers talked about these and other aspects of their jobs in semi-structured or focused group interviews. They were also observed at work. Comparative data was drawn from diaries kept by a number of workers from the NSU and from the home care service in Southey Green (see appendix).

Becoming support workers

Background

There was noticeable diversity in individual backgrounds, but the 'typical' support worker was a married woman in her mid-40s, who worked part-time and contributed jointly to the household income, and whose children were over 16 and/or had left home. She had previously held a number of unskilled or semi-skilled jobs, commonly in the public service sector, before joining the home help service. Her reasons for entering the domiciliary services included the need and/or desire for a job, the convenience of hours and locality, formal and informal experience, and the caring nature of the work.

Bearing in mind the fact that NSUs were intended to be a radical initiative in the field of social care, for what reasons, then, had interviewees taken up the post of support worker? The majority had actually been redeployed, either due to the opening of the centre or to the closure of residential homes. Transference to a new district within Sheffield was not considered a viable option, especially by those for whom the chance to work close to home and to their children's schools was part and parcel of their decision to become home helps/wardens. Only five had actively chosen the job of support worker, including two who wanted to move beyond the limited cleaning role in which, as home helps, they felt themselves to be confined: 'I was a cleaner, that's *all* I did', and 'they said I couldn't care. I wasn't there to care'. Two others wanted to escape what they referred to as the 'conveyor belt' and 'production line' organization of residential care.

Opinions differed as to whether the job met workers' expectations. A number felt that it did not fit its written description, which was rather loosely worded and open to interpretation and, in particular, said that it had overplayed the social work qualities of the role. One woman described the job as 'just an update on home help to get breakfasts and dinners. It's just another name.' On the other hand, a former care supervisor in the voluntary sector said that it had met her hopes of being a 'challenging, worthwhile and rewarding career'. She particularly valued the level of responsibility and the variation in everyday activities which the post had promised.

As for the objectives of the initiative, workers were not always confident in giving details of the policy strategy behind the NSUs, though they were very positive about the operation of the unit: 'Well, I can't say [exactly] what it is but it's got a good aim'. Descriptions of goals were broad: 'Meeting the needs of old people', 'Keeping them out in the community as long as possible, help and support but not to take over' and 'Supporting the whole family'. The aims of their own role, too, were expressed very loosely or generally: 'visiting needy people'; 'everything'; 'caring what counts'; 'Jack of all trades'.

Comparison with traditional home care services

A much clearer picture of their role emerged when support workers were asked to draw comparisons between the new NSU service and the home help service. How the differences were perceived in the main depended upon positions held within the traditional service, which was characterized by the familiar division among staff between home helps and home wardens. As we have seen (Chapter 3), home helps worked formal and rigid shifts – from 9.00 a.m. to 1.00 p.m. or 3.30 p.m. – performing mainly domestic tasks, and were discouraged from fraternizing with service users. Home wardens operated a split early-morning/evening shift, as well as providing weekend cover, and their activities were more likely to encompass 'caring' duties or personal care. Wardens were paid at a higher rate than home helps for 'unsocial' hours and they also received a telephone allowance, since the nature of their work meant that they quite often needed to contact their supervisors.

Responsibility and flexibility

The biggest change for all support workers related to the new levels of responsibility expected of them. Former home helps had experienced little, if any, control over the organization of their workload, typically receiving a weekly schedule in which help was allocated to users in blocks of time: 'We had a worksheet for a week and *we stuck to that worksheet*'. They described themselves variously as having been 'told what to do', 'answerable to everyone' and 'just like a chimp'.

Within the new initiative, staff still had regular or routine tasks to perform, but *they* were responsible for deciding the ordering of their day to day activities. They were also involved in the longer term assessment and arrangement of support to older people, all of which meant increased paperwork in the form of contact sheets, medical cards, care plans and reviews and team diaries. They were encouraged to use their own initiative and, wherever possible, to deal directly with problems as they arose: 'You're like your own gaffer. You know what a client needs and you do it.'

As part and parcel of the increase in responsibility, support workers found themselves switched to a far more flexible work schedule as well as to a broader programme of activities. The working day was split, informally, into three shifts: mornings, afternoons and evenings, and staff were expected to take their turn to provide weekend cover and, if necessary, night-time support. Emphasis was moved from cleaning to caring and the range of 'medical' tasks provided increased (see Chapter 3).

Autonomy

One of the most immediate effects of the change was the greater autonomy enjoyed especially by ex-home helps who described themselves as being 'free[r]' from the oppressive monitoring of activities and unnecessary time-wasting resulting from the rigid timetabling of help:

When they've set you three hours and you've done a job in an hour because they're so clean – some of them were clean – and I just used to come in, I used to stand in this kitchen, just playing with the dish cloth from quarter-past two to half-past three watching this apple tree blossom, apples fall off, year after year. It used to drive me mad.

Under the new NSU regime, support to individual users could be more usefully spread out over the week. Former wardens who had faced a very hectic schedule generally found the transition afforded them more time to complete tasks and, above all, meal preparation. Workers were also able to allocate support more equitably:

> You can give them what's needed more. A lot of people was getting it what don't need it, there was, and them what needed it weren't getting it.

The elements of flexibility and autonomy were found particularly satisfying when of mutual benefit to staff and to users as, for example, when support workers who preferred to start work early were teamed with individuals who liked to rise at an early hour. In this respect, the job of support worker was seen as a combination of the best of the two traditional roles. It ended the two-tier or 'two class' system of care by which wardens were commonly perceived to be of higher status than home helps, replacing it with one which was perceived as being 'a lot fairer' as well as more efficient for workers and users alike. Frontline staff were better able to plan with users what they did for them: 'because no matter how good anybody is in assessing, nobody can go in and talk for quarter of an hour to somebody and assess their needs'. Rather than simply working *for* or giving help *to* users, support workers reported a sense that they were working *with* them.

This is not to say that the job was not demanding; morning shifts, when support workers helped older people to get out of bed, wash, dress and prepare their breakfast, often left little room for the notion of 'flexibility' to be fully implemented or appreciated. Yet staff were still expected to be willing and available to respond to unforeseen changes in users' circumstances. To this end they operated an accounts system with their hours. Frequently they worked with time in hand though, to a limited extent, they were able to structure their day around their own situation, often in order to combine formal and informal caring roles. However, flexibility was ultimately constrained by the availability of resources. Due to its additional cost, the night sitting service was restricted to special circumstances such as terminal illness, for example, while skeleton staffing operated at weekends, resulting in what one respondent judged to be a 'below standard' service. More generally, at any one time workers visited users to whom they would like to have given more support, especially of an emotional kind.

Stress

The clear disadvantage for staff in the new more flexible roles was the added stress that they experienced. Indeed this stress was a direct function of the flexible nature of the support worker role. The work was 'harder graft' in their former posts, but 'more mental' in the support worker service. In addition to coping with the 'unpredictability' of death or the sudden illness of users, support workers felt unable to 'switch off', especially because they could be telephoned at home and asked to cover in an emergency situation, though also because they worried about users who became, in the words of one, like the members of an 'extended family'. A couple of ex-residential care assistants said that they found it particularly distressing to leave older people alone and locked into their own homes. Support workers' families sometimes objected to what they saw as the intrusion of their jobs into their private lives.

Team organization helped to mitigate stress. It enabled a balance of strengths and weaknesses, and reduced the harassment and sense of isolation experienced by former home care workers. However, there was always the possibility that individual members of the team might not contribute what was judged to be their fair share, relying on others to pick things up out of a sense of commitment, concern, duty or responsibility. Staff who worked part-time said they often felt as though they did as much as full-timers. Such factors could lead to the creation of tension and even divisions within teams.

Policy and guidelines

Despite the inclusion of a number of new activities among the tasks performed by support workers, as shown in Chapter 3, other features of the service remained the same. The most notable was the fact that, apart from their basic job description and health and safety regulations, most workers claimed not to have any specific policies or written guidelines which spelt out their duties and the tasks that they were and were not allowed to do as support workers. They either followed 'traditional patterns', sought professional and/or managerial advice and acted on verbal cues, or simply used their 'common sense'.

Some felt that the notion of flexibility precluded the idea of detailed guidelines; policy was thus set or adapted according to circumstances. However, this could work to their disadvantage. For example, support workers were not clear about specific expectations concerning the availability of staff to provide emergency cover. At the same time, it was recognized that important, often demanding, elements of the support worker role could not be defined easily and regimented as 'activities' *per se*. These included social and emotional support, advice, companionship and motivation, which were 'by-products' of visits to users as much as ends in themselves.

Belief in its value to older people as well as the sense of achievement it afforded to staff led some to openly pursue a rehabilitative role, despite frequent resistance to or failure of their efforts: 'I play hell, I always do, I play hell. But I get a lot of satisfaction if somebody'll shift.' However, the fact that such aspects of their role were given little attention in training, could not always be seen to be done or to have immediately measurable benefits, and were commonly experienced as being in competition with practical aspects of care in terms of limitations of time, resulted in other support workers experiencing feelings of anxiety:

> There's practical and emotional, isn't there. I mean, I had one and she wouldn't even let you hoover up. She'd say 'Sit down, talk to me', you know. That made her quite happy. Made me feel guilty, but it made her feel quite happy.

Such sentiments implied potential conflict with the notion of user-led services.

Organization of activities

The process of allocating support to older people was determined at the outset by team leaders who were responsible for initial assessments of new referrals. They then drew up 'care plans' based, as far as possible, on the wishes of the older persons, and detailing the nature and frequency of help to be given. From that point onwards, it was the duty of support workers to monitor the needs of individual clients.

To some extent care plans helped to limit the potential for exploitation arising from the lack of clear guidelines. Nevertheless, concern was expressed about the amount of work done in antisocial hours and as 'emergency cover', and individuals still reported carrying out 'favours' for older people in their own time; visiting people who were sick, taking home their washing or sewing, shopping for special items. Although support workers suffered less than staff in more traditional set-ups from shortages of time combined with the need to be seen to be caring, as the preceding section indicated, these pressures were still evident. In particular, the influence of the familial model of care underpinning traditional patterns of service provision (Warren 1990) was apparent in workers' descriptions of their relationships with older people and the various factors shaping them.

Relationships with older people and their carers

Level of need

In common with domiciliary staff from other local authorities, support workers used categorizations to talk about older people which were useful in understanding the nature of the relationships between them (Warren 1990). Here groupings were based on level of need as well as nature of the person's disability or personal behaviour (Table 7.1).

Users were referred to generally as 'clients'. All support workers were assigned an average of one or two 'main' or 'heavy' clients. These were older people with high levels of need who required 'full' care and to whom individual support workers were directly responsible. Full care was also known

Table 7.1 A classification of support workers' relationships with older people

Main/heavy need clients: Older people requiring 'full' or 'daily' care of a personal and practical nature constituting the core of the support worker role.

Low need clients: Users with lower levels of need, typically requiring weekly errand care or monthly cleaning.

Handicapped/disabled clients: Includes severely disabled older people: e.g. amputees, sufferers of strokes, etc. More likely to require help of personal kind: e.g. getting in and out of bed, dressing, preparing food.

Confused clients: Older people suffering from confusion, dementia or Alzheimer's disease, usually requiring mix of domestic, errand and personal care.

Dirty clients/dirty homes: Older people maintaining low standards of personal hygiene or living in dirty/dilapidated homes. Usually confused or with learning difficulties and requiring 'heavy housework'.

Awkward and/or abusive clients:
Awkward: older people who are 'fussy' or 'demanding' or constantly moaning.
Abusive: older people who are verbally or physically threatening.

Undeserving clients: Includes older people who overplay their disability or who continue to receive help on the basis of tradition rather than need.

as 'daily care' since it usually involved workers paying an average of at least two to three visits per day to a user to provide help of a personal and practical kind. The remaining service users, whom we have called 'low need clients', comprised those users whose needs were not so great and who were therefore visited less frequently and/or regularly. They too were assigned to individual or key workers though, because of the nature and level of support received, were more likely to be shared out among workers from week to week.

Within these two main need categories, workers made further distinctions on the basis of disability or personal circumstances. We report these, sometimes pejorative, descriptions because they represent the operational classifications used by support workers in their day to day work and discourse. They talked of 'handicapped/disabled' clients; 'confused' clients and 'dirty', or in one case 'mucky' clients using much the same criteria as home helps in other parts of the country (Warren 1990). They also referred to 'awkward and/or abusive' clients. A final category of user whom we have called 'undeserving clients' comprised older people who were thought not to need the (degree of) help provided to them.

Team leaders attempted to match support workers and users as closely or harmoniously as possible and teams generally 'shared the load' of those users regarded as being 'difficult' or 'dirty'. If workers showed any objection to the idea of looking after older people in their own homes or expressed support for residential care, it was usually with reference to such groups of users. For example, a handful of individual users were judged as being at too great a risk to be living at home due to physical frailty and/or confusion or depression. Occasionally, staff felt themselves to be at danger, fearing physical attack by abusive older people. All support workers agreed 'if they don't need it they shouldn't have it', though the unpleasantness of withdrawing help was noted.

The setting and nature of care

Support workers did not relate to older people on the basis of levels of need alone; the nature of the care which they subsequently gave as well as the setting for its delivery also played a major part. All of the workers we spoke to recognized the importance to older people of remaining in their own homes. It signified autonomy and independence and also was believed to preserve motivation. Support workers described the meaning of home to older people variously as their 'domain'; 'castle'; 'own four walls'; 'own key in the door'; 'bits and bobs'; 'memories'; 'self-respect'; and 'dignity'. Individuals had a right to 'get up when they want and . . . go to bed when they want', and they could 'say whatever they want'.

It was generally considered to be a duty not to 'overstep that privacy' – 'I wouldn't like anybody coming in [my home] telling me what to do' – and, in this respect, workers described themselves as 'visitors'. Yet a one-to-one level of contact, especially with people living alone and/or requiring help with very personal tasks over a sustained period of time, made inevitable a certain degree of intimacy and trust. Respondents spoke of being treated as agony aunts, members of the family, even second daughters. Occurrences of gift-giving – often in the forms of confectionery or toiletries – were, in part, an expression of affinity.

While it was possible for workers and users alike to get too involved, other relationships were of a more formal nature. Some older people – typically requiring help of a purely practical kind, such as heavy cleaning – saw themselves as 'the boss' and set out very strict parameters for the conduct of activities. While few older people called staff by their new title of 'support worker', this group of users not only used the former title of 'home help' but some had been known to refer to workers as cleaners, and in one case as a 'scrubber'. Workers referred to in this way felt they were being 'taken for granted' or treated as 'skivvies'.

Gender

Gender was another influence on the degree of closeness between older people and workers. It was not simply that caring roles were perceived traditionally by most people as women's jobs. Caring was synonymous with femaleness. Subsequently, when female support workers gave help to an older user which was of a personal nature, such as washing, it was 'natural' for them to perform this role. This was not possible in the case of male support workers, since caring of this kind was not a feature of maleness. It required a level of intimacy which, instead, carried sexual undertones. Increasing numbers of men may have been entering the nursing profession but in the private setting of the user's own home the medical model was not appropriate and some older people – men as well as women – found it impossible to renegotiate rules of intimacy:

> A woman's always related to as a nurse, isn't she? So I think they think when we're washing then they relate to us as like a nurse, whereas a man, they relate to it as sex, don't they?

At the same time, one support worker believed that his gender and youth were an (additional) source of concern to older men as a reminder of their increased powerlessness:

> I think it upsets a man . . . for such a young fellow to go in and wash him. He feels more inferior with a young man as us. You know what I mean, he'll think 'Oh, he's fit and strong and a young fellow and I'm in this wheelchair.'

Attitudes to men doing domestic tasks were acknowledged to be changing, yet a number of female workers still believed it was 'not a man's job' to provide personal care in a one-to-one situation. Male support workers themselves could do very little in response to older people's refusals to accept their help in this context. One commented that he understood and respected the reasons for their objections. He felt a greater sense of frustration regarding other assumptions made about him on the basis of his status, including the fact that he must be gay and that he would not be able to cook.

Despite the suggestion from one group that there were differences in temperament among older people – older men wanted 'more cosseting' when they were 'poorly', and were 'mardy' and more untidy – workers refuted the idea that they had different sets of expectations concerning the support required by men and by women: 'You tailor your visits down to each client and what that client needs'. A handful of women said that they had felt awkward or embarrassed when first required to wash or bath older men, but had overcome this feeling by rationalizing it as part of their job – 'You've just got to do what is what' – which, in turn, was an extension of their feminine/motherly role – 'Like caring for a child, you know'. Likewise, they tended to deal with sexual harassment at an individual level – 'You just say "put it away"' – and as an occupational hazard – 'You have to put them in their place'. However, a couple of references were made to instances where male support workers had taken over the care of older men because of persistent harassment of female staff, and several respondents voiced the opinion that it might be better if male workers cared for violent or abusive male users.

Informal carers: family, friends and neighbours

A number of the characteristics outlined above also featured in support workers' relationships with the relatives, friends and neighbours who cared for older people. Since relatives and kin were the major source of informal support to users, workers commonly referred to 'the family' when asked about carers. The consensus of opinion was clearly that family members should be involved to as great a degree as possible with the welfare of their older relatives. 'Good' families were those that 'pulled their weight'. They were exemplified, at the extreme, by the daughter who provided '24-hour cover' for her mother; she 'did everything', including taking her mother away on holiday for five weeks of the year. 'Bad' families left everything to the support workers, or cared simply for instrumental reasons such as financial gain through the receipt of attendance allowance or in anticipation of inheritance. One person believed that such carers receiving benefits should pay something towards the services provided.

The aim of supporting carers or families was identified as being part of the general objectives of the unit:

> Well, you know, when I first came on the job they told me when they interviewed me that I worked alongside the family, so that's what I do.

Yet, in line with findings noted above, there appeared to be no specific guidelines to recommend how support workers should go about translating the goal into action. A handful said they made a point of contacting informal helpers when an older person was first referred to the service. The remainder left it to the carers to get in touch. The existence of personality clashes or longstanding feuds between carers and older people, as well as the 'burden' of caring, were acknowledged and respondents tried to relieve pressure where possible. Those who had personal experience of being an informal carer appreciated the, albeit temporary, sense of 'non-responsibility' or respite which their support could provide, especially to carers living with the person for whom they cared. In this situation, support workers commonly assisted by offering a sitting service while the carer did tasks outside the home, or relief from certain practical jobs such as shopping if carers themselves appeared to be ill or under stress. Otherwise, approaching families was talked about very generally as, for example, a 'fine balance' between 'taking over completely and backing off' and 'not a straight-away thing' but something 'you build up to'.

In the ideal situation, support workers and carers came together and tried to 'get an understanding' to 'work things out between them' and to 'work as a team'. This was not only for the sake of the carers, in order to 'take a bit of weight off them', it also relieved pressures on workers: 'Well you try and include family don't you because if they can help you, you know, with doing a few dinners, it helps the team.' However, the process was complicated by the varied response of carers towards support workers. While some families welcomed assistance, rewarding workers with presents at Christmas, for example, others were felt to resent outside involvement. Informal carers could be very demanding – 'We have notes left, you know, "You do this and you do that!"' – and even jealous of the attachment to workers which older people developed.

The expansion of the support worker role was judged to have had diverse effects. On the one hand, there had been a withdrawal of informal help:

> It's gone backwards as far as families helping because when we were home helps, if they'd got daughters, they'd got to help and do a bit. They're not now, they are just standing back and leaving us.

On the other, the increased contact which support workers had with older people was believed to have encouraged greater liaison with carers. Yet, despite claims that there were families who now treated individual staff as 'equals', a number of carers still referred to workers as home helps or domestics, assigning them the 'rubbish work'. In turn, support workers' comments on their relationships with the families of older people suggested they had mixed perceptions of their responsibilities to carers. They emphasized the carer's well-being *per se* but their responses also indicated a more instrumental approach, reflecting the ambiguous position occupied by carers within the wider social care system (Twigg 1992).

Relationships with management and other professionals

The details of care arrangements were also shaped by relationships with team leaders and other professionals alongside whom support workers operated.

Team leaders

In comparison with traditional services, the amount of contact between frontline workers and their supervisors had inevitably increased relative to their greater involvement in the organization of care. Support workers saw team leaders at weekly team meetings, for regular supervisory appraisal sessions and whenever new developments in users' situations needed to be discussed. On the whole, relations were of a much more relaxed and informal nature. Both parties were on first-name terms and shared a staff room, for example. Support workers were encouraged to use the building as a base and were free to call into the office with problems or to seek advice at any time. In the same way that support workers were expected to work *with* users and carers, so the emphasis was on team leaders working *with* their respective teams in the organization of care.

Achieving this goal required a similarly fine balance, however. Any action taken by team leaders which suggested a move (back) to the strict disciplinarian nature of the traditional services – for example, covert monitoring of activities – was condemned. Yet neither did support workers like being 'left to sort everything themselves', especially with regard to paperwork which some found particularly demanding and therefore tended to neglect. The failure of one team leader to manage the 'different personalities' of the group had led to the emergence of divisions. The most successful management style was judged by the support workers as being one born of grass roots experience of what the job encompassed and of what individual workers were capable. This was also believed to lead to an improved service for older people since team leaders were better able to assess their needs and to match up users and workers.

Joint collaboration: the health team

Successful relationships with members of the health team likewise depended on 'respect' for the work of staff based on first hand knowledge of the support worker role. As home helps and wardens, respondents had not been called upon formally to liaise with health workers. Meetings took place largely by chance within the homes of older people and were typically with members of the nursing staff, who were described as 'stand-offish': 'they didn't want to know'. Moreover, they came from both within and without the district, so that the chances of achieving some sort of rapport through regular contact were slim.

In Manor, F&CS and health services had made concerted attempts to operate together and in ways which were complementary. Where there were areas of overlap in their activities – the bathing of older people, for example – then discussions, between managers at least, were conducted in a spirit of collaboration rather than demarcation, avoiding any deepening of unmet need. All workers appreciated the ease of communication and referral afforded by the patch-based system of care.

Efforts to build up good cross-agency working relationships at frontline level were still patchy but they were improving steadily. The EMI (Elderly Mentally Ill) day centre was organized by the community psychiatric nurse with the assistance of support workers who also collaborated with nurses in the operation of the bath run. The occupational therapist was singled out as taking a special interest in support workers' activities and the physiotherapist contributed to training sessions. District nurses had begun to turn up to team meetings whenever possible to discuss problems or care plans while a handful of support workers had, in turn, accompanied them for a day out on the patch, but these ideas had been slow to start off.

Support workers viewed members of the health team collectively as a 'good crowd' – friendly and approachable. Nevertheless, they were still seen, and believed to see themselves, on a different level by dint of their professional training and expertise. Some support workers claimed that district nurses had understood collaboration to mean they could off-load a number of the routine practical aspects of care – bathing, in particular – onto their shoulders, freeing nurses to carry out medical tasks. Such misunderstandings were not helped by the fact that the health team was based at premises approximately half a mile from the NSU building, greatly reducing opportunities for the kind of contact necessary to the mutual appreciation of roles and resources.

GPs and social workers

The attitude of other professionals towards the NSU project was judged by support workers as being mixed, and, in a number of cases, in need of far greater enlightenment. Taking doctors as an example, one GP practice on the Manor had kept abreast of changes, and consequently showed workers 'more respect' and 'credibility'. At the other extreme, workers reported that few hospital doctors had ever heard of the term 'support worker'. Social workers were believed to have acted generally very defensively and jealously towards the development of the key worker component of the support worker role: 'I think they're scared of us doing their job'. Interviewees, in their turn, felt the boundary between the posts of social and support worker to have become much finer – 'I think, apart from training, we're unqualified social workers' – the major difference being levels of pay.

The job of support worker as an innovation

Qualities of the support worker role

Despite its expansion, support workers' descriptions of the personal qualities demanded of their role, to a greater or lesser degree, matched those described elsewhere by domiciliary care workers (Bond 1980; Dexter and Harbert 1983; Warren 1990). They included the social and largely feminine attributes of patience and tolerance, concern and compassion, a common sense understanding of caring as well as listening skills, a sense of humour and commitment. Some struggled to spell out distinguishing characteristics, indeed a minority still referred to themselves as home helps: 'I'll say, you know, "I'm home help. New word for it's a support worker, but I'm old fashioned home help."' However, it should be stressed that respondents commonly described themselves in this way in one of two situations; first, when in the company of users who had been receiving support for several years and who did not 'understand' or accept the new changes and second, when introducing themselves to older people who were new referrals to the unit but familiar only with the traditional titles of the service: 'If you say "support worker" they don't know who you mean. They recognize you more as home help.'

According to workers, the problem was that the 'outside was not educated' though it was felt that the next wave of younger referrals to the service who were less familiar with traditional service organization would be able to 'take in [the changes] better'. Informing people by letter of the new aims of the unit had not been enough, and support workers faced 'a lot of aggro' from users with which they were left to deal largely on their own. Older people accused them of using their attendance at meetings as an excuse to skive from their work, and more than one interviewee admitted still doing 'a bit of cleaning' every week so users would not 'get on [their] backs'.

The issue of information was not just confined to users, informal carers and other professionals, however. The introduction of the NSUs was billed as a major innovation in social care yet once the centre had opened, senior management personnel had 'never taken much notice' of the scheme. The majority of support workers had received no more than the introductory two weeks' training provided prior to the centre opening (if that) and that was described as 'squashed in', little different from that which they were given as home helps, and as failing to prepare them for the reality of being 'on district'. They were effectively 'thrown in at the deep end'.

This is not to suggest that workers were not capable of providing adequate care or lacked motivation to develop their skills. A number spoke of in-house talks and training schemes, and day-release courses in which they had participated. One person had attended a two-week 'management-led' course; another had registered for the National Vocational Qualification (NVQ) in social care and hoped to go on to gain a diploma. However, these were general programmes open to workers from a number of fields – community day and residential care – and chiefly attended on a voluntary basis. There had been no follow-up training targeted specifically at support workers in the two years since the unit at Manor had been operating. The problem was that, in the absence of clear new guidelines, experience gained as former home helps and wardens continued to be employed as a reference point by workers, a handful of whom subsequently defended cleaning and rejected the need for further instruction:

> Cleaning is a part of caring because it was drilled into me as a home help: 'If the lady's got a clean window they will sit many an hour looking out of a window. They are not bothered about anything to eat if they've got the window cleaned to sit and look through.'

> When you've been on like Marge 17 years you don't need no training. If you don't know now, you will never know.

Conclusion

From the perspective of frontline providers of care, NSUs had succeeded in achieving a more flexible service which offered a comprehensive range of support, in a number of areas, beyond that outlined as necessary to constitute sufficient domiciliary care (Norton *et al.* 1986: 116). These changes had been facilitated through teamwork and increased levels of autonomy and responsibility among workers. Joint collaboration with the community health team on a geographical basis (while it lasted) also ensured much more efficient referral and feedback systems across the two sectors of care. The combination of these features suggested, moreover, a step forward towards the packaging of care to older people, even if support workers did not speak in this particular language.

Changing services involves not just new activities but new attitudes, however. It was clear that support workers still defined need largely in terms of physical disability and responded to it on the basis of what was available already. Approaches to informal support tended to be based on an implicit conception of carers as 'resources' – part of the taken-for-granted background to provision or, perhaps less often, as 'co-workers' – to be encouraged and supported but in an instrumental fashion (Twigg and Atkin 1991). This is not to say that support workers did not recognize additional needs but both the nature and setting of care made involvement and empowerment a 'threatening business' (Beresford 1992: ii). Other weaknesses in the initiative were inherent to schemes with certain key features: for example, disharmony within teamwork (Renshaw 1988), the defence of professional boundaries within jointly collaborative projects (Webb and Hobdell 1980; Wright *et al.* 1988; Meetham and Thompson 1992) and the exploitation of staff operating within 'familial' models of care (Bond 1980; Warren 1990).

8

User and carer involvement in principle and practice

Introduction

The core aims of the Neighbourhood Support Units (NSUs) – to enable older people to remain in the community for as long as they so desire and to strengthen family, friendship and neighbourhood networks – were informed by the general trend towards more flexible and user-oriented social services (Chapters 2 and 3). These wider objectives were invoked by senior staff, from both health and social services, who were involved in the day to day running of the scheme. As we have shown in previous chapters, however, the manner in which and extent to which support workers put them into practice were constrained by a lack of resources and operational guidelines. Older people and their carers appeared to have very limited say in the organization of their individual support or care packages. The single most frequently given explanation by users of both the traditional home care (HC) and the new NSU services was that, ultimately, decision making powers still lay in the hands of service providers: 'They just give you what they think is essential. There's no frills' (NSU); 'There are too many chiefs and not enough Indians' (NSU); 'You get what they send and that's that' (HC). Some older people believed that staff in general were not really concerned about their welfare: 'When you tell them what type of service you need they won't listen to you' (HC). One man commented sardonically: 'They decide themselves. Well, perhaps to a certain degree. If I said don't come any more, they'd take notice of that' (NSU).

In this chapter we consider the goal of user-centredness from two sets of perspectives. The first, which we have called the management view, draws primarily from semi-structured interviews with more senior staff, comprising social and health care managers and team leaders. The interviews were supplemented by observation of the work of senior staff both at the unit and in the homes of older people (appendix), and by analysis of their work tools, in this case assessment forms. The second set of perspectives is based on a series of case studies of older people and their carers put together in order to explore in more detail whether and how the important objective of involvement was being met (appendix). Pen portraits of two selected households have been included to illustrate the kinds of circumstances, experiences and beliefs that had bearing on the process of user and carer involvement.

The wider context

The relationship between user and carer involvement and service organization could not be fully appreciated without wider consideration of variations in need among older people and their carers and their understanding of the NSU initiative and its aims.

Features of need

Older people have traditionally been assessed for and allocated social care on the basis of health and measurements of incapacity. A less structured exploration of need revealed a complex picture of often interlocking determinants. Older users' assessment of their requirements depended on their individual perceptions of their health, the nature and duration of their illness or disability and on how these factors fitted with their varied personalities and life histories (Shanas *et al.* 1968; Wenger 1984; Warren 1988).

A number of very frail older people described their health as good, dissociating it from their physical fitness or taking pride in their longevity. In contrast, others indicated that particular events, which included withdrawal from long term tranquillizer use and the experience of being burgled, were colouring their overall notion of well-being. One man who was terminally ill with cancer clearly wished to avoid questions of any kind which might lead to the confrontation of this condition, while an older woman with severe dementia was unable to articulate her feelings but tended to express stress or pain through increased disorientation, wandering and incontinence. In both cases, close and frequent monitoring were necessary to obtain an accurate picture of need.

Some individuals, who stressed their independent nature, fought against increased reliance on support, accepting the minimum amount necessary to enable them to live at home. Others were judged by their informal carers to lean on them more heavily than was necessary, in practical terms at least. In three instances, older people were themselves looking after another person. All identified themselves primarily as carers and put the requirements of those to whom they gave support before their own.

Needs were also influenced by certain structural factors such as housing. A number of older people in upper-storey flats were effectively housebound by their fear of negotiating stairs on their own. Adaptations, including bath rails and wheelchair access, had been carried out in some cases, though the provision of alarms appeared of little use to highly confused older people who did not understand their purpose.

While the norm of family care was still very much alive, there were pressures on family members – typically relating to paid employment and to the responsibilities of caring for others. This meant that the normatively approved hierarchical model of family care preferences (Qureshi and Walker 1989) was rarely straightforwardly realized and, where it was, the situation was often highly stressed. A number of carers highlighted their reliance on the telephone to check on the well-being of older people. One carer took turns with her brother in taking their mother to the supermarket to do a 'big monthly shop'. In the absence of family care, neighbourly ties were activated, though support of this kind was generally not as substantial as family care and often was provided by people who were themselves over 65 years of age.

Mrs McAllister

Mrs McAllister had experienced a series of major set-backs to her health including contracting polio when an infant and suffering a brain tumour in middle age. The muscles of both arms and legs were consequently affected and her mobility and manual dexterity considerably impaired. Her fitness was further reduced by arthritis, a chest condition and painful cellulitis covering her legs. Two years previously, she had fallen and broken her wrist and more recently had undergone an operation to stitch her bladder back onto its cradle following a prolapse. Of late, she had also experienced a number of fits which left her trembling and unable to control her limbs or her speech. Mrs McAllister related her life history around these events, stressing her dependence on others, particularly her husband, for support.

Due to the extent of her disabilities, Mrs McAllister had to be carried up and down stairs. However, despite the fact that the only time she ever left her flat was to attend appointments at the hospital, she did not want to move from her flat which had a spare bedroom where her son and daughter-in-law were able to stay and where she had lived happily for more than 18 years. She also claimed that she would feel too vulnerable to the risk of break-ins in ground-floor accommodation. Instead, she thought the council should install lifts to all the upper-storey flats occupied by older people at the same time doubting that it was likely to happen.

As for informal support, in addition to her husband, Mrs McAllister's son and daughter-in-law, Keith and Julie, had an acknowledged caring role. Both worked full-time and they lived on the other side of the city which, without a car, made pop-in visits difficult. Usually, they visited every Sunday for the day, when Julie cooked a full Sunday dinner, did the ironing, washed Mrs McAllister's hair and saw to anything else that needed doing. When Mr McAllister was taken into hospital, they moved into the spare bedroom and Julie took three weeks unpaid leave from work in order to provide Mrs McAllister with the practical and emotional support she needed.

Mrs McAllister also spoke of the neighbours who 'kept an eye' on her and her husband. The nextdoor and upstairs neighbours visited two and four times a week respectively on a social basis. The latter had a spare key in case of emergencies and helped out with shopping when the weather was bad. Another friend, who called in once a week, bathed Mrs McAllister on those occasions when the auxiliary nurse failed to turn up.

Mr Miller
Mr Miller looked outside his own situation in rating his well-being. He had arthritis, heart trouble and a chest condition, walked with the aid of sticks, and struggled to get out of his chair and to wash and dress himself. Since suffering a heart attack two years earlier, he had slept on the settee because he was too scared to go to bed. Recently bereaved and with no close relatives, he spoke tearfully of his loneliness and described life as 'no great joy' as it was. Yet Mr Miller judged his circumstance to be fair given that there were, as he stressed several times, people worse off then he was.

Mr Miller had a number of nieces and nephews but they lived in different areas of Britain and abroad. Only one visited him and then just once every six weeks since he himself was 69 and had a family of six. Mr Miller was estranged from his in-laws. His neighbour, Mrs Hill aged 80, was his chief source of support. She called every morning to check that he was all right. In addition to providing him with a cooked meal five days a week (for which he paid), she did Mr Miller's shopping, fetched his pension and paid his bills, and ordered and collected his prescriptions. Mrs Hill valued her caring role, which gave her a sense of purpose, though she was limited in the amount she could do since she also looked after her three elderly sisters.

The management perspective clearly recognized the variation in user need. However, what was crucial was the fact that opinion was divided on whether the NSU initiative had moved away from providing a general service to as many older people as possible to providing a more intensive service to a smaller number of users, as was its professed goal. In the eyes of one member of the social care staff, the NSUs aimed to do both:

> There are small numbers who need a lot of intensive help and there are other people who perhaps need a shopping trip . . . I think, in a way, we can meet both – if we've got the facilities to do it.

Reasons for, and the potential impact of, differences in views of services emerged in discussion of the initial setting up of the units, especially in relation to the communication of aims.

Communication of aims

At the outset of the initiative, a variety of channels were employed to inform users and carers of the aims of the new unit at Manor, including public meetings, a coffee morning, pamphlets and letters, though most people appeared to learn of the initiative by means of the verbal explanations given by frontline staff and team leaders.

One reason for the intensity of resistance to the changes may have been that policy was not conveyed as successfully as was hoped (Chapter 7). It was certainly the case that a considerable proportion of older people were housebound and unable to attend meetings and/or had difficulty in reading printed materials. Commenting on the first NSU to be opened, one member of the senior staff felt that, in the eagerness to put into operation the new plans for service delivery, not enough time or attention had been devoted to discussion with local people. It seemed the omission had been repeated in Manor, where flexibility was called into question by a number of users:

> The way they go on, I think they please theirselves. I think they make their mind up where they're going and where they're not going.

One senior employee of Sheffield Family and Community Services (F&CS) spoke of making mistakes by 'rushing out' and being 'too straight' with users, and expressed the opinion, in hindsight, that individual changes to services should have been introduced more gradually, especially the reduction in/withdrawal of cleaning support. The view was not necessarily one which implied actively involving users in decisions about the services to be provided, though ultimately managers had acknowledged the voice of users. The pressure of objection – older people were 'going berserk' – meant that the unit was forced to reinstate cleaning support in a number of cases, albeit at a lower level.

Senior staff confirmed the observation (Chapter 7) that, at the point of taking up their posts, support workers too had only partial understanding of the new system. The three-week induction course was judged to have been relatively intensive – 'They might not remember it all but there's paperwork around. They all went home with, you know, a nice bundle at the end of the three weeks' – but at the same time, it tended to concentrate on very general aspects of the care-giving role. Thus, with few guidelines, it was left to the managers of the NSUs to make decisions as they went along on such things as timetabling of shifts, allocation of support and activities to be undertaken, while support workers attempted to translate those decisions to the best of their ability.

The potential for older people to be alienated from service organization and change due to inadequate preparation for the launch of Manor NSU was further compounded by the fact that other local service providers, working in both the health and social care fields, did not have a clear idea of the aims of the unit. Written information had been circulated – 'I don't know whether it goes in the bin or what' – but professionals still phoned asking for a 'home help organizer' to carry out an assessment. Providers based outside Manor and assisting users moving into the area were often ignorant of the existence of the unit and were surprised by what it had to offer.

There were exceptions to the apparent trend for NSUs to operate in relative anonymity or isolation. A couple of team leaders from Manor were members of a housing project group, set up to inform and discuss plans for the building of over 200 new properties in the locality. They were concerned with ensuring that the interests of both workers and potential service users among the new residents be taken into account in the design of the estate. In their various activities away from the units themselves – at workshops, seminars, courses or training sessions, for example – individual support unit staff took pains to communicate information about the NSUs, while within the unit staff had produced a number of booklets and reports about the Manor Neighbourhood Centre.[1]

In her liaison role within the local resource panel, and spurred by the Griffiths' (1988) proposals for the 'packaging of care', the manager of the unit had compiled a programme of all the services, clubs and activities based in the Manor area including those organized by the voluntary sector, which had been distributed to all doctors' surgeries in the locality.[2] At Ecclesfield, a video of the unit's aims and activities had been produced and open days were held to explain various aspects of the services available.

Despite such efforts, it was still believed that 'some kind of formal public relations programme' or 'outreach work' involving team leaders or support workers needed to be established so that other professionals could be better informed about the work of the NSU, though one interviewee was very pessimistic about the likelihood of changing often 'deeply entrenched' professional attitudes towards the role of the social care workers.

Service organization

The complexity of need among older people and their carers combined with general ignorance, uncertainty and ambiguity surrounding service aims raised a number of implications for the notion of participation. Not least, it begged the question of the extent to which support was being given according to the wants of users and their carers and to what extent needs were still being fitted into the existing framework of service provision. The evaluation covered three aspects of NSU service organization which were central to involvement: assessment, provision/choice of services, and monitoring and reviewing of services, plus an additional channel of user group committees.

Assessment

Assessment forms
The assessment form initially employed at Manor was devised by F&CS for use within the support units. It asked for basic information regarding personal details and home surroundings, with an additional set of headings inviting brief notes on health, medication and treatment; interests and activities; financial affairs; and informal support. It also contained an activities of daily living scale to

which staff at the Manor Unit had appended their own 'task-orientated dependency rating' measure. One side of the form was left blank for the assessor to report on the initial interview with space to record the 'client's view of problem(s)'.

On the basis of this information, staff were expected to summarize the problem areas and draw up an 'action' or 'care plan'. A standard letter was then sent to users setting out the services which the unit could offer and informing them of their right to discuss this decision with their assessor. Review sheets containing, where relevant, updated care plans were attached accordingly.[3]

Recognizing the recommendations of the Griffiths report (1988) for a system of case management as well as the movement towards computerization of information systems, F&CS made compulsory a new common assessment form in November 1990. The introduction of the form coincided with the period of study of new referrals to the unit.

In comparison with the NSU form, the common assessment form was much more detailed. It contained standard measures for recording physical and mental state; environment; medical condition; relationships; support by carers; services currently received; and a daily analysis of need. Space was provided under most of these headings for comments and additionally for observations on social activities; stress points for carers; areas of unmet need; and statements from users *and* carers. Assessors were expected to make appraisals regarding short term/day care, to draw up a profile of needs which took into account risks involved both to the person and to others and to propose an individual care plan. They then noted the resources allocated and any resource deficiencies along with a suggested date for reviewing plans. A section was included for the registering of decisions of the resource panel to which users with complex needs were referred, while a final sheet for the recording of revisions to individual care plans was also built into the form. The same standard letter was sent to users to inform them of the services on offer.

In theory, the common assessment form should have elicited a more detailed and accurate picture of need. It paid more systematic attention to people's mental state including morale and, in particular, to their relationships and to the support given by informal carers. It also considered potential or existing care gaps. Indeed, notes on the use of the form stressed its key objective as being to determine the best available way to help the individual rather than focusing only on the user's suitability for a particular service(s), and to this end the users' and carers' contributions were 'an integral part of any assessment'.

However, a comparison of forms revealed that they were used in similar ways: that is, the minimum of data was typically recorded, with very brief comments. Sections were often left incomplete. This was especially the case in respect of the new common assessment form which, in the words of one team leader, tended to be filled in according to what was felt to be useful or relevant. Indeed, responses to the 15-page document suggested that (quality aside) quantity of information had an inverse relationship to the length of the form. While team leaders had smaller caseloads than home care organizers, they did not necessarily have the time to devote to paperwork due to the new demands of their roles such as running the day centres and attending resource panel meetings.[4] Thus, if the forms achieved anything, it was to perpetuate the traditional culture of social care service organization whereby considerable amounts of information about users were passed on verbally and staff operated on the basis of taken-for-granted knowledge of older people.[5]

On the other hand, the determinants of need listed above did not necessarily comprise an exhaustive list. Studies have revealed gaps between the received wisdom of professionals and policy makers who devise, utilize and base their actions upon tools to measure need and the day to day experience of individuals (Percy-Smith and Sanderson 1992). Standard measures used to record information cannot always capture the complexity of need or the challenge it poses to the normative value system underlying social care provision. Given these various issues, it was important to look at the wider assessment interview.

The assessment interview
Examination of the assessment interview showed that it was not simply that assessors, or team leaders, were operating within limited boundaries. They had no regulations or detailed guidelines concerning their approach to older people in assessment. There were no specific procedures or mechanisms to explain the process, or to encourage or secure the involvement of potential users or of their carers. Older people were described by senior staff as 'participating', and observation of the assessment of new referrals to the unit over a two-month period showed team leaders to be very thorough in their consideration of the circumstances of individuals, their life histories and informal support networks. The inclusion of carers (who were not themselves users) was varied though it tended to be linked to level of input. Nevertheless, how people's views were recorded lay very much in the hands of individual team leaders rather than being a joint process.

A number of older people appeared to be unaware that they had been referred for help and/or to be confused about the purpose of the team leader's visit. Even among those who clearly knew of or had themselves made the referral, however, few were active or assertive in setting out directly what they considered to be their needs or the assistance they wanted. No users or carers made reference to the sections of the assessment forms set aside for recording their own views of their situation. Indeed, some did not even know of the existence of the forms.

This is not to suggest that all older people saw themselves as passive recipients of care:

> Well, I always have a say in what I get otherwise I wouldn't ask. It's important to stay in control, be independent. Once I lose that, I'd much prefer that I passed on.

Yet such statements were largely an expression of individual character. They did not necessarily mean that users were active initiators of change. Older people's general failure to assert themselves reflected the traditional role of users within service provision: 'I leave them to get on with it. It's their job, isn't it?'; 'I'm simply grateful towards anybody who helps me. I would never tie them down.' Likewise, few carers expected to have their needs taken into account: 'They are interested in my sister – I never needed help'.

The language of senior staff was equally equivocal. All social care managers claimed to assess every person individually since 'different individuals have different needs'. But there was also talk of 'giving or refusing' a service and of making comparisons with other users – their needs and what they received – as part of the same process. One senior member of staff described the issue of assessment as resting on debate concerning 'the difference between quality of care and quality of life'. While it was possible for older people to argue that cleaning was important to their quality of life, if cleaning support was supplied to all people defining their needs in this way the overall quality of the service would be compromised.

In parallel, a central goal of the health team was described as being in 'partnership' with older people. Here, senior staff spoke of members of the team acting as advocates for older people who were unsure of their wishes and of 'standing between the inflexibility of some services and the clients'. Particular note was taken of users' feelings over matters such as entering hospital. However, many of the more routine day to day medical activities of health care workers were governed by strict guidelines which perforce shaped assessment and provision. At the same time, staff were making decisions based upon the apparent need to ration resources. One member of the team refused to 'start diluting care for people who needed specific nursing duties in order to go and help somebody have a strip wash'.

Senior staff drew attention to older people who, despite being extremely frail or disabled, opted to turn down social care services on the basis that there were others worse off than themselves or from fear of being considered a nuisance. On the other hand, reference was also made to 'people who [were]n't capable of making that decision'. One employee of F&CS was not willing to tolerate a situation where such individuals were left at risk and put in support on the ground that the unit was accountable for their well-being. Comments of this nature suggested that the power of decision as to whether a user received a service, and to the nature and the extent of that service still lay firmly in the hands of staff, and that the actions which they took continued to be shaped primarily by a perception of finite resources and support.

Provision/choice of services

In terms of the 'packaging of care', there was evidence of a shift away from the domestic focus of the traditional home help service towards meeting needs through new activities. As Chapter 3 demonstrated, these included the running of day centres by domiciliary workers, shopping trips, transport and laundry facilities as well as more extensive personal care.

Senior staff commonly and primarily pointed to the expansion in the scope of support worker activities – shopping in town rather than just locally, writing letters, and fetching books from the library – as illustration that older people were being provided with more choice. That needs were being better met was further evidenced by the allocation of a key worker to each individual user rather than operating what was effectively a two-tier system of service delivery, crudely divided between cleaning and caring tasks (Chapters 3 and 7). Close collaboration with the health care team had contributed to a greater sense of continuity of care. Reference was made to situations in which district nurses were able to contact support workers if an older person was taken ill unexpectedly and required help being put to bed.

However, senior staff also acknowledged that certain features of the wider care-giving culture continued to intervene in the attempt to introduce change. Under the initiative, there had been a reduction in the ratio of staff to users so that the 'number and quality of visits' to individual users could be increased. But the effectiveness of the modification, in the eyes of one manager, was compromised by the failure of senior staff to accept the necessity of 'prioritizing in a world which was far from ideal':

> I think that we're bad at prioritizing care. I think what we try to do is to give something to everybody and I'm not sure that's always right. I think sometimes we've got to prioritize and instead of diluting the service and giving quantity, we've got to prioritize and give quality. That sounds a bit glib and a bit flip but at the end of the day I think it's a real issue that we have got to tackle because I cannot see more resources flooding in to us.

Another senior member of staff claimed that, while the unit had initially appeared to break down some of the rigidity of the traditional service – primarily by extending the shifts worked by support workers and team leaders – of late, the service had reverted back to more traditional patterns with the result, among other things, that older people were still being put to bed early and were greeted by an answering machine if they telephoned the unit in the late evening.

In other situations, there was simply no question that cost-effectiveness ruled the day. Thus, while health and social care staff readily agreed that there were a number of confused older people who would have benefited greatly from a 24-hour service, it was deemed too expensive to provide.[6] Intensive services such as the night-sitting service were restricted to terminally ill older people who lived alone or were being supported by carers who required a sitting service.[7] Team leaders no longer staffed the unit at the weekends on the grounds that the number of telephone calls received from users and support workers was not enough to justify the expense of such cover. A bleep had been purchased instead and team leaders took it in turns to be on-call.

Among the case study sample, the amount and nature of support given to individual users varied from fortnightly shopping trips plus Christmas dinner at the Neighbourhood Centre to full care seven days per week. Across this range, users were helped to feel involved in the sense of participating in everyday outside or communal activities and to exercise choice in terms of remaining at home or continuing to care for significant others at home. With daily input from support workers, and twice weekly visits from the district nurse, one woman had been able to return to her flat relatively soon after a major operation where she judged herself to have 'recovered a lot more quickly than in hospital'.

Older people who had received home care prior to the introduction of the NSU acknowledged changes to service provision. Some highlighted the increase in supervisory visits, or what was referred to as 'personal attention':

> Well, I suppose it's psychological, I would say. They make you feel – you know like you feel you're nobody and nobody cares and nobody wants you – they give you the feeling that somebody cares. So I think that's good. I believe that's why they altered it to this way because for some people it's not practical help but it's reassurance. They're too frightened to be on their own. When they know that somebody's going to pop in and look after them, it's a lot better.

Shopping trips and day centre activities were also praised by those who participated in them.

Satisfaction with services was not always about the range of choice, but was also linked to the adequacy of help received within what was on offer. There was a clear sense that aspects of provision had suffered as a result of the shift. In some cases, it was felt that support – especially with housework tasks – had been reduced as a matter of policy: 'there's a lot less attention given to cleaning'. Others saw the problem as lying in the fact that support workers, who were looking after a wider range of users including those who were severely confused, were too stretched:

> I think myself they don't get enough time to do the jobs that want doing. I think it depends on how many they've got to do and how much time they've got to do it in.

There is a risk of explaining older people's lack of reference to areas of support lying outside current service provision solely in terms of the dominance of the traditional model of social care, and thereby to play down the importance of adequate domestic help to their physical and emotional well-being. One older woman had to 'shut out' the thought of the dust under her bed otherwise it would get on her nerves and make her ill. Even among new referrals, who had no personal experience of home care, the desire was expressed for more help with cleaning, while a number of carers indicated a preference for practical assistance so that precious time could be devoted to companionship and emotional support. But comments suggested that neither users or their carers felt in a position to make demands. One carer speaking about her mother observed:

> [We were involved] at first, but that again just seems to have petered out. But I think that's because she refuses help so often – refuses a lot of help. But they don't offer what we would accept – cleaning.

In addition to adequacy, older people indicated how essential it was that flexibility did not compromise reliability and that the careful matching of users and workers mattered. For example, it was crucial to one older man with diabetes that he received a balanced diet, or 'proper' meals. He was very upset at being allocated a key support worker who, by her own confession, did not know how to cook and quite often brought meals from the local take-away. He was also frustrated by the early hour at which support workers commonly called to put to bed his sister-in-law whose home he shared. Whilst acknowledging that she could be 'difficult' and 'obstreperous', he sympathized with her distress caused by the attitude of the key worker who used coarse language and paid her the minimum amount of attention.

Observational studies suggested that where choice was openly offered, it tended to be within containable boundaries. For example, older people determined the selection and ordering of a number of the day centre activities, but it was within a framework shaped by the availability of transport and the provision of lunch at a fixed hour. In their own homes, users appeared to be given little support of a motivational nature, especially when they were severely confused or frail, though support workers were commonly struggling to complete essential practical and errand tasks within their daily schedules.

> To return to our case studies, Mrs McAllister thought it a 'funny idea' when the team leader turned down her request for cleaning assistance, issuing her instead with weekend help with washing herself (a task, until then, carried out by her husband). She was not very happy with her key support worker whom she claimed neglected to wash her legs and feet, and had failed to call to help her to the toilet on occasions during the period when Mr McAllister was ill and had been forbidden by the doctor to help with this activity. According to her daughter-in-law, Mrs McAllister denied the need to go to the toilet if a male support worker called to assist her.
>
> In contrast, Mr Miller explained his satisfaction with the services as arising from the 'very good' relationship he enjoyed with his key worker. She had visited him under the traditional service and Mr Miller asked if she could carry on calling when the support worker system was introduced. Describing her as 'a friend rather than a support worker' he cited the fact that the worker took home his laundry to wash and iron. He also pointed out that the other support worker to call regularly was the daughter of an 'old friend' of his.
>
> On the other hand, Mr Miller's help had been changed from a full day

of housework and shopping once a week to twice-weekly hour-long visits, leading him to state that there was 'a lot less attention given to cleaning' under the new NSU system. Referring again to his key support worker, he commented:

> As a support worker she's not supposed to clean, but that's what we need. She's got so many to see she has to fit them all in. They have to attend a lot of meetings which is ridiculous and unnecessary. They have a lot of paperwork, too much.

Mr Miller had not complained at what he had effectively seen as a reduction because he was 'too independent' and preferred to 'struggle', as he put it.

Monitoring and reviewing of services

Choice should not end at the point of assessment. Not only do users' circumstances change, with implications for their needs, but it is possible for older people to change their minds over time about the suitability of care. This is important to remember as a substantial number of older people come to the service in an emergency situation and are not always in a position to make rational decisions in those circumstances. The role of monitoring was highlighted by senior staff who noted the difficulty of capturing a complete picture of people's needs at the initial stage of assessment. For one staff member, involving people in the ongoing review of their needs lay at the heart of effective and efficient service provision:

> I want to say this because our department are really hung up on initial assessment as the be-all and end-all, and for me it's not. The most important thing is the monitoring. Once you've assessed and you think you know what they need, you've got to put the services in and you've got to monitor very carefully and evaluate and change subject to need changing. And our department in the Griffiths era are moving into the 'assessment will tell them everything' gear. It won't.

However, at the Manor NSU, how the scoring of measures in assessment was translated into the particular services provided was not clear-cut and there was no obvious evidence of the standardized recording of unmet need. Neither did there appear to be any systematic collation of outcomes over time.

Older people whose situation remained more or less constant described checks on their needs as being very informal: '[The support worker] might just say 'Is there anything else?"'. According to one user, 'having a say' in this context meant being able to phone the Neighbourhood Centre if someone was needed to pick up a prescription. Not all users were happy with telephone contact, however. One older man claimed that, more often than not, the team leader called him only when trying to get hold of one of the support workers: 'They don't talk to us really'.

Two new referrals who had required emergency cover following hospitalization reported decreases in provision over a relatively short period of time that were reflective of their recovery. In these cases, revisions had been made in consultation with the respective users and their families. Elsewhere, evidence showed patterns of provision to be sensitive to developments in need among existing users, but largely on the basis of how staff perceived those changes. In respect of the terminally ill user who did not want to confront his imminent death, such an approach was understandable. Otherwise, the failure to consult with users and their carers was left unexplained. For example, one older woman who was also a carer was instructed by support workers simply to inform them when she knew the date of her sister's discharge from hospital and they would 'do the rest'. Of what that might consist beyond the promised provision of the incontinence laundry service the older person in question could not predict, though she was certain that the support workers could be 'relied upon'. A second older woman returned home from an operation to her foot to find she had been allocated daily supervisory visits and extra help with housework. She had not asked for the increase – 'They just come and see what needs to be done and do it' – but she found it 'very welcome'.

Situations still arose where users and/or their carers had to make requests because of the lack of response from service providers, however. A number of people had recently complained about the failure to find a replacement for the auxiliary nurse who had been off sick for several weeks. Various mechanisms existed for registering dissatisfaction with services. Users of the building who were unhappy with the running of the unit had access to a complaints and appeals procedure, details of which were set out in the Code of Practice guidelines (see below). For older people receiving services in their own homes, an official complaints system operated city wide whereby, if an issue could not be settled at the local level, it was brought before a panel at F&CS headquarters.[8] But although it was the general expectation among older people and care staff alike that matters would be dealt with by senior staff at the unit, the expression of grievances was not made easy by limited contact between users and team leaders. While the recently introduced system of care management should in theory alter this situation, the creation of a new relationship between managers as purchasers and workers as frontline providers may remove the benefits of direct line management.

> Our two case studies' experiences with the review/complaints procedures were as follows. Mrs McAllister had taken on a private cleaner over 15 years ago when she found inadequacies in the service which had been allocated to her following her accident; the home help failed to clean her cooker thoroughly or to turn out her cupboards. Domestic assistance was consequently withdrawn. Support was reinstated when Mrs McAllister broke her wrist, though on the switch to the support worker service, cleaning help was again taken away and

attention focused instead on personal care. Although Mrs McAllister had continued to pay for private help throughout the entire period, she still thought that services should provide cleaning help free of charge: 'I think I'm entitled to a couple of hours, don't you? Just little things would help.'

Julie and Keith felt Mrs McAllister to be 'hard to please' at times but expressed dissatisfaction with the failure of services to respond immediately when Mr McAllister fell ill. Sufficient help was provided only when hospital doctors had been contacted. Mrs McAllister was pleased with the two 'good uns' who replaced her former support worker, but despite stating that she and her husband '[couldn't] get a better service really', she still did not feel they had a say in how the service was run.

In between first and second round survey interviews with Mr Miller he was admitted to hospital with a chest infection. Extra supervisory visits were allocated for four months following his discharge, after which, in his words, he was 'told politely' by the team leader that he did not need daily help and was switched back to the original pattern of support. Daily supervisory visits were later reinstated at the request of Mr Miller's neighbour who was prompted to contact the centre when support workers failed to call for three consecutive week days.

User group committees

In addition to the three processes that have been described, there existed a fourth means for user participation in the shape of user group committees. In the belief that users 'should play a big part' in the running of services, and 'feel wanted' at the centre, senior staff had encouraged the setting up of three separate committees, known respectively as the 'Building/Neighbourhood Centre', 'Under-5s', and 'Support Services' groups. A couple of representatives from each of these groups met on a regular bimonthly basis with senior members of staff, the aim of which was 'to ensure community users participation in the development and use of community facilities in the Manor Neighbourhood Centre (The Building)' (Building User Group Code of Practice: 1).[9]

In practice, however, not all meetings were well attended or were attended consistently by the same handful of individuals. The extent of members' participation in management decisions appeared to be concentrated chiefly on the use of the building and the mini-bus by people living locally, and on services run on site, especially those for the under-5s. Users who received support within their own homes, particularly those who were housebound and/or in the 75 and over age range, were severely underrepresented within the groups. Indeed, during the course of the evaluation only one older person who was visited by a support worker attended a user group meeting.

One senior member of staff argued that offering choice to older people in all day to day or 'hands on' caring activities was more important than facilitating their attendance at user group meetings. However, the illustrations of choice given – which included asking users what dress they would like to wear that day, whether or not they were ready to get up or if they wanted cornflakes for breakfast – represented a very limited process of individual decision making rather than any sense of wider collective service choice. Given that none of the case study sample appeared to know of the groups or their purpose, it seems fair to conclude that, in their existing set-up, these groups were clearly not a route to ensure the effective participation of older people in the organization of the NSUs.

Conclusion

The low attendance at user group meetings was not really unexpected. It reflected both the general frailty of older users of services and the well-documented tradition of poor attendance at public meetings which are not organized around a burning issue. People in general tend to adopt a passive stance in relation to the public policy making process, especially if they are sceptical about the proposed pay off (Croft and Beresford 1990; Percy-Smith and Sanderson 1992: 34).

Neither was it surprising, as the model of user-involvement favoured by the government is a consumerist one which concentrates on the delivery of services as a transaction. In this model, older people are at risk of only being listened to if they have the resources (financial and other) to become 'customers'. Even then, control of services does not necessarily follow, since market forces and other externalities are ignored. As we noted in Chapter 2, the model offers a pseudo-market form of empowerment (see also Percy-Smith and Sanderson 1992: 49; Barnes and Walker 1995) in which services are still provider-led.

What was required, if genuine empowerment was to be achieved, was the development of a 'culture of participation' whereby older people and their carers were more fully involved on a continuing basis in the process of service planning and development, an issue that we turn to in the final chapter.

Notes

1 At the time of interviews, the most recent report to have been assembled on the Manor Neighbourhood Centre represented a response to a request from one of the city councillors for briefing information in anticipation of a meeting with health authority representatives. It was intended to present the material to representatives at an impending visit from the Social Services Inspectorate.

2 Regular visits were made to all of the 23 GP practices in the area by members of the health team. Otherwise, the team publicized information about the Manor project through public meetings, informal seminars and coffee mornings, as well as relying on

the grapevine of informal networks. Feedback to health service personnel was carried out by means of quarterly reviews and an annual report.

3 Early on in the course of the evaluation, the Manor NSU switched to using a common assessment form introduced by F&CS. However, the discussion focuses on the NSU form since, with respect to the case studies, those older people drawn from the survey sample were all assessed using the latter.

4 Each page of the new form was produced in triplicate – to ensure that all bodies involved in the provision of services received a written copy of the assessment – and was backed by cardboard (to be inserted between each set of three pages), so that the whole thing measured almost half a centimetre. Not only did the form look formidable, it proved to be extremely time-consuming; in a dummy run, it took one team leader over two hours to complete just the basic sections.

5 The new form was eventually abandoned by F&CS, and staff at the Manor Unit simply reverted to the tools used prior to its introduction.

6 The alternative suggestion of offering very basic night-time cover in the form of pop-in checks on people who wandered or 'toileting' for older people who were incontinent was judged likely to be too disorientating or disruptive to be worthwhile.

7 Night-sitting services were usually provided by the health services. Where support workers stepped in, the care was commonly shared between the two sectors.

8 Complaints about health services were dealt with through a separate system run by the health authority. Those arising from issues such as drug errors were covered by the UKCC (United Kingdom Central Council) professional code of conduct.

9 Members of the health team also participated in their own independent user group meetings. Two to three otherwise housebound people were transported by mini-bus to the meetings in an attempt to make them as representative as possible. Collaborative efforts were made to set up a short series of support meetings for carers with the primary aim of supplying information and a forum for sharing experiences, but they were poorly attended.

9

Conclusion

It is crucial to learn lessons from any innovation. In view of the indeterminacy of aims within the social care sector (Twigg *et al.* 1990), the resource constraints that have bedevilled social services for the last two decades, and the necessity for creative responses to the growing need for long term care as a result of population ageing, it is especially important to squeeze out from demonstration projects the last drop of relevant information that might be of use to those responsible for service development in this country and elsewhere. Thus the primary purpose of this concluding chapter is to distil the main lessons, positive and negative, from the NSU implementation with regard to both the processes of innovation and change within the social services and the important goal of user involvement. We begin by highlighting the main findings of our research.

Impact and effectiveness of the Neighbourhood Support Unit

Older service users took the centre stage in our evaluation and, from their perspective four key findings must be emphasized. First, there was widespread support for the basic community care, or ageing in place, aim of the NSU. There was no doubt that even severely disabled older people preferred to maintain what we have called an interdependent existence in the community rather than to enter a residential home. Second, however, there was a distinct lack of clarity in service users' understanding of the practical implications of the NSU concept, especially the prioritization of critical care needs and the downgrading of cleaning tasks, that is, the shift from 'charring to caring' (Walker 1985b).

This suggests, on the one hand, a failure to fully inform older people about the implications of changing their services and, on the other, a failure to respond to the users' own definitions of their needs, a point we return to below.

Third, in terms of the core aim of enabling older people with substantial care needs to remain interdependent in the community, the NSU worked. Indeed, in comparison with the more traditional home care set-up, the support unit achieved a notable level of success. There was also some indication of success with regard to the subsidiary NSU goal of supporting the informal carers of older people with the greatest care needs. Finally, although the care needs of the vast majority of older people in both areas were being met, there was a significant care gap among those requiring moderate levels of support and a smaller one among those needing substantial support. In both cases – moderate and substantial needs – the care gap was greater under the home care service than the NSU. The biggest gap between care needs and provision, under both new and old service models, though the failure rate of the home care service was nearly double that of the NSU, was with regard to the daytime supervisory needs of older people.

Turning to informal carers we found that, despite the relatively heavy investment in social care represented by the NSU and the high average age of our sample of older people, it was still this group that provided the bulk of care. Furthermore, although there is no doubt that informal care entailed considerable adverse costs, it was clear that it often also produced intrinsic rewards, such as satisfaction, warmth and pride. With regard to the effectiveness of the NSU there are three key points to emphasize from the carers' perspective. First it is important to note that the neo-liberal or neo-conservative case against the social services – which are said to be damaging because they have taken over the functions of the family (Murray 1984; Segalman and Marsland 1989; Willetts 1992) – was not supported by carers in our research. They showed no inclination whatsoever to off-load their responsibilities on to the formal services. This is not a new finding (see for example Qureshi and Walker 1989) but it is remarkable how persistent the erroneous claim about the impact of the welfare state has proved to be – a clear case of ideology crowding out empirical reality. Second, the NSU did not succeed in fulfilling its goal of involving informal carers in decisions about services for the older person they were caring for. Indeed we found that carers were no more closely involved in such decisions than they were under the home care system. Third, the verdict of the majority of informal carers was that both the NSU and the home care system had enabled older people to remain in the community and had supported their own caring activities. However the majority was larger with regard to home care rather than the NSU, which tends to suggest that home carers and wardens were rather more effective than their support worker counterparts at assisting informal carers.

From the perspective of the formal providers of care the NSU had succeeded in achieving a more flexible service than that provided by home care. There were also signs that support workers were creating 'packages of care' even though they did not employ this particular language. On the basis of our interviews with support workers and their service users, however, it is clear that they had not made the quantum leap away from existing service structures and assumptions implied by the NSU concept. Thus, support workers still operated with definitions of need based largely on physical disability while their responses were shaped largely by what was available already. Similarly informal carers were regarded in a very traditional way, as 'resources' that were often taken for granted (Twigg and Atkin 1991) and rarely involved in the operational decisions concerning the care of older people.

The final report on the NSU innovation, therefore, would have to be equivocal; in terms of the key goals of enabling disabled older people to remain in an interdependent community setting the support unit represented a considerable advance over home care. With regard to the interrelated aims of flexibility and user involvement, however, the achievements did not match the aspirations of the senior managers responsible for the innovation.

Lessons for service development

There are two main sets of lessons, both positive and negative, that may be relevant to the development of services for older people needing personal care. They concern the process of innovation and the vexed question of how to involve users and carers in the key decisions concerning care.

We have shown that there was a great deal of uncertainty in the minds of older service users about the implications of the changes that had taken place in their social care services. This uncertainty is a serious indictment of the process by which the NSU was implemented and introduced to the service users and their carers. Part of the blame for this can be laid at the door of local management for its failure to communicate effectively with those most affected by the changes. But it is clear also that there was a lack of commitment to the initiative at various levels within F&CS (and in the health authority) with the consequence that both support unit staff and their health service colleagues felt marginalized within their own departments. Because of this lack of commitment, strongly perceived by some staff of the unit, there was a drift away from the original ideals of the NSU. Some departure from the social service planners' blueprint is inevitable in the innovation process (Hall *et al.* 1975). It is also accepted that 'perfect implementation' is unattainable (Hogwood and Gunn 1984). In the NSU case, however, the distance between ideals and implementation was widened unnecessarily, we believe, by a lack of preparation at the local level and a lack of guidance and ongoing support, such as training, from the social services department. Towards the end of our evaluation there was widespread uncertainty about the future of the Manor Unit and the other NSUs because of the severe resource constraints imposed on F&CS but here we are referring to the very start of the initiative when there was a more favourable financial outlook, at least in the short term. The NSU was a 'top down' innovation (Barrett and Fudge 1981; Hogwood and Gunn 1984), therefore there was a special responsibility on the part of the senior management overseeing it to ensure that preparation was adequate and that the implementation phase was monitored closely. In the light of this experience we would make the following recommendations concerning the process of innovation:

- clarity at all levels – from strategic planning through frontline delivery to users and carers – about the aims and targets for provision and guidelines for implementation which, in turn, requires regular and well-organized channels of communication. Such clarity of purpose and effective communication are important elements of any policy implementation, but when a public sector organization steps outside of its normal bureau-incrementalist planning framework they become indispensable (Lindblom 1959; Walker 1984; Lindblom and Woodhouse 1993);
- a sense of ownership and commitment to the scheme at a senior management level (Meetham and Thompson 1992) and the ongoing encouragement and support of middle managers;
- training for middle managers, frontline workers, carers, and service users. Interdisciplinary training is vital to the understanding of each other's expertise and function (Goldberg and Neill 1972), the identification of overlap of traditional boundaries and the establishment of a common language and terminology, particularly if care management is to be grafted onto multidisciplinary teamwork (Beardshaw and Towell 1990). This training necessitates greater physical proximity to promote face to face contact (Bruce 1980);
- given that GPs are a key point of contact for those with service needs, their involvement should be encouraged (Meetham and Thompson 1992);
- if the above proposals are to be met, the need for personnel resources must be recognized. Time must be set aside for project development, planning, training and liaising with other agencies;
- regular monitoring of the implementation and feedback to the managers responsible for it;
- all of this implies, of course, a certain future for the innovation (though this does not preclude the evolution of its operation) which, in turn, rests on a secure financial environment, a luxury that Sheffield's F&CS department was not, and still is not, able to enjoy.

User and carer involvement and empowerment

As is often the case with top down innovations there was obviously insufficient consultation with service users and potential users about the NSU concept and its implications. However this does not mean that F&CS did not make strenuous efforts to consult on the contrary, there was extensive consultation.

We noted in Chapter 1 that a planned NSU was delayed (terminally) by the consultation process. There is no doubt that the social services department (SSD) and the local councillors went to considerable lengths to try to ensure not only the acceptance of the Support Unit in Manor but also that the residents regarded it as their resource. In one instance this determination to ensure that it was 'owned' by local residents led to a confrontation between the Chair of the Social Services Committee and community representatives. The bone of contention was whether or not the Manor Unit, when it was operational, should have a janitor. The councillor argued that, for democratic rather than financial reasons, the residents should run the building themselves and that the appointment of a janitor would create a gate-keeper. For their part the local residents did not want to be responsible for the building and especially ensuring its security and the regular maintenance of its heating boiler. These different perspectives resulted in a protracted stand-off (which we observed with a mixture of frustration and nervousness) but, in the end, the local residents had their way. Thus there was genuine and painstaking consultation, but this consultation suffered from two defects.

First, it was community consultation rather than user and carer consultation. The management committee included local residents, such as the leader of the Manor Tenants Association, but it did not penetrate sufficiently to the grass roots level. As we noted in Chapter 8, there was a user group, but its meetings were poorly attended. However, this should not have been un-expected, given both the frailty of the older users of the service and the low levels of participation among older people in the UK. People in general tend to adopt a passive stance in relation to the public policy making process, especially if they are sceptical about the proposed 'pay off' (Percy-Smith and Sanderson 1992: 34), while frail and vulnerable service users require tailor-made approaches to involvement. In the absence of specifically targeted consultation with older service users the key messages concerning the NSU simply did not get across.

Second, therefore, there was a failure to take on board older users' own definitions of need and to find ways of reconciling these with the aims of the NSU. Thus, as we saw in Chapter 4, the cause of great dissatisfaction on the part of older people was the decline in help with cleaning associated with the introduction of the NSU. This issue tended to cloud the many positive aspects of the support unit in the eyes of older service users. From the perspective of carers, supervisory checks may have been more highly valued than cleaning though the latter was still important (Chapter 6). But the main issue here concerns the older users themselves and there is no doubt that they gave assistance with cleaning a much higher priority than the NSU concept allowed for. As a result the change in service left many older people confused and angry about what they saw as 'cuts' in services when, in fact, the NSU represented a substantial *increase* in resources. So what general lessons can be learned concerning the goal of user involvement?

As we noted in Chapter 8, the fundamental requirement is to develop a 'culture of participation' whereby older people are more fully involved on a continuing basis in the process of service planning and development (Percy-Smith and Sanderson 1992: 34). Services must be user-led rather than seeing involvement and participation as bolt-on extras (Walker 1992). This is contingent upon the decentralization of power within and from statutory agencies. Croft and Beresford (1990: 24) argue that positive *support* (including skills training, advocacy and resources) and *access* are essential if participation is to be representative and a positive experience:

> Unless both are present people may either lack the confidence, expectations or abilities to get involved, or be discouraged by the difficulties entailed. Without them, participatory initiatives are likely to *reinforce* rather than overcome existing race, class, gender and other inequalities.

Barnes and Walker (1995) have established eight key principles which they argue should underpin attempts to empower users of health and social care services:

1 Empowerment should enable personal development as well as increasing influence over services.
2 Empowerment should involve increasing people's abilities to take control of their lives as a whole, not just increase their influence over services.
3 Empowerment of one person should not result in the exploitation of others, either family members or paid carers.
4 Empowerment should not be viewed as a zero–sum; a partnership model should provide benefits to both service providers and older people.
5 Empowerment must be reinforced at all levels within service systems.
6 Empowerment of those who use services does not remove the responsibility of service providers.
7 Empowerment is not an alternative to adequate resourcing of services.
8 Empowerment should be a collective as well as an individual process; without this people will become increasingly assertive in competition with each other.

Within a principled approach such as this there are a host of practical down-to-earth measures that health social services authorities can take to encourage user involvement and empowerment:

- listening to all users – finding out their views using sensitive tools;
- special recognition of the acute social exclusion of some groups, such as black service users (Ahmad 1990: 32; Askham *et al.* 1995);
- service sampling – where managers experience the service for themselves;
- opening up organizations – giving older people a more active role with appropriate support;
- designing charters – with rights of redress for complaints;
- ensuring regular evaluation of services, with user involvement in such evaluations;
- considering the *how* as well as the *what* of service provision – ensuring that services are received and perceived as involving and empowering;

- providing appropriate advice, information, training, advocacy and resources at all these levels.

There are enough practical examples to confirm that user involvement and empowerment are achievable (Croft and Beresford 1990, Beresford and Croft 1993). Moreover there are working examples of the involvement and empowerment of frail older people within social services (Barnes *et al.* 1994). User involvement does not have to be all or nothing, but should develop in a flexible and organic way. Most frail older people do not want to be full-time participants but they should be consulted properly and empowered to make decisions. Nor is it a matter of health and social services being expected to respond to every demand made by a service user. Instead the aim should be to take on board users' views where possible and to 'negotiate' a consensus about problems and priorities jointly (Percy-Smith and Sanderson 1992).

How will service providers know if a policy of involvement and empowerment is working? Most of what we have been discussing concerns processes but, of course, success is judged on the basis of outcomes. Evidence of empowerment may be measured by a simple checklist that can be modified to fit specific circumstances:

- Are older users/potential users consulted about what package of services is required to meet their various needs?
- Are older people able to exercise any choice about the type of services they receive?
- Are they able to make choices about the level of services they receive?
- Are carers consulted independently of older users/potential users?
- Where older people are unable to exercise effective choice for reasons of disability or frailty are there independent advocates to speak for them?
- Are users, carers and advocates involved in managing agencies, including the setting of goals, and monitoring the operation of services?

Also it is essential to operate a process of user auditing where older people are asked what they think of a service and what they value about it. Indeed the simple process of asking people helps to make them feel more powerful.

The underlying model we are advocating is shared care (Walker 1983; Qureshi and Walker 1989) or co-production (National Board of Social Welfare 1989) whereby formal supporters work in partnership with older people and their family carers. This partnership model places a heavy responsibility on frontline staff to work in new inclusive ways with users, and therefore the provision of training and regular monitoring of activity are crucial. In public services 'street level bureaucrats' usually have substantial discretion in the execution of their tasks (Lipsky 1980; Hudson 1989) and, in doing so, they may subvert the original intentions of the social services planners. In the NSU case the support worker role was purposely designed as a flexible one, which actually increased the scope for 'implementation deficit' (Hill and Bramley 1986).

Did the support workers, in practice, subvert the original ideals of the

NSU? Our view is that such a conclusion would be unfair and far too simplistic. As was reported in Chapter 7 support workers expressed strong allegiance to the NSU concept but, nonetheless, they still operated largely within traditional service provider approaches and categories. Thus older service users and their informal carers were not routinely involved fully in decisions about the appropriate service responses to need. The blame for this failure, however, cannot be laid primarily at the door of the NSU and its staff.

Support workers were inadequately prepared for the challenging tasks of involving and empowering users and their carers. They did not receive training to discharge this difficult duty and there was insufficient operational guidance available to assist them. It is obvious too that both team leaders and support workers had not received sufficient training with regard to the implications of the new form of service for their work and thinking. (There was no formal training programme for team leaders, but support workers underwent a three-week induction course. The unit manager received no specific training.) Because the support workers were endowed with such high levels of street level discretion it was incumbent on their senior managers in F&CS to ensure that they were adequately prepared to exercise it. Having said this it is important to recognize the constraints under which senior management was operating, including the major one of limited resources and also the tight implementation schedule and the need to utilize existing staff resources or risk a dispute with the trade unions.

The future of NSUs

Our final comments take two forms, first we conclude the story of the support units initiative with reference to three ironies and then we return to the European policy context discussed in Chapter 2.

It is ironic that, despite the proven success of the Manor NSU in supporting older people's ageing in place, it was not the impact of the innovation that determined its fate and that of the other NSU, but their financial cost. All of the positive features of the support units with regard to the care of older people were overtaken by events. First there was the tighter and tighter control of local authority expenditure by central government, which started in the early 1980s and has continued to the present time. Because of Sheffield's oppositional politics (see Chapter 3) and the negative financial impact of the decision to host the World Student Games in 1990, these constraints have had a particularly sharp effect on the city's finances. This meant that further NSU buildings could not be contemplated (the Manor NSU cost £0.5 million to build) though it is possible that the *concept* behind the NSU innovation could have survived. Second, however, the NHS and Community Care Act (1990) introduced the purchaser/provider split into social care and set in motion a process that is reducing the role of SSDs as direct providers and the NSUs were a classic case of direct provision. Third, there was a positive desire, on the part of F&CS, to improve the flexibility of the home care service and import some of the features of the support worker role into the home care system. Fourth, there was the creation of primary health care teams which, sadly, resulted in a dilution of joint working between the staff of the two authorities.

What happened to the NSUs? They have been rolled into an enhanced home care system. The irony of this outcome will not be lost on those who have read our comparisons of the two services, particularly in Chapters 4 and 5. There were positive aspects to this policy change – again, a top-down one – as noted already, but it is clear that the main motivation behind it was a drive to reduce financial costs. The cost effectiveness imperative triumphed once more over the care effectiveness aspiration (Davies 1981, Walker 1985a), the main culprit being the government and its policy towards local authorities rather than the city council or SSD. F&CS instigated a review of both NSUs in 1993 with the open aim of including them in a single status, extended hours, home care service. The review concluded, in February 1994, that the NSUs should remain distinct but with some cuts in staffing to reduce their costs but this was merely the first major step in the demise of the NSU concept.

The second ironic element of the final twists and turns of this story is that, when the department investigated the costs of NSUs compared to home care, it did not find a major difference between them. True, support workers were more expensive to employ than home care workers, but when their outputs and the benefits to users were included, the cost difference was small. Support workers provided day care, meals, laundry and so on and when these services were included they brought the costs of the two services much closer together. However the main focus of attention was the staff costs not the care benefits and, with the added pressure from central government to involve the voluntary and private sectors, there was an opportunity to contract out non-personal care tasks and reduce costs by diluting the support worker role. Of course the financial cost of the full-blown support worker service was still substantially less than that of residential care (one-fifth of the cost). Thus the real cost of replacing the NSUs with home care may be higher for both the individual older people entering residential care as a result and, therefore, the state. It is only a cheaper option in terms of the direct financial cost to the local authority and under the current one-dimensional policy towards local spending that proved to be the major criterion.

The third and final irony is that, although the NSU initiative is effectively dead in Sheffield, the concept lives on elsewhere. The Elderly People's Integrated Care System (EPICS) that has been developed in several parts of the UK was informed by the NSU innovation as well as the ON LOK model in California (Bland 1994; Hudson 1994).

Towards a European policy on the care of older people

Shifting our sights back to the wider European policy context, is there a chance that the EU might be able to encourage a more reasoned, needs-led and research-informed approach to social care planning than that which is ascendant in the UK at the present? What hope is there that the EU will act as a source of pressure towards convergence in user-oriented home care? The main difficulty is that the Commission has no legislative competence in this field. Indeed until very recently it had taken hardly any action at all with regard to older people. In discussions concerning the Internal Market of 1992 older people have been largely invisible and the Social Charter or Chapter is primarily concerned with those in employment.

Moreover the agreement on Union social policy at Maastricht shifted the emphasis on social security from harmonization to convergence. Thus the principle of subsidiarity is likely to rule out the granting of any powers to the Commission with regard to the care of older people. This does not mean that the Commission has no role to play however – far from it. The Maastricht Treaty gave the Commission some competence in the field of public health and the second programme on ageing (still to be ratified) includes specific mention of good practice with regard to the care of disabled older people. Thus the Commission has a vital task to perform in publicizing examples of good practice – in service provision, training and so on – and encouraging the standardization of vocational qualifications, in order to facilitate the convergence of social services towards a model that enhances the status of older people in the Community by ensuring that they are treated with respect and dignity. The Commission also has an important contribution to make in research and monitoring and the encouragement of knowledge transfer. The sharing of knowledge between the North and South is particularly important in order to ensure convergence within the EU, in so far as convergence is possible in the context of very different cultures.

As we illustrated in Chapter 2 some considerable convergence has already taken place in the social services of the EU member states towards an increased emphasis on community care. This will undoubtedly lead to improvements in care for some older people but provision in most countries is likely to remain minimal. There is little realistic hope of a massive and widespread growth in home care, for example to harmonize with Danish, Dutch or Swedish levels of provision. There is even less chance of the voluntary sponsorship of user empowerment by national governments, or in the medium term, by the EU Commission. The best that we can hope for in the short term is to build on good practice in service innovations such as the NSU project, while, in the long term this cumulative knowledge may combine with the growing political confidence of older people in different European countries, including the UK, to produce demands for more extensive and empowering home care provision. Although it was short-lived, the NSU concept contained many examples of good practice which, in a more enlightened social policy context than that operating in the UK at present, could provide the foundations of a high quality, user-oriented support service.

Appendix

Methodology

Introduction

The methodological approach adopted in the study was pluralistic in nature. Our desire was to avoid the narrow confines of social surveys and to respect the importance of contextualizing key concepts such as old age, dependency and care (Warren and Walker 1991). The evaluation therefore employed a triangulation of methods to obtain data from a number of key groups. Those groups comprised older users of services, their carers, support workers, members of the health team, management and administrative staff involved in the day to day running of the NSUs, and senior management within F&CS.

Older people

Surveys

Since the unit had been running for a year prior to the commencement of the evaluation, it was not possible to conduct a quasi-experimental before/after series of interviews with users. The survey therefore took the form of a comparative study of those getting NSU services and a group in receipt of more traditional home care. The comparison group was drawn from another area in Sheffield – Southey Green – matched with Manor in respect of social class and housing, as well as numbers of older people and the level of need for social care (as measured by F&CS and Sheffield Health Authority).

Samples of older people were obtained, in consultation with team leaders and home care organizers, from the lists of service users in the two areas. The focus of the evaluation was on the most disabled users of services, though interviews in Manor included older people simply visiting the day centres or going out on shopping trips. Where team leaders and home care organizers were confident of a proxy being available, older people classed as being 'mentally infirm' were included.

Letters outlining the nature and aims of the survey and requesting individuals' participation in the project were sent to 134 households in Manor and 94 households in Southey Green. The original target figures were 150 and 100 households respectively. The revised numbers can be accounted for by the relatively fluid nature of service-using populations. That is, sample lists were affected by deaths, illness, confusion, house moves and entry to hospital and residential care. These factors continued to deplete sample size throughout the evaluation. Nevertheless, in the first round, interviews were secured with 96 older people in Manor, including 12 by proxy and five with the help of a proxy; and 84 older people in Southey Green, four by and six with the help of a proxy. Counting proxy interviews, these figures represent response rates of 71 per cent and 88 per cent respectively.

The questionnaire used in interviews with older users was designed to evaluate the effectiveness of the NSUs through the examination of outcomes and so-called 'quasi-inputs' (Challis 1981). Outcomes were judged in terms of the receipt of needed services and older people's general well-being and covered morale; anxiety and depression; loneliness; boredom; felt capacity to cope; care shortfalls and care overlaps; and social contacts and social activities. Specific measures employed included the Philadelphia Geriatric Centre Morale Scale (PGCMS) and the 12-item General Health Questionnaire (GHQ), both of which have been used successfully with older people (Bergmann *et al.* 1975; Wenger 1984; Davies and Challis 1986; Challis *et al.* 1989). Questions on loneliness and relationships drew on the work of Wenger (1984), supplemented by a question on neighbours taken from the Family Care of the Elderly Survey (Qureshi and Walker 1989).

Quasi-inputs refer to 'descriptions of client state' (Challis 1981), which, in this case, covered the circumstances and personal characteristics of older people. They included physical health; mental health; informal support; personality/attitude to help; and housing, environmental and material factors. Various objective and subjective self-rating items were used to assess these quasi-inputs. A measurement of functional disability and an 'interval' measure of dependency were derived from measures originally developed by Isaacs and Neville (1976) and used in the Kent Community Care Project (Challis 1981; Davies and Challis 1986); questions on 'care overlaps' drew on the Family Care of the Elderly questionnaire (Qureshi and Walker 1989); and the Survey Psychiatric Assessment Schedule (SPAS) was used to gather information about organic mental impairment. A couple of catch-all questions were also included to make it possible for older people to raise items of current significance to them which had not been covered in the rest of the questionnaire.

A number of social gerontologists have indicated the importance of time dimensions in research into older people (Abrams 1978; Johnson 1978).

Table A.1 Characteristics of the two matched samples

	Manor	Southey Green
Widowed (%)	83	76
Age	81.2	80.4
PGCMS	2.1	2.1
Mean no. health problems (maximum of 12)	3.8	4.2
Activities of daily living: (and requiring help)		
Getting into/out of bed	32	25
Washing self	11	17
Dressing	30	28
Getting around indoors/using toilet	24	32
Feeding self	7	7
Getting around outdoors	74	68
Light housework	45	49
Cooking hot meal	41	58
Heavy housework	89	100
Shopping	96	96
Laundry	84	96
All (maximum of 22 items)	9.4	10.3
Intensive informal care (%)	17	13
Housebound (%)	42	23
Incontinence – urinal (%)	21	29
faecal (%)	8	12

Although, for resource reasons, the time period in the evaluation was relatively brief, follow-up interviews were conducted with older people some 12 to 16 months after the first round of the survey in an attempt to detect any significant changes in their circumstances and to allow comparisons to be made between the two respective services in their response to needs, especially to crises (which may or may not be directly attributable to the ageing process). Sixty-seven people were interviewed in Manor, 11 by proxy. In Southey Green the numbers were 47 and three respectively. New items were included in questionnaires asking about such things as increases in informal support as the result of illness, admission to hospital, and revisions in the amount of formal help received.

Matched samples

The use of proxies clearly meant that a number of the self-rating questionnaire items had to be left out of those interviews. Even where proxies were not used, not all schedules were completed fully due to fatigue or distress on the part of the older person. This incompleteness, along with the degree of variability in need and support received, had obvious implications for the analysis of data and the generalizability of findings. This being so, it was decided that a more accurate picture of the extent to which the NSU had shifted away from traditional service provision and the impact of this change on older people would be obtained through the examination of matched groups of older people.

Drawing on the work of Davies and Challis (1986) 53 pairs of older people from each of the two samples were matched on five variables comprising age, sex, household status, need and degree of confusion. Household status referred to whether individuals were living alone or with one or more other people. Need was approached using a four-point measure originally developed by Isaacs and Neville (1976) which was modified slightly to accommodate the pair-wise matching procedure. An additional variable of the older person's attitude to help (Davies and Challis 1986) was not used. A comparison of the two matched groups is contained in Table A.1.

The two groups of older people were reasonably similar across a range of factors, particularly the global measures of mental and physical health. The only two significant differences were the greater number of housebound people in Manor and the more frequent incidence of incontinence in Southey Green.

Carers

First round survey

It was also the intention of the evaluation to examine the views and experiences of the informal carers of users of services. Despite the recent expansion of interest in the subject of carers, research tends to have concentrated on accounts or ethnographies of caregiving and there is a relative paucity of evaluative work on the needs and situation of caregivers and the impact of services directly in relation to them (Twigg 1989).

Older people were asked at interview to volunteer the name of their main carer, defined as a relative or friend who provided practical assistance at least once a week, or social support at least three times a week (Qureshi and Walker 1989). A list of 70 carers was obtained from older people in Manor and 51 in Southey Green. Where relevant, in-house carers were asked directly if they were willing to be interviewed, otherwise, as in the case of older people, they were contacted by letter. The outcome at the first round was 55 carer interviews in Manor and 37 in Southey Green, representing response rates of 79 per cent and 73 per cent respectively.

The questionnaire for carers covered five main areas: the care tasks performed; the older person's behaviour; the costs of caring; support for the carer; and the relationship between carer and older person. Outputs concen-

Table A.2 Categories of carer interviewed at the second stage

Category of Carer	Manor		Southey Green	
	N	%	N	%
Continuous carers	30	65	22	76
Bereaved carers	9	20	3	10.5
New carers	5	11	1	3
Carers of older people in hospital/residential care	2	4	3	10.5
Total	46	100	29	100

trated on the effect of caring on carers in terms of emotional and physical health, financial and employment costs, and family relations and social life, while quasi-inputs considered factors which might play a mediating role in the experience of caring including support from others, formal support, and attitude to caring. The only specific measure contained in the questionnaire was the Malaise Inventory, used in research on carers of older people to assess emotional stress (Levin *et al.* 1983; Bebbington *et al.* 1986; Challis *et al.* 1989). However, other questions were shaped by the findings of various studies: for example, physical health (Levin *et al.* 1983; Charlesworth *et al.* 1984), material costs (Townsend 1963; Isaacs *et al.* 1972; EOC 1980, 1982; Nissel and Bonnerjea 1982; Levin *et al.* 1983; Rimmer 1983; Brody and Schoonover 1986; Wright 1986, 1987; Lewis and Meredith 1988; Glendinning 1989).

Second round survey

It was also the aim of the evaluation to include a second round of interviews with carers in order to record any significant changes in their circumstances and the effects (if any) of the services on the stability and reliability of informal care networks and the support they offered. However, it soon became clear that it was not possible to administer a standard questionnaire – and consequently to achieve a rigorous and detailed longitudinal perspective on carers' lives – since a number of important subgroups had emerged between the two surveys with implications for the size and continuity of the two samples.

The subgroups included carers of older people who had been admitted to (and were still in) hospital or residential care, or who had died between the first and second round of interviews. Where they were willing to be reinterviewed (Table A.2), these respondents were asked retrospectively about their experiences in a more informal interview setting. In addition, a number of 'new carers' had turned up. They comprised people who had only recently started looking after the older person on a regular basis or as a 'main' carer, in some cases replacing original carers who had died or moved away from the area between survey rounds. The category also embraced a number of carers whose names and addresses were refused or not known by the older person at the first round of interviews but were given at the second. Members of this group were included in the survey chiefly because of the back-up information they could provide about the older person's circumstances. However, in many instances they passed important comments on the response of services to changes in their own situations which were duly recorded.

Case studies

A number of case studies were put together as a further part of the evaluation directly involving older people and their carers. A key aim of the studies was to explore, in greater detail, the extent to which the NSU aims of flexibility and user-centredness were met. Older people from 18 households in Manor were included. They comprised two groups: the nine households to which help was allocated during the period of study of new referrals to the unit, which were compared with nine households selected from those participating in the survey. Since many older people's views of Manor NSU were shaped by their previous experiences as users of home help, inclusion of the former group – consisting solely of first time users – helped to highlight any residual difficulties associated with a change in the form of service received.

New referrals were made up of six people living alone, one woman who lived with her son, and two couples. The average age of the group was 73. Four households were in receipt of support from formal carers, all of whom were included in the study. The group drawn from the survey sample consisted of eight people living alone and one couple, and had a mean age of 82. Three households were visited by informal carers and, again, all took part in the study. In one instance, the spouse of the carer was also included since she proved to provide the bulk of practical support.

The case studies were based on material collected from the survey questionnaires, and from informal unstructured interviews with older people and, where present, their carers. These additional unstructured interviews were intended to complement the tightly structured format of the survey questionnaire, providing greater insight into user's biographies and rationalizations of their social worlds. Interview material was supplemented by notes from users' records as well as observational data (see below).

Support workers

Group interviews

It was decided that semi-structured interviews would be conducted with frontline staff on a group basis. This involved tape-recording discussions which

Figure A.1 Notes for filling in time diaries

| DAY 1 | *Day:* | The diaries will be kept for two separate weeks each starting on |
| | *Date:* | Day 1 and ending on Day 7. *For each day, please record the day of the week and the date on **every** sheet used.* |

Activity

Time/arrived/began activity: **Time departed/ended activity:**

Things done:

Comments/ observations:

Activities include:
Visits to an older person/client; trips to the shops for groceries, to collect pensions or to pick up prescriptions; trips to the launderette; group meetings; supervision with organizers; days off.

NB When recording visits to an older person, please note whether that person is a 'main client' or if you are covering for someone else.

Times
Please make a note of the time you began and ended each activity or, if visiting an older person/client what time you arrived and departed. This will help us to work out roughly how much time you spend doing certain things and also how much time you spend travelling between visits/activities.

Things done include all the different things you do as part of an activity.
e.g. If you are visiting an older person, list *all* the things you did for them – including supervisory checks and sharing a cup of tea or having a chat.
Also make a note (in brackets) of roughly how long you spend on each task.

Comments/observations
Note any comments or observations which you think are of importance or interest.
e.g. If an older person is feeling poorly and you decide to put in an extra supervisory check make a note of this (and the consequent reshuffling of your timetable).
Or If a member of an older person's family is particularly helpful/ unhelpful you may wish to make a note of this.

were led by members of the group prompted by key questions. This focused group approach was taken not simply because it helped to meet the difficulties posed by limited resources of interviewing workers individually, but because it has been shown to be a fruitful method of talking to people who spend a large proportion of their time working in relative isolation (Warren 1988). Consensus and difference are highlighted while any fears that reports of 'irregularities' in activities or criticisms of supervisors may reach management ears are lessened by the anonymity of 'the group'. Indeed, the success of the group interviews with support workers was attested to by the several requests that they be held on a regular basis. Each respondent was also asked to complete a very brief questionnaire asking for basic personal, employment and training details to supplement the interview data.

In total, six group interviews were conducted at the Manor NSU, each of the three teams having been divided into two. Out of a possible 40 workers, a total of 34 (32 women and two men) took part, with a variation in group size from five to eight. A draft copy of a working paper on the role of the support worker, based on the transcripts, was sent to respondents inviting them to make comments, additions and amendments and every effort has been made to take these into account in the final chapter.

Time diaries

Time diaries were designed as a means of obtaining detailed comparative data on services. It was the intention that the diaries would be filled in over two separate weeks: from Saturday 2 November to Friday 8 November 1991, and from Monday 2 December to Sunday 8 December 1991. The time gap was a deliberate feature of the exercise, its goal being to minimize the chances of unusual events – e.g. a flu epidemic or severe winter weather – influencing patterns of activity.

Eight workers from each service – in Southey Green, four home carers and four home wardens – were recruited for the exercise. Volunteers were supplied with a sheaf of empty diary sheets, a set of instructions on how to fill them in (Figure A.1) and an example of a mock diary account. Individual participants were given the option of submitting their records anonymously with the obvious reassurance that all data would remain strictly confidential.

In the end, diaries were received from three workers from the home care service in Southey Green – two home carers and one home warden – and from six support workers in Manor. The intervention of union officials in Southey Green prevented the full participation of all volunteers. In Manor, one support worker found herself under too much stress to complete the exercise. A second jumped the gun by starting her own diary before the agreed dates and without the standard diary sheets. The information she provided was useful but, since it was not in the standard format, could not be considered for the construction of the time diary diagrams (see Chapter 3).

Key actors in the day to day operation of the NSUs

As well as interviewing support workers for the purposes of the NSU evaluation and higher management staff to obtain details of the policy development process, researchers spoke to management and other staff involved in the day to day operation of the NSU. The latter included the current and previous managers of the Manor NSU, three team leaders, the clerk and senior clerk, the current and previous senior nurses on the Manor project, and the manager of the Ecclesfield NSU. Participants were involved individually in taped interviews which were guided by a list of key questions. Transcripts of the interviews were sent to respondents who were invited to comment on, add to and amend their respective versions as desired.

Interviews were also conducted with practitioners and frontline workers within the health team. Unfortunately, the lack of resources meant that a detailed analysis of the health component of the project was not possible, though findings from these interviews have been incorporated to as great an extent as possible in writing up the evaluation.

Observation

In addition to the separate methods used for each of the groups above, information was gathered through the general observation of the day to day activities of the NSU. At the Manor Centre itself, researchers sat in on team, user group and resource panel meetings and were able to observe general administrative and managerial activities, especially while spending time accessing information from user files which were held in the main offices. The 'elderly persons' day centre was attended once a week over a period of two months, and researchers were also present at less regular events such as the launch of the new assessment form and the Christmas show.

Away from the NSU, researchers accompanied team leaders on assessment visits to new referrals. Frontline workers were often encountered during the course of interviewing, giving researchers the albeit brief chance to observe them at work in older people's homes. This is not to suggest that users were interviewed in the presence or hearing of a worker. It was usually the case that interviews were temporarily suspended or, in some cases, terminated on the understanding that researchers would return to complete the interview at a later date. In a handful of cases, where users were particularly nervous or frail, arrangements were made for frontline workers to be present at the older person's house to let in the researcher though again, reassurances were made that the interview which followed would be in strict confidence and that details would not be reported back to service providers. In a couple of cases, researchers also accompanied support workers on visits to older people who were very confused, lived alone and relied on neighbours as their sole source of informal support.

References

Abrams, M. (1978) *The Elderly: An Overview of Current British Social Research*. London: NCCOP and Age Concern.

Ahmad, B. (1990) *Black Perspectives in Social Work*. Birmingham: Venture Press.

Alber, J. (1995) A framework for the comparative study of social services. *Journal of European Social Policy*, 5(2): 131–50.

Allen, I., Hogg, D. and Peace, S. (1992) *Elderly People: Choice, Participation and Satisfaction*. London: Policy Studies Insitute.

Askham, J., Henshaw, L. and Tarpey, M. (1995) *Social and Health Authority Services for Elderly People from Black and Minority Ethnic Communities*. London: HMSO.

Association of County Councils (1979) *All Our Future*. London: ACC.

Atkin, K. (1991) Health, illness, disability and black minorities: a speculative critique of present day discourse. *Disability, Handicap and Society*, 6(1): 37–47.

Audit Commission (1986) *Making a Reality of Community Care*. London: HMSO.

Baldwin, S. (1985) *The Costs of Caring: Families with Disabled Children*. London: Routledge.

Barclay Committee (1982) *Social Workers: Their Role and Tasks*. London: Bedford Square Press.

Barnes, M., Cormie, J. and Crighton, M. (1994) *Seeking Representative Views from Frail Older People*. Fife: Age Concern Scotland.

Barnes, M. and Walker, A. (1995) 'Consumerism versus empowerment: a principled approach to the involvement of older service users', unpublished paper. University of Sheffield, Department of Sociological Studies.

Barnes, M. and Wistow, G. (1992) *Researching User Involvement*. Leeds: Nuffield Institute.

Barrett, S. and Fudge, C. (eds) (1981) *Policy and Action*. London: Methuen.

Barritt, A. (1990) *Innovations in Community Care: A Review of County Council Strategies for Elderly People and Family Carers*. London: Family Policy Studies Institute.

Bayley, M. (1973) *Mental Handicap and Community Care*. London: Routledge and Kegan Paul.

Bayley, M. (1982) Helping care to happen, in A. Walker (ed.) *Community Care.* Oxford: Basil Blackwell/Martin Robertson: 179–96.

Bayley, M., Parker, P., Seyd, R. and Tennant, A. (1981) *Neighbourhood Services Project, Origins, Strategy and Proposed Evaluation.* University of Sheffield, Department of Sociological Studies.

Beardshaw, V. and Towell, D. (1990) *Assessment and Case Management: Implications for the Implementation of Caring for People.* London: King's Fund Institute.

Bebbington, A.C., Charnley, M., Davies, B.P., Ferlie, E.B., Hughes, M.D. and Twigg, J. (1986) *The Domiciliary Care Project: Meeting the Needs of the Elderly,* Interim Report to the DHSS. Personal Social Services Research Unit, University of Kent at Canterbury.

Beresford, P. (1992) 'Expert' involvement. *Community Care,* 26, March: ii–iii.

Beresford, P. and Croft, C. (1993) *Citizen Involvement: A Practical Guide for Change.* Basingstoke: Macmillan.

Bergmann, K., Gaber, L. and Foster, E.M. (1975) The development of an instrument for early ascertainment of psychiatric disorder in elderly community residents: a pilot study. *Gerontopsychiatrie,* 4: 84–119.

Bernard, J. (1971) *Woman and the Public Interest.* Aldine: Atherton.

Bland, R. (1994) EPIC – a Scottish Case Management Experiment, in M. Tatterton (ed.) *Caring for People in the Community.* London: Jessica Kingsley: 113–29.

Bond, M. (1980) 'Women's work in a woman's world', MA dissertation, Warwick University, Department of Applied Social Studies.

Bond, M.E. and Bennett, D. (1987) A community support unit: analysis of records. *Social Services Research,* 4: 13–21.

Bond, M.E. and Ferrari, P. (1987) *Ecclesfield Support Unit 1984–1987 – A Report.* Sheffield: Family and Community Services.

Booth, T. (1985) *Home Truths.* London: Gower.

Bradshaw, J. and Gibbs, I. (1988) *Public Support for Residential Care.* Aldershot: Avebury.

Brody, E.M. and Schoonover, C.B. (1986) Patterns of the parent care when adult daughters work and when they do not. *The Gerontologist,* 26: 372–81.

Bruce, N. (1980) *Teamwork for Preventive Care.* New York: John Wiley & Sons.

Bulmer, M. (1987) *The Social Basis of Community Care.* London: Allen & Unwin.

Challis, D. (1981) The measurement of outcome in social care of the elderly. *Journal of Social Policy,* 10(2) April: 179–208.

Challis, D. and Davies, B. (1980) A new approach to community care for the elderly. *British Journal of Social Work,* 10(1): 1–18.

Challis, D. and Davies, B. (1986) *Case Management in Community Care.* Aldershot: Gower.

Challis, D., Darton, R., Johnson, L., Stone, M., Traske, K. and Watt, B. (1989) *Supporting Frail Elderly People at Home.* The Darlington Community Care Project, Canterbury: University of Kent, PSSRU.

Charlesworth, A., Wilkin, D. and Durie, A. (1984) *Carers and Services: A Comparison of Men and Women Caring for Dependent Elderly People.* University of Manchester, Department of Psychiatry and Community Medicine.

Cicirelli, V. (1983) A comparison of helping behaviour to elderly parents of adult children with intact and disrupted marriages. *The Gerontologist,* 23: 619–25.

Clarke, C. (1984) *Intensive Home Help and Home Care Services: A Directory.* London: Age Concern.

Clarke, L. (1995) Family care and changing family structure: bad news for the elderly, in I. Allen and E. Perkins (eds) *The Future of Family Care for Older People.* London: HMSO: 19–49.

Croft, S. and Beresford, P. (1990) *From Paternalism to Participation: Involving People in Social Services*. London: Open Services Project and Joseph Rowntree Foundation.

Cumberlege, J. (1986) *Neighbourhood Nursing – A Focus for Care: Report of the Community Nursing Review*. London: HMSO.

Dalley, G. (1983) Ideologies of care: a feminist contribution to the debate. *Critical Social Policy*, 8: 72–81.

Davies, B. (1981) *The Cost-effectiveness Imperative, the Social Services and Volunteers*. Berkhamsted: The Volunteer Centre.

Davies, B. and Challis, D. (1986) *Matching Resources to Needs in Community Care*. Aldershot: Gower.

Dexter, M. and Harbert, W. (1983) *The Home Help Service*. London: Tavistock.

Dooghe, G. (1991) *The Ageing of the Population in Europe*. Brussels, CBGS.

Durward, L. and Morton, J. (1980) *A Catalogue of Developments in the Care of Old People*. London: Personal Social Services Council.

Equal Opportunities Commission (EOC) (1980) *The Experience of Caring for Elderly and Handicapped Dependants: Survey Report*. Manchester: EOC.

Equal Opportunities Commission (EOC) (1982) *Who Cares for the Carers? Opportunities for Those Caring for the Elderly and Handicapped*. London: EOC.

Ermisch, J. (1983) *The Political Economy of Demographic Change*. London: Heinemann.

Evers, A. (1991) Introduction, in R. Kraan *et al. Care for the Elderly – Significant Innovations in Three European Countries*. Frankfurt: Campus/Westview: 1–6.

Family and Community Services (F&CS) (1980) *Department Newsheet* (supplement). Sheffield: Family and Community Services Department.

Family and Community Services (F&CS) (1984) *Manor Neighbourhood Project: Better Services for Children, Families and Elderly People on Manor Estate, Proposals for Public Consultation*. Sheffield: Family and Community Services Department.

Family and Community Services (F&CS) (1987) *Neighbourhood Support Schemes*. Sheffield: Sheffield City Council/Family and Community Services Department.

Family and Community Services (F&CS) (1989) *Programme Committee Progress Report*. Sheffield: Family and Community Services Department.

Fatimilehin, I. and Nadirshaw, Z. (1994) A cross cultural study of parental attitudes and beliefs about learning disability. *Mental Handicap Research*, 7(3): 202–27.

Ferlie, E. (1983) *Sourcebook of Initiatives in the Community Care of the Elderly*. Canterbury: University of Kent, PSSRU.

Finch, J. (1984) Community care: developing non-sexist alternatives. *Critical Social Policy*, 9: 6–18.

Finch, J. and Groves, D. (1980) Community care and the family: a case for equal opportunities? *Journal of Social Policy*, 9(4): 487–514.

Fisher, M. (ed.) (1989) *Client Studies*. Sheffield: JUSSR.

Friedmann, R., Gilbert, N. and Sherer, M. (eds) (1987) *Modern Welfare States*. Hemel Hempstead: Harvester Wheatsheaf.

Glendinning, C. (1989) *The Financial Circumstances of Informal Carers: Final Report*. SPRU Discussion Paper. York: Social Policy Research Unit, University of York.

Goldberg, E.M. and Connelly, N. (1982) *The Effectiveness of Social Care for the Elderly*. London: Heinemann.

Goldberg, E.M. and Neill, J. (1972) *Social Work in General Practice*. London: Allen & Unwin.

Griffiths, R. (1988) *Community Care: An Agenda for Action*. London: HMSO.

Grundy, E. (1989) Living arrangements and social support in later life, in A.M. Warnes (ed.) *Human Ageing and Later Life*. London: Edward Arnold: 96–106.

Hadley, R. and McGrath, M. (eds) (1980) *Going Local: Neighbourhood Social Services*. London: Bedford Square Press.

Hall, P., Land, H., Parker, R. and Webb, A. (1975) *Change, Choice and Conflict in Social Policy*. London: Heinemann.

Henwood, M. and Wicks, M. (1984) *The Forgotten Army: Family Care and Elderly People*. London: Family Policy Studies Centre.

Herzog, A.R. and Dielman, L. (1985) Age differences in response accuracy for factual survey questions, *Journal of Gerontology*, 40(3): 350–7.

Hill, M. and Bramley, G. (1986) *Analysing Social Policy*. Oxford: Blackwell.

Hogwood, B. and Gunn, L. (1984) *Policy Analysis for the Real World*. Oxford: Oxford University Press.

Howell, N. and Boldy, D. (1977) Establishing a method to equalise provision of hours. *Health and Social Services Journal*, 25 November, 1621–2.

Hoyes, L. and Means, R. (1991) *Implementing the White Paper on Community Care*. Bristol: SAUS.

Hudson, B. (1987) Collaboration in social welfare: a framework for analysis. *Policy and Politics*, 15(3): 175–82.

Hudson, B. (1989) Michael Lipsky and street level bureaucracy: a neglected perspective, in L. Barton (ed.) *Disability and Dependency*. London: Falmer Press.

Hudson, H. (1994) Case Management: The EPIC Model, in D. Challis, B. Davies and K. Traske (eds) *Community Care: New Agendas and Challenges from the UK and Overseas*. Aldershot: Ashgate: 149–59.

Isaacs, B., Livingstone, M. and Neville, Y. (1972) *Survival of the Unfittest, a Study of Geriatric Patients in Glasgow*. London: Routledge and Kegan Paul.

Isaacs, B. and Evers, H. (eds) (1984) *Innovations in the Care of the Elderly*. London: Croom Helm.

Isaacs, B. and Neville, Y. (1976) *The Measurement of Need in Old People*. Scottish Health Services Studies No. 34, Edinburgh: Scottish Home and Health Department.

James, G.A. and Saunders, M.N.K. (1988) Assessment criteria in the home help service. *Social Services Research*, 4(2): 22–7.

Jamieson, A. (ed.) (1991) *Home Care for Older People in Europe*. Oxford: Oxford University Press.

Jamieson, A. and Illsley, R. (eds) (1990) *Contrasting European Policies for the Care of Older People*. Aldershot: Avebury.

Johnson, M. (1978) That was your life: a biographical approach to later life, in V. Carver and P. Liddiard (eds) *An Ageing Population*. Sevenoaks, Hodder and Stoughton in association with the Open University Press: 99–113.

Johnson, N. (1987) *The Welfare State in Transition*. Brighton: Wheatsheaf.

Johnson, N. (1990) *Reconstructing the Welfare State*. London: Harvester Wheatsheaf.

Kraan, R.J., Baldock, J., Davies, B., Evers, A., Johansson, L., Knapen, M., Thorslund, M. and Tunissen, C. (1991) *Care for the Elderly – Significant Innovations in Three European Countries*. Frankfurt: Campus/Westview.

Land, H. (1978) Who cares for the family? *Journal of Social Policy*, 7(3): 357–84.

Levin, E., Sinclair, I. and Gorbach, P. (1983) *The Supporters of Confused Elderly Persons at Home*. London: National Institute of Social Work.

Lewis, J. and Meredith, B. (1988) *Daughters Who Care: Daughters Caring for Mothers at Home*. London: Routledge.

Lindblom, C. (1959) The science of 'muddling through'. *Public Administration*, 19, 79–99.

Lindblom, C. and Woodhouse, E. (1993) *The Policy-Making Process*. 3rd edn, Englewood Cliffs, NJ: Prentice Hall.

Lipsky, M. (1980) *Street-level Bureaucracy: Dilemmas of the Individual in Public Services.* New York: Russell Sage Foundation.

MacDonald, R. (1982) Accommodation and services for elderly people who are frail or handicapped. Supplement to *Newsheet 59.* Sheffield: Family and Community Services.

MacDonald, R., Qureshi, H. and Walker, A. (1984) Sheffield shows the way. *Community Care,* 18 October, 28–30.

Mayer, J. and Timms, N. (1970) *The Client Speaks.* London: Routledge.

Meetham, K. and Thompson, C. (1992) Setting up the Scarcroft Project: the problems of joint working. *Caring for People,* 9: 6–7.

Murray, C. (1984) *Losing Ground.* New York: Basic Books.

National Board of Social Welfare (1989) *Clients or Co-Producers? The Changing Role of Citizens in Social Services.* Helsinki: Government Printing Centre.

Nijkamp, P., Pacolet, J., Spinnewyn, H., Vollering, A., Wilderom, C. and Winters, S. (1991) *Services for the Elderly in Europe.* Leuven: HIVA.

Nissel, M. and Bonnerjea, L. (1982) *Family Care of the Handicapped Elderly: Who Pays?* London: Policy Studies Institute.

Norton, A., Stoten, B. and Taylor, H. (1986) *Councils of Care: Planning a Legal Government Strategy for Older People.* London: Centre for Policy on Ageing.

Oliver, J. (1983) The caring wife, in J. Finch and D. Groves (eds) *A Labour of Love.* London: Routledge and Kegan Paul: 72–8.

Pacolet, J., Versieck, K. and Bouten, R. (1994) *Social Protection for Dependency in Old Age.* Leuven: Hoger Institute.

Parker, G. (1985) *With Due Care and Attention: A Review of Research on Informal Care,* Occasional Paper No. 2. London: Family Policy Studies Centre.

Percy-Smith, J. and Sanderson, I. (1992) *Understanding Local Needs.* London: Institute for Public Policy Research.

Phillipson, C. and Walker, A. (eds) (1986) *Ageing and Social Policy.* Aldershot: Gower.

Pollard, S. (1959) *A History of Labour in Sheffield.* Liverpool: Liverpool University Press.

Pollard, S. and Holmes, C. (eds) (1976) *Essays in the Economic and Social History of South Yorkshire.* Barnsley: South Yorkshire County Council.

Qureshi, H. and Walker, A. (1989) *The Caring Relationship: Elderly People and Their Families.* London: Macmillan.

Renshaw, J. (1988) *Care in the Community: the First Steps.* Canterbury: University of Kent, PSSRU, Gower.

Rimmer, L. (1983) The economics of work and caring, in J. Finch and D. Groves (eds) *A Labour of Love.* London: Routledge and Kegan Paul: 131–47.

Robbins, D. (ed.) (1993) *Community Care: Findings from Department of Health Funded Research 1988–1992.* London: HMSO.

Sainsbury, E. (1980) Client need, social work method and agency function: a research perspective. *Social Work Service,* 23: 9–15.

Salvage, A. V. (1985) *Domiciliary Care Schemes for the Elderly: Provision by Local Authority Social Services Department and Recommendations for their Introduction,* vols 1 and 2. Cardiff: Research Team for the Care of the Elderly, University of Wales College of Medicine.

Sargeant, T. (1979) Joint care planning in the health and personal social services, in T. Booth (ed.) *Planning For Welfare.* Oxford: Blackwell and Robertson: 173–86.

Segalman, R. and Marsland, D. (1989) *Cradle to Grave.* London: Macmillan.

Shanas, E., Townsend, P., Wedderburn, D., Friis, H., Milhøj, P. and Stehouwer, J. (1968) *Old People in Three Industrial Societies.* London: Routledge and Kegan Paul.

Sheffield Community Health Care Services (1991) *Health Care Services for Life,* IHSM Consultants Final Report, Community Nursing Service Review. Sheffield Community Health Care Services.

Smith, D. (1982) *Conflict and Compromise. Class Formation in English Society 1830–1914: a Comparative Study of Birmingham and Sheffield.* London: Routledge and Kegan Paul.

Tinker, A. (1995) Housing and older people, in I. Allen and E. Perkins (eds) *The Future of Family Care for Older People.* London: HMSO: 181–200.

Townsend, P. (1962) *The Last Refuge.* London: Routledge and Kegan Paul.

Townsend, P. (1963) *The Family Life of Old People.* London: Routledge and Kegan Paul.

Twigg, J. (1989) Models of carers: how do agencies conceptualise their relation with informal carers? *Journal of Social Policy,* 18(1): 43–66.

Twigg, J. (ed.) (1992) *Carers: Research and Practice.* London: HMSO.

Twigg, J. and Atkin, K. (1991) *Evaluating Support for Informal Carers.* York: University of York.

Twigg, J., Atkin, K. and Perring, C. (1990) *Carers and Services: A Review of Research.* London: HMSO.

Ungerson, C. (1983a) Women and caring: skills, tasks and taboos, in E. Gamarnikow, D.H.J. Morgan, J. Purvis, D. Taylorson (eds) *The Public and the Private.* London: Heinemann: 62–77.

Ungerson, C. (1983b) Why do women care? in J. Finch and D. Groves (eds) *A Labour of Love.* London: Routledge and Kegan Paul: 31–50.

Ungerson, C. (1987) *Policy is Personal.* London: Tavistock.

Victor, C.R. (1991) *Health and Health Care in Later Life.* Buckingham: Open University Press.

Waerness, K. (1986) Informal and formal care in old age? Paper presented to the XIth World Congress of Sociology, New Delhi, July.

Waerness, K. (1990) What can a promotive orientation of health and care services mean for women as professionals and family carers?' Paper No. 8, Vienna Dialogue V, European Centre.

Walker, A. (1981) Community care and the elderly in Great Britain: theory and practice. *International Journal of Health Services,* 11(4): 541–57.

Walker, A. (ed.) (1982) *Community Care – The Family, the State and Social Policy.* Oxford: Basil Blackwell and Martin Robertson.

Walker, A. (1983) Care for elderly people: a conflict between women and the state, in J. Finch and D. Groves (eds) *A Labour of Love.* London: Routledge and Kegan Paul: 106–28.

Walker, A. (1984) *Social Planning.* Oxford: Basil Blackwell and Martin Robertshaw.

Walker, A. (1985a) *The Care Gap.* London: Local Government Information Unit.

Walker, A. (1985b) From charring to caring, *The Guardian,* 2 October: 13.

Walker, A. (1987) Enlarging the caring capacity of the community: informal support networks and the welfare state. *International Journal of Health Services,* 17(3): 369–86.

Walker, A. (1989) Community care, in M. McCarthy (ed.) *The New Politics of Welfare.* London: Macmillan: 203–24.

Walker, A. (1990) The economic 'burden' of ageing and the prospect of intergenerational conflict. *Ageing and Society,* 10(2): 377–96.

Walker, A. (1992) 'Increasing User Involvement in the Social Services', in T. Arie (ed.) *Recent Advances in Psychogeriatrics 2.* London: Churchill Livingstone: 5–19.

Walker, A. (1993a) Community care policy: from consensus to conflict, in J. Bormat, C.

Perieva, D. Pilgrim and F. Williams (eds) *Community Care: A Reader*. Basingstoke: Macmillan: 204–26.

Walker, A. (1993b) *Age and Attitudes*. Brussels: Commission of the EC.

Walker, A., Alber, J. and Guillemard, A-M. (1993) *Older People in Europe: Social and Economic Policies*. Brussels: Commission of the EC.

Walker, A., Guillemard, A-M. and Alber, J. (1991) *Social and Economic Policies and Older People*. Brussels: Commission of the European Communities.

Wall, R. (1984) Residential isolation of the elderly: a comparison over time. *Ageing and Society*, 4: 483–503.

Warnes, A.M. and Ford, R. (1995) Migration and family care, in I. Allen and E. Perkins (eds) *The Future of Family Care*. London: HMSO: 65–92.

Warren, L. (1988) *Home Care and Elderly People: The Experience of Home Helps and Old People in Salford*. PhD thesis, University of Salford.

Warren, L. (1990) We're home helps because we care: the experience of home helps caring for elderly people, in P. Abbott and G. Payne (eds) *New Directions in the Sociology of Health*. London: Falmer Press.

Warren, L. and Walker, A. (1991) Neighbourhood Support Units: a new approach to the care of older people, in F. Laczko and C. R. Victor (eds) *Social Policy and Elderly People*. Aldershot: Avebury.

Webb, A. (1991) Coordination, a problem in public sector management. *Policy and Politics*, 19(4): 29–42.

Webb, A. and Hobdell, M. (1980) Co-ordination in the health and personal social services, in S. Lonsdale, A. Webb and T.L. Briggs (eds) *Team Work in the Personal Social Services and Health Care*. Croom Helm: London.

Wenger, C.G. (1984) *The Supportive Network; Coping with old age*. National Institute, Social Services Library No. 46. London: George Allen and Unwin.

Westergaard, J., Noble, I. and Walker, A. (1989) *After Redundancy*. Oxford: Polity Press.

Willetts, O. (1992) *Modern Conservatism*. Harmondsworth: Penguin.

Willmott, P. (1986) *Social Networks, Informal Care and Public Policy*. London: PSI.

Wright, F. (1986) *Left to Care Alone*. Aldershot: Gower.

Wright, J., Ball, C. and Coleman, P. (1988) *Collaboration in Care: An Examination of Health and Social Services Provision for Mentally Frail Old People*. Mitcham, Surrey: Age Concern.

Wright, K. (1987) *The Economics of Informal Care of the Elderly*. York: Centre for Health Economics.

Index

OLDER PEOPLE AND COMMUNITY CARE
CRITICAL THEORY AND PRACTICE

Beverley Hughes

Older People and Community Care sets social and health care practice with older people firmly in the context of the new community care arrangements and the consequent organizational trends towards a market culture. However, it also questions the relative lack of attention given by professionals to issues of structural inequality in old age, compared for example to race and gender. Thus, the book tackles a double agenda:

* How can community care practice be suffused with anti-ageist values and principles?

Addressing this question the book sets out the foundation knowledge and values which must underpin the development of anti-discriminatory community care practice and examines the implications for practitioners in terms of the essential skills and inherent dilemmas which arise.

Older People and Community Care is essential reading for all those working with and managing services to older people, and who aspire to make empowerment for older people a reality.

Contents
Series Editor's Preface – Understanding the NHS and Community Care Act – PART ONE: Knowledge and values – Theories of ageing – The social condition of older people – Ageism and anti-ageist practice – PART TWO: Skills – Communicating with older people: the professional encounter – Assessment – Implementing and managing care – Direct work with users and carers – Protection – Conclusion: challenges and priorities – Bibliography – Index.

176 pp   0 335 19156 8 (Paperback)   0 335 19157 6 (Hardback)

IMPLEMENTING COMMUNITY CARE

Nigel Malin (ed.)

This introductory text provides a unique overview of the implementation of community care policy and the process of managing changes in the field. The central thesis is an expansion of the theme of integrating policy and professional practice in order to assess the requirements for providing models of care based upon a user and care management perspective. The book analyses the impact of changes for community nurses, social workers, those employed in residential and home-based care and discusses anticipated new roles and functions. Its examination of changes in policy and planning both at national and local level makes it a valuable sourcebook for health care, social work practitioners and planners, but the volume is designed for use by students and professionals alike. The emphasis throughout is on the design and delivery of services and providing an overview of research findings, particularly in relation to measuring service effectiveness.

Contents
Preface – Section 1: The policy context – Development of community care – Management and finance – Community care planning – Care management – Section 2: Staff and users – The caring professions – The family and informal care – Measuring service quality – The consumer role – Section 3: Models of care – Residential services – Day services – Domiciliary services – Index.

Contributors
Andy Alaszewski, Michael Beazley, John Brown, David Challis, Brian Hardy, Bob Hudson, Aileen McIntosh, Steve McNally, Nigel Malin, Jill Manthorpe, Jim Monarch, John Rose, Len Spriggs, Gerald Wistow, Wai-Ling Wun.

224 pp   0 335 15738 6 (Paperback)

COMMUNITY PROFILING
AUDITING SOCIAL NEEDS

Murray Hawtin, Geraint Hughes, Janie Percy-Smith with Anne Foreman

Social auditing and community profiles are increasingly being used in relation to a number of policy areas, including: housing, community care, community health, urban regeneration and local economic development. *Community Profiling* provides a practical guide to the community profiling process which can be used by professionals involved in the planning and delivery of services, community workers, community organizations, voluntary groups and tenants' associations. In addition it will provide an invaluable step-by-step guide to social science students involved in practical research projects.

The book takes the reader through the community profiling process beginning with consideration of what a community profile is, defining aims and objectives and planning the research. It then looks at a variety of methods for collecting, storing and analysing information and ways of involving the local community. Finally it considers how to present the information and develop appropriate action-plans. The book also includes a comprehensive annotated bibliography of recent community profiles and related literature.

Contents
What is a community profile? – Planning a community profile – Involving the community – Making use of existing information – Collecting new information – Survey methods – Storing and analysing data – Collating and presenting information – Not the end – Annotated bibliography – Index.

208 pp   0 335 19113 4 (Paperback)

14.99